THE SEARCH FOR AMELIA EARHART

THE SEARCH FOR
AMELIA
EARHART

FRED GOERNER

1966

DOUBLEDAY & COMPANY, INC.
GARDEN CITY, NEW YORK

To Merla and Gary
for their love and encouragement
and the late Fleet Admiral Chester W. Nimitz
without whose help and guidance
this book would not have been written.

Foreword

The Search for Amelia Earhart is the chronological story of the six-year, 1960–66, investigation conducted by the Columbia Broadcasting System, the Scripps League of Newspapers, the San Mateo *Times,* and Associated Press into a mystery which began in the summer of 1937, and it is the story of my own personal involvement over those six years.

The effort has involved four expeditions to the islands of the Western and Central Pacific Ocean, literally thousands of interviews with people closely associated with Amelia Earhart and her navigator, Frederick Noonan, or somehow connected with the events surrounding their disappearance. The research now fills three filing cabinets at KCBS in San Francisco. In addition, the transcript of hundreds of conversations and interrogations are preserved on tape recordings. The dialogue and detail the reader finds in this book has been drawn from those sources, and every attempt has been made to make it authentic, and in character with the personalities involved.

For the help of many individuals at various levels of our government and the cooperation, encouragement, and assistance of my friends at CBS, Scripps League, and Associated Press, I am deeply grateful. To those who could not or would not offer information at various times, I express my understanding.

To Walter Bradbury, the Doubleday editor who valiantly accepted the challenge of making an author of a radio newsman, goes my special thanks.

Amelia Earhart changed or affected the lives of millions of Americans and others the world over, and my life in particular. It is my hope that this book brings her and Fred Noonan closer to all persons, and produces the justice of truth, which I believe their accomplishments and their memories deserve.

Fred Goerner

THE SEARCH FOR AMELIA EARHART

1

"Dave, did you see this thing about Amelia Earhart in the San Mateo *Times?*"

It started that simply.

Dave McElhatton now does the 6 to 10:00 A.M. *McElhatton in the Morning* program for KCBS Radio in San Francisco. In 1960, however, he and I were working together on an afternoon show of topical news and interviews, and each day was a scramble to come up with something unusual. The article I referred to had appeared in the May 27, 1960, issue of the *Times,* and seemed to suit our needs. It told of a San Mateo, California, woman, Mrs. Josephine Blanco Akiyama, who had related a weird yarn about having seen two American fliers, a man and woman, on Saipan Island in the Marianas in 1937. The descriptions given by Mrs. Akiyama fit Amelia Earhart and her navigator, Captain Frederick Noonan, who had been lost under mysterious conditions in the Pacific during their around-the-world flight the same year.

The story held special interest for us. Dave and I do some private flying, and almost anything about aviation receives extra attention. I recall, however, that we were both highly skeptical of Mrs. Akiyama's revelations. Over the years there had been many stories which purportedly gave answers to the Earhart disappearance, but none of them had withstood investigation. In any case, Mrs. Akiyama qualified as an interesting interview, and I called her to see if she would appear on the program that afternoon.

I got a surprise. Mrs. Akiyama hung up on me before I could extend the invitation. Several other reporters had already been at her, and their doubting attitudes had upset her.

Intrigued, I called Linn Day, the *Times*' newsman who had written the story. He was convinced Mrs. Akiyama was telling the truth, and said I might be able to get to her through a San Mateo attorney named William Penaluna, who was representing Mrs. Akiyama and her husband, Maximo, in a war reparations case against Japan for damage done to their Saipan property during the war. As a simple precaution, I checked on Penaluna through some friends at the San Francisco Bar Association, and found him to be one of the most respected attorneys in northern California. In addition to his private law practice, he was area inheritance tax appraiser for the state, and was highly regarded by Governor Pat Brown of California.

When I talked with Penaluna, I found he not only believed Mrs. Akiyama's tale, he had been responsible for it reaching the *Times*. In the course of questioning the Akiyamas in regard to the aforementioned case, he had gleaned the Earhart information and relayed it to the publisher of the paper. Penaluna arranged for me to see Mrs. Akiyama.

Maximo and Josephine lived with their young son in a modest house in San Mateo. They had come to the United States from Saipan in 1957, hoping for a better life. Maximo was working as a dental technician while Josephine served as a nurse in a nearby hospital. They were quiet and reserved and it was not easy to start them talking. Finally, after thirty minutes of get-acquainted amenities, Mrs. Akiyama told her story.

One day in 1937 she had been riding her bicycle down the beach road on Saipan taking lunch to her brother-in-law José Matsumoto, who worked for the Japanese at their secret seaplane base at Tanapag Harbor on the western shore of the island. As she neared the gate to the facility, she saw a large, two-motored plane fly overhead and disappear in the vicinity of the harbor. A little while later, when she reached the beach area, she found a large group of people gathered around two white persons. At first she thought they were both men, but someone told her that one was a woman.

"They were both thin and looked very tired," said Mrs. Akiyama. "The woman had short-cut hair like a man and she was dressed like a man. The man, I think I remember, had his head hurt some way."

"Why are you sure it was 1937?" I asked.

"Because that was the year I graduated from Japanese school," Mrs. Akiyama answered. "I was eleven years old that year."

"Why are you sure they were American fliers?"

"That's what the people said and later the Japanese guards said it."

The guards, according to Mrs. Akiyama, had taken the pair away, and later there was rumor they had been executed by the Japanese. Her memory of the plane was hazy. She could remember seeing it in the water by the shoreline, but she could not recall if it was damaged or what happened to it after that day.

Maximo Akiyama knew nothing that would support his wife's story. His father had worked in the Japanese government on Saipan before and during the war, but Maximo had heard no mention of the incident.

When I questioned Mrs. Akiyama about the long delay in telling her story, she replied she had revealed the information in 1945 to a U. S. Navy dentist on Saipan whom she served as an assistant.

"His name was Dr. Casimir Sheft," she said. "He went back to the United States after the war, so he must be here now."

"Just a few months ago," she continued, "I also told an Air Force captain named Briand. He told me not to say anything to anyone else, but Mr. Penaluna told me to tell anyway, so I've talked to several news people about it."

What Mrs. Akiyama had said tumbled through my mind as I drove back to San Francisco. It sounded like truth, but there was only her word. Even if it were true, there could be a thousand other explanations of "the two white people" on Saipan before the war.

The next day I checked the registry of the American Dental Association and found a Casimir Sheft, D.D.S., in practice in Passaic, New Jersey. A phone conversation with Sheft gave some corroboration to Josephine's statements. Sheft had served with the U. S. Navy on Saipan during 1945–46, and Josephine Blanco, a native girl, had been his nurse. One day the doctor had been talking with a Navy flier who was in the office to have his teeth checked and the subject got around to Amelia Earhart and where she might have been lost in the Pacific.

"At that point," said Dr. Sheft, "Josephine came into the conversation and told us about having seen two American fliers, a man and a woman, on Saipan before the war."

Sheft proceeded to tell me almost exactly the same story Mrs. Akiyama had told.

"What did you do about it?" I asked.

"I told some other officers about it, but no one seemed interested in starting an investigation. Everyone was thinking about getting back to the States."

"Did you file a report?"

"No. I thought that military intelligence surely had the information. It never occurred to me they didn't, but I guess now they didn't."

"Over the years have you tried to tell anyone else?"

"Well, a couple of years ago I saw one of those *Omnibus* television programs. It was about Amelia Earhart and I was surprised they didn't mention Saipan as a possibility. Spencer Tracy was the narrator, I think. He just left it that Earhart and Noonan had probably crashed into the ocean. Afterward I wrote a letter to the producer of the program, but I guess it was too late for him to do anything about it."

Sheft felt that Josephine had told the truth.

"After all," he said, "she couldn't have had any reason for inventing such a story back in 1945."

The phone call established Mrs. Akiyama's 1945 conversation with Dr. Sheft, but it could hardly be considered substantiation that Amelia Earhart and Fred Noonan were Saipan's "two white fliers."

A study of a map of the South Pacific made me doubt that Amelia Earhart and Fred Noonan could have flown their plane to

Saipan. At the time of the disappearance, they were on the second to last leg of the around-the-world flight. They were bound for Howland Island, a distance of 2556 miles, mostly east and slightly north of Lae. To hit Saipan—with Howland Island as intended destination—would have represented navigational error of between ninety and one hundred degrees, as Saipan lies 1500 miles almost due north of Lae, New Guinea. Frederick Noonan had been a navigator of international reputation. Such an error seemed unthinkable, until I talked with two friends, one a check pilot for United Airlines, the other a flight captain of Pan American Airways. Both have made record long-distance flights in private planes over the Pacific. I asked them if Noonan could have made such a mistake.

"Possible, if not probable," was the consensus.

"You can look at it this way," said one. "Two international airliners have made worse mistakes within the last seven years, and they were using modern navigational aids. One of them landed 2100 miles off course and the other 1700 miles from destination. If the circumstances are right, anything can happen in the air."

But were the circumstances right, or more properly, wrong, for Amelia and Fred in 1937?

I learned that Paul Mantz, who owned an air service at Orange County Airport in Santa Ana, California, had been a technical adviser for Amelia's final flight. I flew down to get his opinion.

In aviation, you name it, and Mantz had piloted it, from biplane to jet, in every part of the world. In his early sixties, he could still put a converted B-25 bomber down on a runway so smoothly there was not the slightest jar. Motion pictures had provided the greater part of his living over the years. He was the only man ever to land a B-17 bomber by himself. He accomplished it in a harrowing crash-landing sequence for the Gregory Peck film *Twelve O'Clock High*. He was also responsible for the extraordinary aerial photograph for the Cinerama productions *Seven Wonders of the World* and *How the West Was Won*. Tragically, Mantz was killed during the filming of a motion picture in 1965.

Keen senses keep a flier alive, and they also help with success in Hollywood. Paul Mantz's sense for publicity had been honed to an exceptionally sharp edge. He had already gotten into the Akiyama story by the time I reached him in 1960.

"Sure it's possible," he said. "I've thought for a long time that Amelia and Fred must have been off course during that flight."

"But could they have gotten as far off course as Saipan?" I persisted.

"Yes. It's possible. With the extra gas tanks I put aboard her plane she had a range of well over four thousand miles. She could have flown a good part of the way toward Howland and still would have had enough fuel to make Saipan."

"What could have caused Noonan to make such an error?"

"Hell, how much flying have you done, boy? Up there"—Mantz gesticulated toward the ceiling—"everything can go against you and I don't give a damn how good you are, you're going to be in plenty of trouble."

Mantz went over to a cabinet and took out a large file folder. "Here's a copy of the radio log of that Coast Guard cutter, the *Itasca*, that the government stationed at Howland Island in '37 to be AE's homing vessel. Look at a few of the messages received from the plane during the flight and you'll know what kind of trouble Noonan had."

Paul pulled a half-dozen photostats from the file. "Eleanor Roosevelt sent these to me the year after AE disappeared. Look at this one. AE reported they were flying in heavy overcast. That meant Noonan couldn't shoot a celestial and he was primarily a celestial navigator. He would have had a hell of a time gauging his drift, too. All he could do was guess."

"What about their gyro compass, or the magnetic?" I cautiously asked. "Without a star fix, wouldn't they have flown dead reckoning?"

"That's right. They were probably doing just that, but a lot of things can go haywire flying DR. In those days, a gyro would tumble in rough air and the caging mechanisms were so primitive that it was tough and sometimes impossible to get them caged again."

"What about the magnetic compass, though? Aren't they pretty dependable?"

"Sure they're dependable—to a point—but there's still plenty that can happen. A mechanical pencil or a camera or anything metal hung close to the compass can cause the needle to home on the object. I've known, too, of lightning striking a plane in flight and magnetizing the ferrous metals in the wings and then the compass goes crazy."

"But even then," I continued, "wouldn't there still have been one means of navigation left? What about the radio homing signals sent out by the *Itasca?*"

"Look for yourself," Paul replied, throwing the file into my lap. "AE acknowledged only once receiving the *Itasca*'s signals and then she couldn't get a minimum. Either there was something wrong with her radio or they were goofing-off aboard that boat."

"Paul, doesn't it stretch your imagination to believe something went wrong with all four navigational aids during the one flight?"

"Sure it stretches. But you asked if such a thing was possible. Well, it was possible; not probable, but possible."

As I read over the yellowing copies of the *Itasca*'s log, I saw that the last message received from Amelia's plane had been conspicuously circled.

"What does this final message mean, Paul? 'We are 157–337 running north and south. Wait listening on 6210.'"

"It means Noonan was lost. The figures 157–337 simply represent a sunline he had shot in the early morning hours. See, the message came at 8:43. After flying all night with overcast, he finally got a crack at the sun after dawn, but without a reference point he couldn't have told where he was along two thousand miles of that sunline."

"What about the 'running north and south' and 'wait listening on 6210'?"

"'Running north and south' means they were flying up and down that sunline trying to pick up Howland Island. And the '6210' just represents their daylight radio frequency. They had been working 3105 kilocycles through the night and were switching to 6210."

"I wonder why they weren't heard on 6210?"

Mantz was silent for a moment, then said, "It could have been they were too damn far away to be heard. And 6210 doesn't have a fraction of the range of 3105. Signals on 3105 at night can skip thousands of miles across an ocean, but 6210 is usually good for just a couple hundred miles."

"Paul, condense it for me. How tough was the flight?"

"Tough. Plenty tough. I warned AE about the Howland Island leg. With perfect weather conditions, they would have had a good chance to make it. But the weather wasn't perfect; a typhoon had just blown out of the Caroline Islands and they undoubtedly hit plenty of turbulence. With that overcast, too, they needed more than luck."

Mantz walked over to a huge map of the Pacific Ocean hanging on the wall of his office.

"Look at that, Lae, New Guinea to Howland Island . . . more than 2500 miles over open water, and Howland is a peewee, about two miles long and a half mile wide. It would be like our taking off from my field here at Santa Ana, flying clear across the United States without once seeing the ground or anything we could check our position by, and then trying to find the eighteenth green of a golf course in New Jersey where we're supposed to land. How would you like to try to navigate that one?"

I was hooked; not completely, but there was a fairly large barb working in me. Some of the best fliers in the world had said it was possible, if not probable, that Earhart and Noonan could have flown their plane to Saipan, and Josephine Akiyama's story had stood its first test.

At KCBS I began writing a series of six- to ten-minute features for the afternoon program. Each gave some background on Earhart and Noonan and probed into the mystery of their disappearance. The response was immediate and more than any of us could have imagined. Letters and phone calls came from every part of northern California from people who had met or known Amelia or Fred. Some people had positive ideas of what had happened to them. Others contributed wild guesses.

By that time it certainly had occurred to me that if Josephine Akiyama as an eleven-year-old on Saipan had witnessed a scene in 1937 in which two American fliers were in custody of the Japanese, there must be others living on Saipan who knew as much or more, but it took some competition to get us going.

On June 5, 1960, several stories moved on the wire services about the U. S. Air Force officers, Captains Robert Dinger and Joseph Gervais, from Naha Air Force Base, Okinawa, who called themselves "Operation Earhart" and who were headed for Saipan to write a final answer to the mystery. Dinger and Gervais reportedly had convincing information that Earhart and Noonan had perished at the hands of the Japanese.

I called the Akiyamas and asked them if they knew of anyone living on Saipan who could give additional testimony should I visit the island. "Yes," was their answer, but they were not willing to disclose the names. If I would take Maximo Akiyama along with me to Saipan, it was stipulated, then the names would be revealed to me and Maximo would assist me with interrogation and interpretation.

"Do you want to be paid for the trip?" I asked.

"No. Just the expenses," Mr. Akiyama answered. "But I would like an agreement to be signed with Mr. Penaluna."

Persuading CBS to send me and a former native of Saipan six thousand miles on the slim hope of solving a twenty-three-year-old mystery should have been a difficult job. Actually, it was surprisingly easy. Sy Whitelaw, KCBS's sales manager, was acting manager of the station while Maurie Webster was in New York for network meetings. Sy, a former Navy flier, latched onto the idea immediately, and gave me the go-ahead. In New York, Maurie was delighted and John Day, then director of CBS News, and William Paley, Chairman of the Board of CBS, both agreed the story warranted the expenditure. The tough job was gaining permission to visit Saipan.

Saipan is one of several thousand small islands that make up the United Nations Trust Territory of the Pacific now under control of the United States. Most of the islands are administered by the U. S. Department of Interior, so it was with some surprise we found Saipan under U. S. Navy authority in 1960. Our surprise was nothing compared to the reaction of the Navy's Department of Information in Washington, D.C., when we asked to visit the island. At first there was shocked silence, then apparently disbelief that a search for Amelia Earhart could really be our reason. After a week's delay, Sy Whitelaw called a friend in Washington who finally got the clearance. Sy has never divulged his friend's name, but I know now he must have had considerable power. Saipan required top security clearance in 1960.

Maximo Akiyama then became the center of a small controversy: if Max turned up additional witnesses, to whom would the information be exclusive?

The San Mateo *Times* had declared itself "in," and rightly so as it had broken the first story. The *Times*, however, did not seem anxious to finance its own reporter for the expedition. Finally I sat down in William Penaluna's office with representatives of the paper and signed an agreement whereby CBS would pay Mr. Akiyama's expenses to and from Saipan and the *Times* would reimburse him for salary lost while away from his job. Maximo would temporarily become a *Times* reporter. CBS would then have exclusive radio and television rights to anything produced by the trip and the *Times* would get the newspaper beat.

I smile with embarrassment now as I remember concocting with the paper's representatives a code phrase to be cabled from Saipan to San Francisco if Maximo and I were successful in gathering more information.

"Big Hatchet Ready to Fall" was the purple prose selected, although I do not remember voting. I should have cast a negative ballot because the code later produced a scene both funny and considerably troublesome.

On June 16, 1960, Max Akiyama and I left San Francisco via Pan American Airways for Guam, thence to Saipan.

And of the two people whose fate we pursued . . . who were Amelia Earhart and Frederick Noonan? What place do they hold in the history of America and the world?

2

There is an Amelia Earhart Lane in Harrison, New York, and an Earhart Road at Oakland, California, International Airport. Memorial plaques and markers are conspicuously placed in Boston, Honolulu, Miami, Washington, D.C., and twenty other American cities and towns, as well as Burry Port, Wales, and Howland Island in the Pacific Ocean. Elementary schools in Chicago and Houston bear Amelia Earhart's name, and the United States Air Force operates the Amelia Earhart Hotel for Women in Wiesbaden, Germany. Exhibits of her medals, pictures, and books can be seen in a hundred libraries, and there are major displays at Purdue University and the Smithsonian. The American Legion has the Amelia Earhart Post Number 678 in Los Angeles, and the Lockheed Vega airplane she used to solo-fly the Atlantic Ocean thrills school children at the Franklin Institute in Philadelphia. She greatly influenced the development of two of the largest and most powerful women's organizations in the world, Zonta International and the Ninety-Nines, and they yearly give scholarships in her name to women aeronautics students. A commemorative airmail stamp was issued by the United States Post Office, July 24,

1963, and there is even a flower named "Amelia Earhart," a hybrid yellow rose-giant buff dahlia. Eighth-grade students still write poetry to her memory; tough managing editors remember her in nostalgic editorials; U.S. astronauts acknowledge her exploits with awe; a million Americans tote Amelia Earhart luggage, and a hundred million people the world over carry the Earhart legend in their hearts.

Why and how did this girl attain such a position? Among other things, what continually drove Amelia to search out and accept challenges filled with danger, that brought her to such peaks of fame?

One answer lay in her attitude toward security. It bordered disdain. She felt that the potential of many women was being destroyed by their attempts to get through life in the safest, most comfortable way. She also felt the security demands of women were in turn causing men to lose their creativity and abandon their dreams. Her deep desire to "dare to live" grew from the unhappy relationship of her mother and father.

In 1895, Edwin Stanton Earhart, a talented young lawyer with hopes of one day reaching the U. S. Supreme Court, had married Amy Otis, daughter of an influential Kansas judge. From the beginning, money was a major problem for Edwin. Judge Otis, a rich man by turn-of-the-century standards, had done a thorough job of spoiling Amy, and he expected Edwin to continue the practice.

Edwin tried. Settling claims for railroads was the best paying, steadiest work he could find. Although it took him away from the career he had planned, he accepted the job to give his wife the security she wanted. Judge Otis bought them a house in Kansas City, Kansas, and showed little faith in Edwin by extending parental protectiveness in other ways. When the first child arrived, Amy went home to Atchison, Kansas, to be more comfortable; thus Amelia Mary Earhart was born July 24, 1898, in her grandparents' big, white ante-bellum house located on a high bluff overlooking the Missouri River.

With Amelia's birth, the money pressures on Edwin increased, and two years later when a second daughter, Muriel Grace, arrived, he began to believe he would never achieve any of his original dreams. He accepted responsibility as defeat rather than challenge.

During childhood, Amelia sensed her father's unhappiness. He felt cheated of the future he had planned; worse, he was forced to endure the judge's berating of his professional and financial progress. Even when the Earhart income improved, frustration remained. To ease his tensions, Edwin began to have a few drinks after work with friends, and by the time the railroad fired him, he had a real alcohol problem.

He fought to control it, but the wagon was hard to mount. There were moves to Des Moines, Iowa, then St. Paul, Minnesota, but the bottle followed and jobs vanished. One sad day, Amy took the children to live with friends in Chicago, while Edwin returned to Kansas City to recover himself if he could.

Amelia decided she would help rather than burden her father. In spite of having changed schools three times in four years, she graduated from Chicago's Hyde Park High School on schedule in 1916. She had already developed a hunger for accomplishment and a determination never to be dependent on anyone but herself.

Filled with zeal to improve the world, Amelia went to Toronto in 1917, and nursed World War I wounded in a Canadian military hospital. The experience motivated her to begin a premedical course in 1919 at Columbia University in New York. She was beginning to discover she could do well with anything in which she was interested. Her first report card at Columbia listed A's in Zoology and French, and B's in Chemistry and Psychology. One of her professors, Dr. H. J. Muller, later said, "She had great curiosity and fine ability to synthesize. She'd often be through with an experiment by the time I had set it up. With her stamina, determination, and ability to concentrate, who knows what she would have discovered if she had chosen the research laboratory rather than aviation as a career?"

I don't agree with Dr. Muller. Amelia could never have endured a life in science or education. It would have been too restrictive, too regular, too secure. What she was to choose would need to offer freedom, personal challenge, opportunity to accomplish, and hopefully but not necessarily—excitement.

Above anything else Amelia wanted happiness for her parents.

Edwin Earhart moved to Los Angeles, and with the help of friends who conducted a version of Alcoholics Anonymous, he escaped the bottle for a while and opened a law office. In 1920, Amy risked her precious security again and Amelia went along to California to be a cohesive force if she could.

The marriage failed. But in California Amelia found the way of life she had been seeking. She found it at an air show. Her father arranged a trial flight for her, from which she returned with a determination nothing could sway. Neta Snook, the first woman graduate of the Curtiss School of Aviation, gave her lessons on an installment plan, and a few months later Amelia took advanced training from John Montijo, an ex-Army instructor.

In 1921, she soloed.

Amelia loved the role. She wore boots and khaki pants, with a scarf wrapped around her throat and folded inside a knee-length, leather flying jacket which had been properly "aged" with the right amount of grease and simulated wear. A leather helmet with goggles completed the uniform. The costume had a practical side. Dresses and high heels were seldom seen at airfields in the 1920s, and certainly were not worn by pilots, who invariably spent more time on the ground with grease-caked engines than they did aloft in the open cockpits of their planes. But practicality had little to do with Amelia's initial reaction. She liked the girl she saw in the mirror. The image was daring, courageous, independent. In short, Amelia Earhart found her identity as a flier, and she never relinquished it.

Winning acceptance, however, from those she admired, was another matter. Because she was a woman, she had to prove her ability many times. As hours in the air increased, she ceased to act the part of a flier and became one. The flying jacket no longer had to be "treated"; the scuff marks and discolorations were real. Gradually, and sometimes grudgingly, male fliers began to recognize her skill, willingness to work, and more than anything else, her coolness under pressure. She never showed or spoke of fear.

Was Amelia Earhart feminine? Many people ask that not surprising question. Most photographs show her with a short haircut, clad in flying gear, and more than a few writers have drawn her without sexual dimension.

Let there be no misconception. Amelia Earhart was a woman. It is true she rejected the established female techniques of attracting the opposite sex. She never flirted or feigned helplessness, because she felt it blocked any real communication or friendship with a man. She believed that woman should share with man, not surrender to him. Her attitude confused men and disconcerted women, but it should never have been construed as a lack of femininity. Under all that flying paraphernalia was a tall, slim, attractive body with enough curves to satisfy any man. At first glance, her features appeared plain, but like a good painting, the longer one looked, the deeper the appreciation. The mouth was full and sensitive. The eyes were penetrating, yet compassionate.

Amelia needed and wanted a man who could command her respect, yet would never attempt to dominate her; a confident, bold man, too filled with the love of freedom ever to restrict another's liberty; a gentle, loving man, whose values matched her own.

She never found him.

A few men tried to meet the standards. There was a young engineer who rented a room in her parents' house in Los Angeles. He courted Amelia for several years, introducing her to the theater, creative writing, and various liberal causes of the day, including labor's attempt to wrest social security laws from the federal government. She retained a love for the arts and continued to champion the rights of the individual all her life, but his own needs made him an early casualty. He proposed marriage several times, and even followed Amelia to Massachusetts, but he demanded too much. He wanted her to give up flying and settle in a permanent home.

In 1922, Amelia, with the help of her father, bought a sport biplane built by William Kinner, and began in earnest to build her hours in the air, learning the right reactions to every emergency. She practiced stalls, spins, forced landings, and even challenged vertigo by flying through fog without instruments. There were to be four crashes during her career, and the first came that year. The engine of a borrowed plane failed on take-off at fifty feet. Amelia calmly cut the switches and dumped the craft into a cabbage patch. As with the crackups of the future, she escaped without injury. A few days after the incident, she set her first record, an altitude mark for women, by climbing her plane above 14,000 feet.

Aside from admiration for her skill, another kind of respect accrued to Amelia. By the standards of any generation, the fliers, mechanics, ground crewmen, and airport kibitzers of the '20s were a lusty, sometimes brutal lot. They drank, brawled, and tried to outdo each other in telling smutty stories. There was an unspoken agreement, however, that Amelia was not to be subjected to any of it. When she appeared, language and behavior improved or the offender received a sharp elbow in the ribs. It was not that she asked to be treated differently. Rather it was something in her manner that said, "I'm familiar with all the four-letter words, and they don't frighten or distress me. Be comfortable. Use them if you want to, I choose not to simply because there are better words to express what I mean."

Edwin and Amy Earhart were divorced in 1924. The pressure was too great, and Ed had begun to drink again. With deep disappointment, Amelia sold the plane, and bought a yellow Kissel sport car in which she drove her mother across the country to Medford, Massachusetts, where sister Muriel had prepared a house. With flying temporarily curtailed, Amelia returned to her pre-medical studies at Columbia University, but records indicate that she withdrew from school April 25, 1925, after failing to complete courses in mathematics and physics. She later said to friends, "That semester convinced me I didn't have the qualities to be an M.D. For one, I lacked the patience. I wanted to be doing something, not preparing for it."

Amelia next began to teach courses in English under Massachusetts University's extension program. Most of her pupils were foreigners, and classes were held in factories in Lynn and other industrial towns near Boston. Her transportation costs, however, nearly matched the meager salary, and in the spring of 1926, she accepted a position as a social worker at Denison House, second oldest settlement house in Boston, which at least saved carfare. The first year she directed the evening school for foreign-born men and women and did follow-up work in their homes. Again she had the opportunity to view the qualifications and frustrations of marriages in which great pressures for security were present. Half of her cases were women with alcoholic husbands.

By the spring of 1928, history had produced a drama with a role exactly suiting Amelia's desires and talents. The world, spearheaded by America, had gone out of its collective mind for aviation. New heroes were emerging almost daily, and the public's clamor for them appeared to be increasing. Lieutenant Commander Cummings Read had begun the parade in 1919 by piloting the U. S. Navy flying boat NC-4 and his crew of five across the Atlantic to Portugal via the Azores, and Commander John Rogers had provided a fantastic adventure story in 1925 as he and his crew attempted to fly another Navy plane from San Francisco to Hawaii. Then came the exploits of Lester Maitland and Albert Heggenberger, Sir Charles Kingsford-Smith and the flight to Australia of *The Southern Cross,* and a hundred other "firsts," topped by the heroics of Colonel Charles A. Lindbergh's May 20, 1927, solo flight from New York to Paris. It was time for a woman to get into the act.

Mrs. Frederick Guest of London, whose husband had been in the Air Ministry of Lloyd George, decided she was going to be the first woman to fly the Atlantic Ocean and purchased the trimotored Fokker aircraft named *Friendship* from Commander Richard E. Byrd. Because she had been born in Pittsburgh, Pennsylvania, Mrs. Guest saw herself as a good-will ambassadress, flying from her native land to England forever to cement Anglo-American *Friendship.* However, after carefully assaying the chances of success, the British socialite prudently withdrew from the passenger list, and allowed another "American girl with the right image" to be selected as her representative.

About this time George Palmer Putnam, of the well-known G. P. Putnam's Sons publishing company, had scored a journalistic coup by persuading Charles Lindbergh to write the story of his flight. George figured the saga of the first woman to fly the Atlantic would sell as well, but Mrs. Guest's second thoughts left the project without its main attraction. A female with a flier's license, an extraordinary amount of courage, amenable to the modest terms of a Putnam publishing contract, was desperately needed. George Putnam came up with the name Amelia Earhart. His call to Denison House ended a promising career in social work, but gave America one of its greatest heroines. Putnam was more than pleased with his candidate. In addition to meeting the existing requirements, Amelia had promising writing facility, and best of all, she somewhat resembled Charles Lindbergh. A "Lady Lindy" exceeded even George Putnam's dreams.

Amelia's enthusiasm lessened slightly when she learned she was to be nothing more than a passenger on the flight, but the adventure of the project was still sufficient to make her join it. Wilmer L. Stultz was selected as pilot and Louis "Slim" Gordon as flight mechanic, and early in June 1928 Mrs. Guest's three hired hands flew her *Friendship* to Trepassey Bay, Newfoundland, and began what proved to be a long wait for the right weather conditions for the hop to England. Almost at once Amelia knew that Bill Stultz had a problem with which she was familiar; he was well advanced toward alcoholism. Each day he downed more than a fifth of brandy, and as the weather reports continued to be adverse, he grew more restless and dependent upon the bottle. Amelia drew from the long experience with her father and her days at Denison House, and managed to keep him fairly sober and to ease his apprehensions and fears.

On Sunday, June 17, 1928, the weather cleared and Amelia became the first woman to fly the Atlantic Ocean, landing, with less than an hour's fuel remaining, at Burry Port, Wales. Wilmer Stultz got her there with a superb display of flying ability. With her missionary ardor, Amelia tried to continue the rehabilitation program, but Bill was too far gone. He drank himself into a stupor every day aboard the ship that brought them back to the United States, and less than a year later killed himself when he tried to land his plane a half-mile short of Roosevelt Field, Long Island.

Serving as Mrs. Guest's proxy brought Amelia many of the things she had always wanted and a few she had hoped to avoid. There was enough money to give her mother security and help her father, who had remarried, buy a house. There were abundant opportunities for her own future in aviation and chances to meet many of the important people of the world on equal terms. But there was also the overwhelming burden of notoriety. Fame had been instant and incredible. Overnight she had become one of the best known women on earth. In open cars she had ridden through blizzards of confetti in New York City and Boston; hundreds of thousands of people surged forward to glimpse their darling, their wonder woman. *AMELIA EARHART ARRIVES* screamed six-inch headlines, and her name emerged at least once a minute from a million radio speakers. The adulation and hysteria at times surpassed that which had been accorded Lindbergh.

Hundreds of offers for personal appearances, speaking tours, radio programs, motion pictures, articles, books, business affiliations, and advertising endorsements bombarded and confused her. She needed guidance and protection, and George Putnam made himself very available. He sorted out the proposals and gave his counsel in a manner that convinced Amelia she was making the decisions. The approach was a sound one. He wanted to marry her, and he knew the only way it could be accomplished was by making her increasingly more obligated to him. There was also the complication of his wife, New York socialite Dorothy Binney Putnam, and their two sons.

Amelia, unaware of the plans being made for her, accepted George's invitation to stay at the Putnam mansion in Rye, New York, while she wrote *20 Hrs., 40 Mins.*, the story of the Atlantic flight. The degree of Amelia's innocence is reflected by the fact she dedicated the book, published in 1929, to Mrs. Putnam, in thanks for her hospitality.

When the manuscript was completed, Amelia set out on a demanding but profitable lecture tour, then accepted a job as aviation editor with *Cosmopolitan* magazine. George, meanwhile, engineered a separation from his wife, and in 1930, Dorothy Putnam obtained a divorce and moved to Florida with the children.

Although a man of considerable accomplishment, George Palmer Putnam II was not liked by many. Feared and grudgingly admired perhaps, but not liked. There are those who say his ego eclipsed the sun, feeding on publicity and personal aggrandizement. He pushed, cajoled, trampled, and suckled to get his way.

He left many enemies, but seldom showed remorse or sought to soothe the wounds his methods inflicted.

How then did this man finally manage to marry Amelia Earhart?

The answer in part derived from Putnam's supreme self-confidence. He had no fear of life. George believed he could do or have anything if he desired it enough.

He had inherited the Putnam publishing firm from his father, and many predicted he would destroy it. His intense need to succeed, however, caused the company to prosper. The novels of Ben Hecht, Alexander Woollcott's first books, and Rockwell Kent's *Wilderness* were issued under the Putnam imprint. Then came a long list of best sellers based on adventure and exploration. Sir Hubert Wilkins, Roy Chapman Andrews, Charles A. Lindbergh, Richard E. Byrd, Martin Johnson, William Beebe, William A. Robinson, Merion Cooper, Robert Cushman Murphy, all were Putnam authors.

"GP," as he wanted to be called, was never content with a single role in any venture. Along with publishing adventure books, he wrote them; in fact, lived them. In 1925, he explored Greenland for the American Museum of Natural History, then helped his elder son, David Binney, write *David Goes to Greenland,* which was a phenomenally successful boys' book. During his lifetime, George wrote ten books of his own, including a biography of Amelia; each concerned adventurous people and places. He displayed little interest in the classics or works of deep social import. Action was GP's milieu, and he enjoyed seeing himself as protagonist.

George went about winning Amelia as he had gone about dominating his publishing business; he dedicated himself to a goal, and nothing could deter him. In 1929, he helped her enter the first Women's Air Race, promptly dubbed the "Powder Puff Derby," from Santa Monica, California, to Cleveland, Ohio. Louise Thaden of Pittsburgh was the winner, followed by Gladys O'Donnell of Long Beach. Amelia placed third, but was happy merely to have participated.

Then George really turned on the charm. He was tall, almost distinguished-looking in his rimless glasses, and he knew more famous people than President Hoover. He brought Ignace Jan

Paderewski, Walter Damrosch, Robert Benchley, Ben Hecht, Heywood Broun, and a dozen other luminaries into Amelia's life, and Amelia was impressed. Great satisfaction came to her through a close friendship with the immensely talented actress and satirist, Cornelia Otis Skinner.

George oozed confidence, dependability, love of freedom and adventure. He had studied Amelia well. Never once did he show any fear of the challenges of life. He was always there with money, encouragement—and an offer of marriage. By his own admission, GP had proposed six times by July 6, 1930, the date Amelia set a women's speed record of 181 mph. in a Pratt & Whitney powered Lockheed Vega. Again George had handled the business details and further indebted her to him. The refusals of marriage grew less definite.

The death of Edwin Earhart from throat cancer probably was a deciding factor. Amelia had loved him very deeply. GP, twelve years older than she, appeared on the surface to be all the things her father might have been had Edwin found the courage to face life. Thus, on February 7, 1931, over the objections of her mother and many friends, she became Amelia Earhart Putnam.

Along with the father image, there were other precipitating factors. She appreciated their common interests, and believed George was capable of giving her the freedom she would need. But, in spite of the case GP had built, she still had reservations. The morning of the marriage she gave him a letter asking for his promise to free her in a year if they found no happiness.

George got what he wanted, but along with it came a mammoth blow to his ego. Amelia was much more popular and admired than he. She had the international fame, and he was often relegated to the role of just another admirer. Unconsciously and compulsively George sought to make his presence felt. In the years that followed, he became known to newspaper photographers as "the lens louse." When pictures of Amelia were being taken, GP always found some reason to include himself. The same was true of interviews. Many reporters complained that it was nearly impossible to get a few words from Amelia without enduring a few thousand from George. Amelia, however, never seemed to mind. Instead she felt relieved of an uncomfortable burden.

In 1931, GP sold his interest in G. P. Putnam's Sons to a cousin, Palmer C. Putnam, and became head of the editorial board for Paramount Pictures, a position which gave him plenty of time to promote his favorite project, Amelia Earhart. He raised money and handled details while AE did the flying. Advertising, promotion, and public relations were not then up to the present Madison Avenue computerized, cost-per-thousand level, but it is likely that George could have succeeded in the 1960s, too. He capitalized on Amelia's name and fame with imagination and little conscience. There were cigarette endorsements (although she did not smoke). She was made to turn designer, and created "recklessly gay" sport clothes for plane travel. Then she was induced to fashion lounging pajamas and mannish-tailored suits and coats with weird buttons shaped like bolts. The biggest success was Amelia Earhart Lightweight Airplane Luggage. On several occasions the race to capitalize grew too thick for Amelia, and she vetoed some schemes. The gambit of the Amelia Earhart Friendship Flight Hats is a good example. George had negotiated with a manufacturer of children's hats to produce a smaller-scale likeness of the fetching cloche Amelia had worn on her return from the Atlantic junket. A small ribbon decorated with Amelia's signature was going to be the bait in the sale of the twenty-five-cent item for three dollars. AE told GP, "Forget it George. I won't be a party to cheating youngsters. Adults are supposed to know better, but not kids."

One business deal with the Beechnut Packing Company brought her two new flight records, this time in an autogiro, forerunner of today's helicopter. For a considerable fee, Amelia flew the windmill-powered oddity about the country, and puffed the excellence of Beechnut products. During one demonstration, she set a new altitude mark of more than 18,000 feet, and when she reached Los Angeles, newspapers made much of the fact that she was the first woman to cross the country in that type of aircraft.

With Amelia's need for accomplishment and George's hunger for publicity, other challenges were inevitable. Because she had been only a passenger on the *Friendship* flight, Amelia felt guilty about the fame accorded her. On May 20, 1932, therefore, five years to the day after Lindbergh's feat, she took off from Harbor Grace, Newfoundland, in her red, high-wing Lockheed Vega monoplane, and 14 hours and 56 minutes later, after experiencing storms, wing icing and a fractured manifold ring which threatened destruction, she landed in a cow pasture outside Londonderry, Ireland, to become the first woman to solo-fly across the Atlantic Ocean.

She was a valid heroine now, and her fame tripled. There were audiences with the Prince of Wales, King Albert of Belgium, the Senate and Foreign Minister of France, and dinner with President and Mrs. Herbert Hoover at the White House. Before a joint session of the U. S. Senate and House of Representatives, she was awarded the Distinguished Flying Cross, the first woman in American history to be so honored. Medals, citations, and plaques came faster than she could accept them. From states, cities, towns, from civic officials, from colleges and universities, from organizations, the praise mounted and compounded itself. Even the Columbia Broadcasting System gave her a medallion for bravery and accomplishment.

The most satisfying recognition, however, came from her father's alma mater, Thiel College of Greenville, Pennsylvania, in the form of an honorary Doctor of Science degree. She wished with all her heart that Edwin Earhart had been standing in her place. She had always believed him capable of it.

The parade continued. Three months after the Atlantic solo, Amelia established the women's non-stop transcontinental speed record from Los Angeles, California, to Newark, New Jersey, flying the distance of 2448 miles in 19 hours and 5 minutes. Less than a year later, July 7, 1933, she lowered the mark to 17 hours, 7 minutes, and 30 seconds.

The day before Christmas, 1934, Amelia's Lockheed Vega was loaded onto the forward deck of the S.S. *Lurline* bound for Hawaii, and the world learned that she was going to try to collect a ten-thousand-dollar purse guaranteed by a group of Hawaiian businessmen to the first person, man or woman, to fly alone across the 2400 miles of Pacific Ocean between the Islands and California.

Newspapers around the world began to headline the effort

long before Amelia, GP, and Paul Mantz, who had been selected
as technical adviser, arrived at Honolulu. A rival Hawaiian organization started a rumor campaign to discredit the venture,
implying that Amelia had sold out to Hawaiian sugar interests
who expected her to use her prestige with the U. S. Congress
for passage of lower tariff rates. The charge so frightened the
sponsoring committee that they suggested the flight be called
off rather than risk more adverse publicity. Amelia, not GP,
settled the matter. With her usual calm manner, she met the
sponsors in a private dining room of the Royal Hawaiian Hotel.

"Gentlemen," she said, "there is the aroma of cowardice in
this air. You know as well as I that the rumor is trash, but if
you can be intimidated, it might as well be true. Whether you
live in fear or defend your integrity is your decision, I have made
mine. This week I will fly to California."

The embarrassed sponsors found courage. The rumor died. And
the afternoon of January 11, 1935, Amelia's heavily loaded Vega
rolled down a muddy runway through a steady downpour at
Wheeler Field, broke ground at the last possible moment, and
climbed awkwardly over Diamond Head. Eighteen hours and
fifteen minutes later, shortly before noon, January 12, the Vega's
wheels touched down at Oakland's Bay Farm Island Airport, and
10,000 Californians forced their way through police lines to
glimpse their idol.

Three months later, on April 19, 1935, Amelia became the
first to fly solo from Los Angeles to Mexico City. Then on May
8, after three weeks of rest, she soloed from Mexico City to
Newark, New Jersey.

The image reached a zenith. Society hostesses schemed and
even fought to get Amelia's name on a guest list. She was asked
to speak, write or simply stand and be admired. The scene bored
her, and when Dr. Edward C. Elliott, the enterprising and
progressive president of Purdue University, suggested she join
the faculty as a visiting counselor for women students, Amelia
gratefully accepted. George disliked the idea because it took
her away from more profitable ventures, but AE, as nearly always, had her way.

She loved the new role, and 800 Purdue girls found a champion
to help them to equal status with the 3200 male students. Soon

Amelia was spending most of her time on campus, meeting individuals, or lecturing to small groups on the advantages of a career.

"Many divorces are caused by the complete dependence of the female," Amelia would say in a typical discussion, according to some who were undergraduates there at the time. "At first there is the strong sexual attraction that sometimes masquerades as love. Everything goes well until the first financial crisis jars the man's confidence and threatens the woman's security. The woman can't help. All she can be is dependent, because that's what she has been trained to be. Instead of standing beside the man, giving him encouragement by contributing her own efforts, she becomes accusatory and sullen and the sex drive that passed for love is no longer enough to satisfy either of them . . . If we begin to think and respond as capable human beings able to deal with and even enjoy the challenges of life, then we surely will have something more to contribute to marriage than our bodies. We must earn true respect and equal rights from men by accepting responsibility. . . ."

President Elliott showed his pleasure with the work of his new vocational guidance counselor by establishing a special fund for aeronautical research. The Trustees of Purdue University ostensibly pledged fifty thousand dollars which was given to Amelia to purchase a plane. She chose the most advanced, long-range, non-military aircraft in the 1936 world: Lockheed's twin-engined, ten-passenger, low-wing, dual-control model 10-E Electra airliner, named for the "lost" star of the Pleiades. Amelia ordered the cabin seats removed from the transport and fuselage gas tanks inserted. The purchase order, dated March 20, 1936, called for a total capacity, including wing tanks, of 1204 gallons, giving the plane a maximum range of 4500 miles. Aft in the main cabin, a navigation room with complete instrumentation was constructed. When Amelia first saw the gleaming, all-metal ship at Lockheed in Burbank, California, she called it my "Flying Laboratory."

On her thirty-eighth birthday, July 24, 1936, she officially took ownership of the plane from Lockheed, and three days later, she filled out and signed in Los Angeles the Department of

Commerce application for a restricted aircraft license. "Long distance flights and research" are the words typed into the space marked DETAILED DESCRIPTION OF PURPOSE FOR WHICH AIRCRAFT WILL BE USED.

One great challenge remained—aviation's Everest—a flight around the world.

3

Preparations moved quickly.

Paul Mantz was hired as technical adviser to ready the plane. GP worked out deals with Standard Oil and Pratt & Whitney to cache fuel and spare parts at various stops around the world, and then arranged clearances with the U. S. State Department for the countries to be visited. Of course George turned a few dollars, too; twenty-five thousand dollars to be exact. He arranged with Gimbel's in New York to sell 10,000 letter covers to collectors to be carried on the flight.

They decided to fly from east to west, and Clarence S. Williams of Los Angeles prepared maps and charts for the entire flight, plotting dead reckoning with compass courses, distances between points, and the specific times to change headings. Because of the navigation complexity, Captain Harry Manning and Commander Fred J. Noonan were selected to accompany Amelia at least as far as Australia. As captain of the S.S. *Roosevelt*, Manning had met AE when she returned from Europe after the *Friendship* flight, and had offered his services as navigator for future flights, if she should need them. A Congressional Medal of Honor winner for having heroically rescued thirty-two men from the stricken steamship *Florida,* he was considered one of the finest navigators in the world. Noonan had almost as glittering a public reputation. In aerial navigation, he was more experienced than Manning.

Everything was ready March 17, 1937, for the first leg of the flight from Oakland, California, to Hawaii. At the last moment, Mantz was included as co-pilot. Among other things, he wanted to join his fiancée who was vacationing in Honolulu. Rain kept the Electra in a Navy hangar until late afternoon, then, about 4:30 P.M., the sky cleared, and Mantz taxied the transport to a small administration building where Manning and Noonan climbed into the passenger compartment. As Mantz ran engine checks, Amelia was driven to the plane in a Navy car. She settled in the left cockpit seat and took over control, moving the big ship to the end of the runway. The bright Hamilton Standard props spun by the powerful Wasp engines chewed great holes in the air, sending a hurricane blasting back against the vibrating fifty-five-foot wingspan. With a smooth, positive motion, Amelia pushed both throttles forward to full open, released the brakes, and the "Flying Laboratory" lunged forward as if eager for adventure. Mantz kept his eyes on the tachometer and air-speed indicator as the plane gained momentum.

"In the green," he shouted, as the needle moved from the red portion of the dial.

"In the white," he shouted again.

Amelia eased back on the yoke, and the Electra was airborne with a run of less than three thousand feet. At five hundred feet, Paul retracted the landing gear, and Amelia banked the plane out of the Oakland pattern, heading toward the Pacific through the Golden Gate. Only a few hundred people witnessed the take-off, but a San Francisco *Chronicle* photographer got a picture that made front pages across the country. From a rented plane circling high over San Francisco Bay, he photographed the Electra at the moment it passed over the Golden Gate Bridge. The bridge was nearing completion and scheduled to open in two months.

The flight to Honolulu was perfect. Fifteen hours and fifty-two minutes after leaving Oakland, Amelia landed the Lockheed at

Wheeler Field, Honolulu. While Manning, Noonan, and AE rested, Mantz moved the plane to Luke Field to take advantage of a longer runway. Nine hundred gallons of fuel would be needed for the next leg of the flight to tiny Howland Island, where an emergency landing field had recently been constructed by the U.S. government. The weight of the additional gasoline demanded as long a take-off run as possible.

At dawn, March 20, Manning and Noonan settled themselves in the Electra's navigation room while Amelia fastened her seat belt in the cockpit, started the engines, and checked the rpm's and magnetoes. Satisfied with the performance of both engines, she signaled the groundcrewmen to remove the chocks from the wheels. The Lockheed did not gain speed as quickly as it had on the Oakland take-off, and halfway down the runway, AE knew they were in trouble. The plane lurched awkwardly to the left, then sluggishly the nose began to swing to the right. To compensate, Amelia pulled back on the left engine throttle, but the correction was too firm. Careening in a wide circle, the Electra groundlooped, collapsing the landing gear and badly damaging one wing. Amelia's calmness paid off again. Before the plane came to rest, she had cut the switches, preventing a possible fire from fuel which poured from ruptured wing tanks. Manning and Noonan were shaken, but not hurt; Amelia sustained only injured pride. Her "Flying Laboratory" however, was a mess. Surgery at the Lockheed factory in California would be necessary. Everyone had an opinion about what caused the accident. Some said one of the tires had blown out. Others claimed Amelia simply lost control of the plane. Amelia believed the extra gasoline had been poorly distributed throughout the Electra, causing a weight imbalance. Sidney V. Bingham, a U. S. Army Corps Intelligence Officer, wrote in his report to Washington, "Due to unexplained circumstances . . ."

In record time, the Electra was shipped to Lockheed at Burbank for repair and reinstrumentation. It was decided to reverse the direction of the flight. Amelia would now fly around the world from west to east. No public announcement of the change was made. Later, the switch in plans would be attributed to "seasonal weather conditions."

Captain Manning's leave would expire soon, so he excused

himself from the flight, and returned to his vessel. Fred Noonan elected to continue. Amelia liked the tall, dark Irishman, who, in forty-four years, had adventured enough for a dozen men. There was a shy, warm quality about him, yet he was capable of sudden, enigmatic flashes of anger.

As a boy Fred had attended public schools in Chicago, then a private military academy and the London Nautical College, but at fifteen, his restlessness drove him to the sea. In 1910, he served aboard the *Compton,* largest square-rigged ship under the Union Jack. On one voyage from the Pacific Northwest to Ireland, the vessel was weatherbound for 152 days. During World War I, Fred became an officer aboard a munitions carrier between New York and London, and then joined the Royal Navy, surviving three torpedo sinkings. On one trip from London to Montreal, he helped rescue five French soldiers adrift on an ice floe. On another, he was credited with saving the crew of a floundering Portuguese fishing schooner. In twenty-two years at sea, he made the trip around Cape Horn seven times, thrice in a windjammer.

Since the first days of aviation, Fred had been fascinated by its potential. During his stays ashore in the late 1920s, he learned to fly, and began to apply his knowledge of maritime navigation to the sky. Finally he quit the sea and served as an instructor in aerial navigation for several airlines. In 1930 a young company known as Pan American Airways offered him a job with the kind of challenge he had always wanted. He was first flier, then navigator, then teacher of both. A few years later he was assigned to manage the airport at Port-au-Prince, Haiti, then he became inspector of all Pan Am airports. In 1935 he was sent to San Francisco to plan the Pacific routes which would take Pan Am to Hawaii, Midway Island, Wake Island, Guam, the Philippines, and Hong Kong. Then, November 22, 1935, he served as navigator for the huge Pan American four-engined Martin flying boat *The China Clipper* as it began its flight from San Francisco Bay, opening the era of commercial air transportation across the Pacific.

Fred Noonan was a talented and handsome man. Only one major flaw disturbed the image. He could drink a bottle of whiskey in the afternoon, and get through the better part of another in the evening. "Boozer," "drunk," "lush"—are hard words, and none of them fit Fred. He was hooked on liquor, yet somehow he always managed to function. He fought his adversary with courage and conviction, but sometimes he lost, and those defeats were costly. One of them caused Pan American to let him go.

Then along came Amelia Earhart with a flight plan that needed a man with ability, guts and an empty billfold, and Fred qualified on all counts. However, gossip of his problem preceded him, and several of Amelia's close friends attempted to convince her that he was a risk not worth taking. Their comments only made AE sure she should help him. Ghosts from the past and her own latent missionary urges made her give Fred a place on the flight.

At first the decision was not critical because Fred served as assistant navigator to Manning, but when the captain withdrew Amelia's belief in rehabilitation and the second chance was tested.

"Do you feel up to staying with me?" she asked him the day after the Honolulu mishap. "Harry is going back to his ship."

"I do," said Fred. "I need this flight."

"I mean all the way," said Amelia, "as the only navigator. I've decided I don't want to try to make even a part of it alone."

"Do you trust me?" asked Fred.

"I believe in you," said Amelia.

Fred's expression did not change, but there was a note of gratitude in his voice as he said, "Then I'll give you the best I have."

GP received Amelia's decision unhappily, but not for expected reasons. He felt that including Noonan on the entire trip would dilute the publicity, thereby reducing the stature of the accomplishment. He pleaded with her to make at least the last leg of the flight solo, but Amelia's answer was a firm "No."

George knew better than to argue further. Instead, he had a contract drawn stipulating that Fred would not sell stories or photographs from the flight or make himself available for interviews, endorsements, radio programs or motion pictures. George was already concerned with the results of the flight rather than the accomplishment of it.

One afternoon aboard the ship returning them from Honolulu to California, Fred stood on deck, staring at the horizon, thinking of the girl he hoped to marry. Amelia joined him at the rail, but he remained lost in thought.

The conversation that follows was related to me by the woman who that day occupied Fred's thoughts.

"Where is she now?" asked Amelia.

"Where is who?" said Fred, startled.

"Don't kid me," said Amelia. "I've never seen your face that soft. She must be someone very nice."

"She is," grinned Fred. "She's the most wonderful woman I've ever met."

"What's your problem then?"

"I'm just trying to decide if I should ask her to marry me. I'm not very good husband material, you know. I don't even know if I would be able to support her."

"Well, what about that navigation school you're planning to start? You should do well with it. I think it's a good idea."

Fred hesitated, then said, "I . . . I don't think that will work out now."

"Why?" said Amelia. "I thought you were counting on it."

"I was, but GP sort of put a crimp in it."

"What did he do?"

"It's not your concern," said Fred. "GP runs the business end. I know that."

"Never mind who runs what," snapped Amelia. "What's he been up to?"

"It's legitimate," said Fred. "I don't blame him."

"Let me judge that. What's he trying to pull?"

"He had me sign a contract that I'd stay strictly in the background on the flight, and not try to capitalize on the publicity in any way. I was counting on a bit of it to get the school off the ground."

Amelia was silent for a moment as if embarrassed, then she shook her head and said, "That . . . unfortunately . . . is GP. He's an intelligent man, but he can't resist the lust for fame and celebrity status. Did you actually sign a contract?"

"Yes."

"Well, I'll solve that problem for you right now," said Amelia. "GP isn't running this flight. I am, and as far as I'm concerned there's no star billing. We'll share the dangers and the same goes for any credit."

Fred nodded, then said, "That makes my decision harder if

anything. You know I have another problem that's been around for a while."

"Does she know about your battle with the bottle?" said Amelia.

"Yes, and she's willing to fight with me. I think I could win with her."

"Then stop letting fear rip you apart. Make a decision, and see what freedom it brings you."

Mary B. Martinelli and Frederick J. Noonan were married in Yuma, Arizona, March 27, 1937. A few days later, as they drove through California, their car smashed head-on into another automobile on a highway near Fresno. The investigating police officer cited Fred for driving in the wrong lane. A notation at the bottom of the traffic ticket said: *"No injuries. Driver had been drinking."*

May 17, less than two months after the Luke Field crash, the Electra was ready to fly again. Amelia tested the plane on the eighteenth, and the next day hopped to Oakland to pick up Fred.

Miami, Florida, is fond of claiming that the around-the-world flight began there, but the starting point actually was Oakland, California, as it had been for the first attempt. Events of the next few weeks were logged as follows:

May 20, 1937—Flight began.

May 21—Tucson, Arizona—Left engine caught fire after refueling. Blaze quickly extinguished, and only small repairs necessary.

May 22—New Orleans, Louisiana—Overnight.

May 23 to June 1—Miami, Florida—Final repairs and adjustments to Electra.

June 1—San Juan, Puerto Rico—First 1000 miles of flight and first stretch of ocean crossed.

June 2—Caripito, Venezuela—Overnight.

June 3—Paramaribo, Dutch Guiana—Overnight.

June 4—Fortaleza, Brazil—Reached after flying over 950 miles of jungle and 380 miles of ocean.

June 5—Fortaleza, Brazil—Engines overhauled and instruments checked by Pan American Airways mechanics.

June 6—Natal, Brazil—Electra loaded with 900 gallons of gasoline for 1900 miles leg over South Atlantic.

June 7—St. Louis, Senegal, French West Africa—Overnight.

(Destination had been Dakar, but Amelia chose to reverse a direction heading given her by Noonan during the last hour of the flight. As a result, they landed at St. Louis, 163 miles north of Dakar. Amelia accepted responsibility, saying she used her judgment instead of Fred's.)

June 8—Dakar, Senegal—Two-day layover to rest and study weather conditions and maps.

June 10—Gao, Mali—1140 mile flight from Dakar. Overnight.

June 11—Fort Lamy, Chad, French Equatorial Africa—1000 miles from Gao. Overnight.

June 12—El Fasher, Anglo-Egyptian Sudan—Overnight.

June 13—Assab, Eritrea (Ethiopia)—Two day layover after brief stops at Khartoum, Sudan, and Massawa, Eritrea.

June 15—Karachi, India (Pakistan)—Two-day stop after Electra spanned two seas—the Red and Arabian—on 1950 mile flight from Assab. Mechanics from Imperial Airways and Royal Air Force instrument specialists put the plane back into top condition.

June 17—Calcutta, India—Overnight. After 1400 mile flight from Karachi.

June 18—Akyab, Burma—Overnight.

June 19—Akyab, Burma—Overnight. Forced back on flight to Rangoon because of monsoon storm.

June 20—Singapore—Overnight. Reached after battling torrential rain storms. Stops at Rangoon and Bangkok.

June 21 to June 27—Bandoeng, Java, Dutch East Indies—An American engine specialist, F. O. Furman, and a crew of mechanics, worked three days on Electra's engines. (On June 24, Amelia and Fred flew to Surabaya, but returned to Bandoeng because of engine and navigation-instrument difficulties. The repairs took two more days. There was no indication of the exact nature of the work of Furman, or of why he happened to be stationed at Bandoeng.)

June 27—Koepang, Island of Timor (Indonesia)—Overnight. After five-hour flight from Bandoeng.

June 28—Port Darwin, Australia—Two-day layover. (Parachutes were shipped back to States because they would be of no use on long over-the-water flights. No other reasons were given for the two-day stop at Darwin.)

June 30 and July 1—Lae, New Guinea—About seven thousand miles remaining.

The next hop to Howland Island would be the most difficult: 2556 miles over open water. Howland is approximately two miles long in a north-south direction, about one half mile in an east-west direction, and rises to a maximum elevation of twenty feet. Three emergency runways had been constructed on the island by the U.S. government with no other apparent purpose than receiving the Earhart plane. Amelia and Fred wished to take off on July 1, but weather conditions looked bad. At 10:30 A.M., July 2, 1937, the Electra roared down the 3000-foot Lae, New Guinea, airstrip, breaking ground with plenty to spare in spite of the fact that the plane was carrying every ounce of gas possible. The U.S.S. *Swan* was stationed halfway between Honolulu and Howland, the U.S.S. *Ontario*, halfway between Howland and Lae, to serve as plane guards. The Coast Guard cutter *Itasca* lay alongside Howland to send and receive homing signals.

Amelia and Fred were actually flying into yesterday because of the international date line. Their take-off time was 12:30 P.M., July 1, aboard the *Itasca*.

In the United States, it was a fairly light news day. Secretary of State Cordell Hull announced that he had conveyed to the Soviet government an apology by Admiral William D. Leahy for referring to the Russian people as "virtually slaves of the central organization." The Soviet Union agreed to pull its troops out of islands in the Amur River, the dividing line between Eastern U.S.S.R. and Manchukuo, averting the threat of war between Russia and Japan. James Young, a U.S. correspondent in Japan, filed a report that Japan was preparing for war. "Tokyo," he wrote, "has the feeling of a city that knows war is inevitable and imminent." A great steel strike was ending in the Middle West and furnaces were being fired again. Several Senators and Congressmen had made speeches in different parts of the country calling for strict isolationism on the part of America, and pledging their support to a "no foreign entanglement" policy. The biggest social wedding of the year had taken place the day before. Franklin D. Roosevelt, Jr., and Ethel du Pont were married in Wilmington, Delaware.

There were lighter notes in the news, too. Carl Hubbell spun a 7-hitter at Boston and the New York Giants beat the Bees 6–2. Joe DiMaggio clouted his seventeenth homer of the 1937 season at Washington, but the Yankees lost 8–3. At San Diego, a young, lean, tall outfielder had a big day at the plate for the Pacific Coast Leagues Padres; four for five, including a home run. The boy's name was Ted Williams. In Los Angeles, circus freaks organized for the first time, joining John L. Lewis' CIO, and at Merced, California, a mechanic named Jesse Zelda sued William Randolph Hearst for $40,000. Zelda claimed he was attacked and injured by a "vicious, wild, and dangerous ostrich" at the Hearst estate at San Simeon. New automobiles were selling for less than $1000, and the big comedy in the nation's movie houses was *A Day at the Races* with the Marx Brothers. An RKO film, *New Faces of 1937*, introduced Milton Berle, Harriet Hilliard, Joe Penner, and Parkyakarkus. On Broadway theatergoers were crowding in to see *You Can't Take It with You* which had won the 1937 Pulitzer Prize for the best play of the year.

Into that quiet news day burst what many journalists have referred to as "one of the ten most reported news stories of the twentieth century."

LADY LINDY LOST!
EARHART DOWN IN PACIFIC
EARHART DISAPPEARS
AMELIA'S PLANE VANISHES
PACIFIC CLAIMS EARHART

For the next thirty days, the nation talked about little else. The search for Amelia and Fred was the largest and most expensive in history. The Navy, at the request of President Roosevelt, sent the carrier *Lexington*, battleship *Colorado*, and a dozen other vessels. Some 262,281 square miles of Pacific Ocean were searched by ships and planes, but no clue was found. In due course the U. S. Navy officially abandoned Amelia and Fred as "lost at sea." At that moment a mystery was born in millions of minds.

GP accepted the Navy's decision, and in 1939 he took possession of the estate as a probate court adjudged Amelia "dead." The same year he married Jean Marie Cosigny, only to divorce her in 1944 and marry Margaret Haviland. After the Pacific war in which he served in the China-Burma-India theatre as an Army Air Corps major, he purchased the Stove Pipe Wells Hotel in Death Valley. In December 1949 he became very ill and was taken to Trona Hospital in Trona, California, where he died at 6:05 A.M., January 4, 1950, from internal hemorrhages and uremic poisoning.

Hollywood did its share to keep the mystery of Amelia and Fred alive. In April 1943 RKO Studios released a film titled *Flight for Freedom* starring Rosalind Russell, Fred MacMurray, and Herbert Marshall, which followed the events of the last flight almost perfectly to the point of the Lae, New Guinea, take-off. According to the movie, the aviatrix, on a mission for the U.S. government, was to fly to "Gull" Island in the Pacific and pretend to be lost while U. S. Navy planes, ostensibly searching for her, photographed the Japanese Mandates. At Lae, New Guinea, however, the script writer had the heroine learn the Japanese were wise to the trick and would pick her up at the island. Thereupon, Rosalind Russell intentionally crashed her plane at sea so the search could take place anyway. Amelia's name was never used in the film, but the events portrayed left no doubt she was intended as the central character. Even the plane was identical to the Electra. The only concession the film company made was to change the "Flying Laboratory's" identification number from NR16020 to NR 16055.

GP supposedly was incensed and filed a suit for damages, but after a flurry of publicity, he dropped the case. A studio publicist later said it was planned as part of the advertising campaign, and George was paid for his assistance.

The script writers were guessing in 1943. The real story would have been deemed almost too fantastic even for a motion picture.

4

Commander George York, the Navy's Public Information Officer at Guam, met Maximo Akiyama and me when we arrived at that island, and immediately began a long series of questions about our reasons for visiting Saipan. He seemed to have difficulty accepting a search for Amelia Earhart as a legitimate purpose. When his probing produced no other admissions, he informed us we were to have an audience with Admiral Wendt in a few hours, and our air transportation to Saipan was scheduled for that afternoon. There were only two Navy flights a week to Saipan; we had hit the right day.

As York drove us to the Navy mess hall for breakfast, I pondered the unique similarity between the conversation with the Navy in Washington as we asked for permission to visit Saipan and the greeting we had just received from the commander. Both had implied that a newsman must have other reasons than Amelia Earhart for wanting to reach the island.

Later, York told us of a news story that had broken the morning before on Guam. Two Japanese military stragglers had come out of the jungle and surrendered themselves. Sixteen years after the

U.S. invasion of Guam and nearly fifteen years after the end of the war, the two finally decided they'd had enough; the Emperor was apparently not going to send forces to retake the island and rescue them. It was especially interesting to me, as I had spent more than a year on Guam with the Navy Seabees in 1944–45. We had guessed at that time that there were probably hundreds of Japanese still roaming the jungles.

Rear Admiral Waldemar Wendt, Commandant of the Marianas Sea Frontier, proved an urbane sort, pleasant and cordial.

"You know, I'm an Amelia Earhart fan myself," he began. "Followed her accomplishments for years. You think she went down at Saipan, do you?"

"We have some testimony indicating that's a possibility," I replied.

"Seems I recall she was lost somewhere around Howland Island. That's a long way from Saipan."

"I've talked to some experts, Admiral, including a man connected with the flight, who believe it was technically possible for her plane to have reached Saipan."

"Mr. Goerner, I'd like you to be frank with me. Is your mission to Saipan really to investigate the disappearance of Amelia Earhart?"

"Yes, sir, it is. Would you be just as frank with me? That's the third time that question has been asked of me. What's going on at Saipan that has the Navy spooked?"

Admiral Wendt smiled but not with humor. "Nothing terribly exciting, Mr. Goerner. There are some restricted areas on the island that you and Mr. Akiyama will not be permitted to visit. This is primarily for your own safety; there's still a lot of live ammunition strewn about from the war."

"Will I have a free hand in questioning the natives?"

"Of course you will. The restricted areas are on Saipan's north and east sides, but almost all the natives live on the south portion of the island. You'll be met this afternoon by a Commander Bridwell who heads our Naval Administration Unit there. He'll give you any help he can and also clearly define the rules; I hope you'll follow those rules as closely as possible."

"I put in better than three years with the Navy, Admiral," I smiled back. "I think I know what you mean.

"Admiral Wendt," I continued, "did a couple of Air Force officers come down here from Naha, Okinawa? They called themselves 'Operation Earhart.'"

"Yes, they were here a week or so ago."

"Did they go over to Saipan?"

"No. They wanted to, but I didn't grant them permission. They didn't have clearance from Washington."

"What did they do on Guam?" I asked.

"I think they questioned some natives who had lived on Saipan at one time."

"What did they find out?"

"I don't know. They went back to Okinawa by Air Force transportation."

On the way to Saipan that afternoon aboard a groaning old Navy DC-4, I asked Maximo Akiyama why the Navy was so secretive about Saipan.

"I do not know for sure," he said, "but it has been going on for many years; since not long after the end of the war with Japan. Not many people except officials are allowed to go to Saipan."

Saipan lies 115 miles north of Guam, about forty-five minutes flight time. It is good sized compared to most other Pacific islands; more than twelve miles long and five miles wide, bordered on the east by the Pacific Ocean, the Philippine Sea on the west. Three miles to the south, across a narrow channel, lies Tinian, a smaller, flatter island than Saipan.

Japan controlled the islands from 1914 to the U.S. invasions in 1944. The cost of taking Saipan was brutal: 15,525 casualties for the U.S., 29,000 of 30,000 Japanese killed.

Mount Tapotchau rises about 1500 feet at the center of the island and from the air the rest appears to be nothing but jungle. There is beauty in the thousand shades of green within the protective reef and through the jungle, but with it is something evil, hostile.

Our DC-4 made a straight-in approach over the southern tip of the island, landed on one of the old bomber strips the Navy had kept serviceable, and taxied over to Saipan's airport complex, two quonset huts and a shed. Plenty of natives were out, however: plane day is a happy day; there's mail, cargo, and curiosity as to who is arriving. Max and I, loaded down with cameras and tape recorders, must have been a diverting surprise.

Commander Paul W. Bridwell and Lieutenant Commander Leroy Hippe, his executive officer, were at the field to meet us. Both gave us disarming smiles and extended a warm welcome. Max had decided he was going to stay in Chalan Kanoa Village with his brother-in-law, José Matsumoto, the same man to whom Josephine had been taking lunch in 1937 when she had seen the white fliers. I had decided that Max was not going to get out of my sight and I would stay where he stayed. Commander Bridwell was having none of that, though, at the moment.

"Let Hippe take Akiyama into the village. I want you to come up to my quarters for a drink and a chat. If you decide later that you want to stay at Matsumoto's, I'll see that you're brought back."

Bridwell drove slowly north on the western side of the island, pointing out scenes he wanted me to see.

"We're passing through a part of Chalan Kanoa Village now. Most of the natives live around here. It's quite a job for us to keep up the roads, but we do it."

"How many natives on the island?" I responded.

"Between seven and eight thousand. Over there you'll notice one of our model experimental farms. We've done a lot of that for the natives, and we're starting to work on a new hospital and a new elementary school, too."

"Commander, why is the Navy the administering authority on Saipan rather than the Department of Interior?" I asked, as innocently as possible.

Equally casually, Bridwell replied, "Oh, it just happened that we drew the mission out here . . . Over there on the right is our model slaughterhouse."

Two large quonsets, with a screen porch tacked on, served as the un-elaborate quarters for Bridwell, his wife and two children. Considering that he was the commanding officer it was anything but posh, but what it lacked in comfort was partially made up by a spectacular view overlooking Tanapag Harbor about halfway up Saipan's western shore.

"That's the harbor where the Japanese had their seaplane base," Bridwell offered, as he broke out a bottle of Canadian Club.

"And that's the place Josephine Akiyama says she saw the two American fliers."

"I didn't know you'd heard about that."

"Sure, I've heard of it," he returned, handing me a drink. "We're not as isolated as all that. I've known about it now for a couple of weeks, but I didn't think anyone would come all the way out here on the strength of it."

"Then you don't think there's anything to it?"

"Frankly, I don't. If it were true, we'd have known about it a long time ago."

"How long have you been out here, Commander?"

"Call me Paul . . . Only about a month. But the Navy has been here a good many years, and I was here on this island during the war and didn't hear anything about it."

"Have you questioned any of the natives?"

"No, not really. Oh, I broached the subject to a few who work for us, but they didn't know anything. Another drink, Mr. Goerner?"

"Call me Fred . . . thank you, I will."

"No, Fred, I'm afraid you're out here on a wild goose chase. That Akiyama fellow you came with . . . you'd better be careful he doesn't get with some of his friends and have them tell you some more stories."

"I've thought of it. That's why I want to stay in the village with him."

"No! . . . No, I wouldn't do that if I were you," said the commander. "You wouldn't be comfortable. Most of the houses in the village are pretty dirty, and the sleeping accommodations are rough. You'll be better off up here on the hill with us."

"So you can keep an eye on me, Commander?"

"Why do you say that?"

"Well, Admiral Wendt said there were certain parts of the island I couldn't see, and I was to get the rules from you and obey them. Is where I stay one of the rules?"

"No, of course not. Nothing as stringent as that. I just thought you'd be more comfortable up here. You can see anyone you want to and stay where you want to; just be sure to let me know where you are."

"What are my boundary lines?"

"Well, under no circumstances are you to go north of our administration area here without my permission, and do not go over to the east side of the island. Care for another drink, Fred?"

"No thanks, Commander, but I will take you up on transportation into the village. I've decided to stay there."

"All right, Mr. Goerner, that's fine. I warn you, though, you won't be comfortable. By the way, I'll come into the village and pick you up tomorrow morning. I'll personally take you to some natives who should know if Amelia Earhart was ever on this island."

Commander Bridwell was right about one thing: living in the village wasn't comfortable. Chalan Kanoa is a labyrinth of deeply rutted coral-surfaced streets and trails. When it rains, which it does several times a day, the surface turns to goo which oozes over one's shoes, so most of the natives wear open Japanese sandals. Within a few hours, the sun dries the coral to a fine powder which blows against houses, vehicles, clothing, and eyes. Dirt and heat are the ways of life, and the cockroach is king. I soon learned to stamp my foot periodically on a floor during evening hours to keep the king at a respectful distance.

José Matsumoto's house was of two-story frame and fairly well screened, which turned out to be the major attraction. Saipan's mosquitoes, I'm sure, were mothered by a B-29 and mosquito repellent is their favorite fuel.

Maximo Akiyama was waiting for me and quite excited.

"Matsumoto remembers the incident. Matsumoto remembers the two American fliers!"

"What does he remember, Max? Did he see them?"

"No, he did not see them. The Japanese police had taken them away before he got there that day, but he remembers the people at the seaplane base talking about it and he remembers the Japanese talking about the woman and man fliers, the Americans, the spies."

"Why has he been so long in telling the story?"

Max shrugged. "He says nobody ever asked him."

J. Y. Matsumoto is a small, sharp-witted but retiring Japanese in his late fifties. He's one of a half-dozen Japanese who were permitted to remain on Saipan after World War II because they had married native Chamorro women. Matsumoto's wife is sister to Josephine Akiyama; I was not sure I could give much credence to his testimony because of that relationship. Matsumoto is one of the richest men on Saipan, which does not make him wealthy by U.S. standards. He runs the motion picture theater in Chalan Kanoa, housed in one large quonset hut, and the natives love the films. Even at the low prices Matsumoto charges, he has done well; enough to afford a car and one of the better houses in the village.

Without much sleep, I managed to get through that first night, and early the next morning came a break. The Monsignor and Fathers at the Catholic mission in Chalan Kanoa had heard I was on the island and came by Matsumoto's for a chat. The natives of Saipan are almost all Catholic. A Baptist mission had been established a few years before but with little success for the Baptist minister.

Monsignor Oscar Calvo is a native of Guam, part Chamorran, as are most of the natives of Saipan, but almost all his life has been spent in an area under U.S. control while the Saipanese have lived under many different governments. Monsignor Calvo is best known in the Marianas as the priest who defied the Japanese and who was finally able to recover the remains of his fellow priest, Father Duenas, who had been beheaded by the Japanese just before the U.S. return to Guam in 1944.

Father Arnold Bendowske comes from Milwaukee, Wisconsin, but has spent most of his adult life in the Marianas. He was captured by the Japanese at Guam in 1941 and spent most of the war in a prison camp in Japan.

Brooklyn, New York, was home for Father Sylvan Conover. A younger man, he has served on Saipan for the last ten years. All are of the Capuchin Order, and I quickly learned that none had served on Saipan before or during the war.

"Father Tardio, a Spanish Jesuit Priest, was the only one to survive the United States invasion of Saipan in 1944," said Monsignor Calvo. "After the war he was sent back to Spain and has since passed away. There was one lay brother, a Brother Gregorio. I think he's assigned to Yap Island in the Carolines now."

The Monsignor and the Fathers had heard vague rumors on Saipan over the years about some white people who might have been on the island before or during the war, but none of the three had been sufficiently motivated to trace the rumors and determine who the white people had been.

I explained why I was on the island and asked Monsignor Calvo and the Fathers for their help.

"I want to make sure any testimony that is given is truth. All of you speak the language and I'd like to ask you to interpret; in fact, I'd like you to do the questioning. Will you assist me?"

I am not sure why they agreed, but they did. Each had more than enough work of his own. Perhaps it was something new, a change from the predictability of Saipan's days. Perhaps, too, they caught the Amelia fever. I had a particularly virulent form in 1960.

In any case, I didn't question, but immediately established some strategy for the questioning. We would not start by asking a native if he remembered the white people who were on the island before the war. Monsignor or one of the Fathers would begin by talking about the post-war era, then the period during the war, and finally the years before the war. Sometime during the latter conversation the question, "Did you ever see any white people on Saipan during Japanese times?" would be inserted. If the answer was negative, we would drop the questioning and move on to the next person. If the answer was yes, the questioning would be pursued, but the individual being questioned would have to establish a date when the white people were seen, before the testimony could be accepted. The date or year could be tied to a birth or death in the family, a marriage, graduation from school, or other event.

Monsignor, the Fathers, Maximo Akiyama and I would start to work that afternoon.

5

Monsignor Calvo and the Fathers left as Commander Bridwell drove up to the Matsumotos'.

"Did the Fathers know anything about your mystery?" the commander inquired after we had exchanged greetings.

"They said they had heard some rumors but nothing definite. I prevailed on them though to help me with the questioning."

"Oh . . . Well, I don't think that'll be necessary," he said. "I thought I might take you around this morning to see a few of the natives who should know, if anyone does, whether Amelia Earhart was ever on Saipan."

Bridwell seemed eager, so I went along with him. In the next few hours we talked with six Saipanese men, all of whom were old enough to have been adults in 1937. Elias Sablan and Vicente Galvan worked at the Land Claims Office just north of Chalan Kanoa. Both were in their fifties and both had held some sort of job under Japanese administration. Their nervousness was apparent as Bridwell questioned them.

"I do not know of such a thing," replied Sablan.

"No . . . no . . . wh-wh-white lady and man," stuttered the other.

Juan Ada lived in Chalan Kanoa and had been a native judge under the Japanese.

"To my knowledge that did not happen," was his answer.

Oswald and Manuel—two more of the many Sablans—had both worked for the Japanese.

"No American. No white lady on island," said Oswald.

Manuel replied, "Sorry, I do not know of this."

Juan Villa-Gomez had served the Japanese at the prison.

"There was no white woman and man. I know nothing."

As we returned to the Matsumoto's, Commander Bridwell seemed to feel the investigation was completed.

"I'm sorry the testimony wasn't more promising," he offered, "but those men should know. They all worked with the Japanese. I'm afraid you've come a long way for nothing."

"That's all right, Commander," I returned. "I'm after the truth whatever the answer may be."

"Would you like me to get you scheduled for the next flight back to Guam?"

"No, I think not yet. I want to give Monsignor and the Fathers a chance, and Akiyama has some ideas, too."

"All right, Fred. We want you to be satisfied. Just remember that some of these people will tell you what they think you want to hear."

After Bridwell left, I considered his last statement. There had been something pat about the six men we had interviewed that morning. They hadn't liked saying anything and all of them had strong ties with the Japanese or were now working for the U. S. Navy. There was the possibility they were telling the commander what they thought *he* wanted to hear.

In the days that followed, we worked in shifts. Father Arnold or Father Sylvan would go out with Max and me in the morning and Monsignor Calvo accompanied us in the afternoons and evenings. After talking with more than two hundred Saipanese, we found that the testimony of thirteen could be pieced together into a story that apparently supported the contention of Josephine Akiyama.

A white woman and man, Americans and fliers according to

what the Japanese had said, either came ashore or had been brought ashore at Tanapag Harbor sometime in 1937. The woman resembled a man, at least she was dressed as a man and had short hair. The man was injured; his head was bandaged. Under guard, they had been held at the dock area until a Japanese military car arrived from Garapan and took them away. (Garapan was the Japanese city on Saipan just south of Tanapag Harbor. It was completely destroyed during the U.S. invasion in 1944, and the rubble has been swallowed by the jungle.)

The pair were next seen being taken into the Japanese military police headquarters in Garapan. Ostensibly for questioning. A Gregorio Sablan had been summoned to serve as interpreter. The interrogation had lasted several hours, and then the woman was taken to Garapan prison, the man to the Muchot Point military police barracks. The woman was held at the prison for only a few hours, then transferred back to the city and placed in a hotel the military police had taken over in 1934 to house political prisoners. None of the witnesses knew what had finally happened to the mysterious white people, although several felt that either one or both of them had been executed.

Here are more-or-less typical samples of the testimony I tape-recorded in June 1960.

Gregorio Camacho is a farmer living in San Roque Village.

QUESTION: Where did you see the white people?
ANSWER: Tanapag Harbor and later in Garapan.
QUESTION: How did you know they were fliers?
ANSWER: The Japanese said so.
QUESTION: What did the Japanese think of them?
ANSWER: The Japanese were very surprised to see a lady flier because at that time it never would happen that a lady would fly.

Jesús Boyer also farms and lives in San Roque.

QUESTION: Where did you see the white people?
ANSWER: I was working at Tanapag Harbor. I see them there.
QUESTION: What do you remember about them?
ANSWER: I remember well the lady. Her face, arms, posture—

all looked American. But the Japanese kept them. They were very suspicious.

QUESTION: Do you remember her hair color—anything like that?

ANSWER: I don't remember so well except her hair was cut short.

QUESTION: Did you see anything published in a Saipan-Japanese newspaper about this?

ANSWER: No, it was kept very secret.

QUESTION: Why did the people never talk about this before?

ANSWER: During the Japanese time, it is very unsafe to disclose information.

Jesús Salas is a farmer and lives in a hut outside Doné Village. Jesús was put in Garapan prison in 1937 after he fought with a Japanese soldier who had spit on a religious processional. He remained in prison until American Marines released him in 1944. Sometime during 1937 a white woman was placed in the next cell, but kept there only a few hours. He saw the woman only once but gave a description of her that fitted those given by the other witnesses. The guards told him the woman was an American pilot the Japanese had captured. Salas also told another unhappy story. A few weeks before the invasion in 1944, the Japanese shot down an American plane, captured the two crewmen, and put them in Garapan prison. One of the fliers was killed in the pre-invasion bombardment when a U.S. shell exploded behind his cell. The attack so infuriated the Japanese they beheaded the other American in the prison corridor, placed the body in a blanket, and after pouring gasoline on it, burned the remains on the prison steps. Commander Bridwell confirmed Sala's story and added that one of the fliers later had been identified from a class ring.

A portion of the prison still stands, although completely hidden by jungle. It takes about ten minutes to hack a path to it from the road, but so dense is the jungle one can be within a few yards and not see it. Garapan prison must have been a brutal torture for unfortunates kept there. The cells were literally holes with bars, no sanitary facilities, open to mosquitoes and weather.

There was other testimony. Josepa Reyes Sablan of Chalan

Kanoa saw the two white people taken into the military police headquarters in Garapan. She was a distant relative of the Gregorio Sablan who had been the interpreter. This Sablan was regarded as the most learned man on Saipan; he spoke Chamorran, German, Spanish, Japanese, and English. His ability made him useful to the Japanese, but also suspect. Gregorio might have been able to identify the two white fliers had he lived; he died in 1945 of tuberculosis without divulging to his family what he had been compelled to do by the Japanese police.

Manuel Aldan is a native dentist practicing in Chalan Kanoa. In 1937 his work was restricted to Japanese officers. He had not seen the two white people, but he had heard much about them from his patients. The American man and woman, according to the Japanese, were fliers who had been captured as spies. "The officers," said Aldan, "made jokes about the United States using women as spies. They said that American men did not have the courage to come and spy themselves."

Eight other Saipanese gave testimony in 1960: Antonio Díaz, José Rios Camacho, Juan Guerrero Reyes, Pedro Sakisag, Maria Ohashi, Francisco Tudela, José Basa, and José Matsumoto, my host. All, with the exception of Matsumoto, had not been anxious to provide information. I knew that without the help of Monsignor and the Fathers I would have got little.

"Why," I asked Monsignor Calvo, "haven't these people come forward before with this story?"

"You have to understand the people and their history," replied Monsignor. "It has been many centuries since they've had self-determination. The Spaniards conquered them first and introduced the Catholic Church. The Germans bought them from Spain in 1899, and then the Japanese took them in 1914 and held them under a harsh administration until the United States came in 1944. During that invasion, the island was torn apart. Many Saipanese were killed, caught between Japanese and Americans, and others killed themselves because the Japanese had convinced them the Americans would torture and maim them if they surrendered. After such experiences, you can't wonder why most of the Saipanese are not willing to become involved in something that is not really their business."

"Are you convinced they are telling the truth?"

"Yes, Fred, I am; for several reasons. They will not lie to their Monsignor; their faith in their religion is too strong. Then, nothing has been paid to them. Also, these simple people living in different villages couldn't concoct a story like this. If it were fabrication, there would be great elaborations and some serious discrepancies. No, they tell the same story; they're telling the truth."

"But what about these names, Guerrero, Sablan, Camacho, and the rest? Wouldn't families stick together on a story?"

"A family sharing a house might, or if they lived next to each other, but not spread out through different villages. There is similarity in names because of the small population, but some of these people don't see each other for months or years."

From many of the Saipanese questioned, we had heard one name repeatedly mentioned. If we wanted answers about things that happened during Japanese times, it was suggested we see a man I shall call Francisco Galvan in this account. Most of the natives seemed to be afraid of him, and Monsignor believed there was good reason for their fear. Galvan had worked with the Japanese police before and during the war. His responsibility had been to keep the rest of the natives in line and his methods hadn't been gentle. Francisco lived in a small house near the edge of Chalan Kanoa and his privacy was closely observed. Twice we stopped by to violate that privacy, but the word had evidently reached Galvan that Monsignor and the Fathers wanted to see him about something that happened before the war and he absented himself in a hurry; the second time, we saw him running out the back door. On our next visit, Father Sylvan stationed himself at the rear exit and Francisco ran right into the Father's chest. Father Sylvan is six feet, three inches tall and weighs 240 pounds. Mr. Galvan stopped.

His encounter with the Father did not make him verbose. He sat, sullenly shook his head as answer to every question, and glowered at me. Francisco, in his mid-to-late fifties, is a tough, bitter, hatred-filled man who looks his reputation. We got no information from Galvan that evening, but I met him again, more than once, in frightening circumstances.

6

Had Amelia and Fred flown their Lockheed to Saipan? That one bothered me, and there was no sure answer in the natives' testimony. All it established was that a man and woman, matching the descriptions of Noonan and Earhart, supposedly American fliers and spies, had been on Saipan sometime during the latter part of 1937. Some of the witnesses felt the pair had come by air and mentioned a plane; others had seen the man and woman at the harbor or in Garapan and did not know how they had reached the island. Those who remembered a plane could not clearly describe it or tell if it had been damaged.

From some of the older natives, I learned the Japanese had begun construction of their naval seaplane base at Tanapag Harbor in 1929 or 1930. By the mid-1930s, there were regular flights, both civilian and military, from Japan and other islands of the Mandate. No one could recall, though, if Aslito Field, the Japanese fighter-bomber base at the south end of Saipan, had been operational at any time during 1937. It was under construction then, but most felt it had not been ready to receive aircraft until a year or two later.

If that was true and if AE and Fred had flown the Electra to Saipan, they would have had no choice but to try to land in the sheltered harbor area or along a beach. Further to limit the possibilities, there are almost no beaches along the eastern shore of the island and those of the western shore are narrow and inclined; only the protected harbor would have remained, and with seaplanes at rest in Tanapag and rescue nearly certain, they might have chosen it.

What of the Japanese? Would they have salvaged the plane, or kept the matter quiet as possible, leaving the Lockheed where it had gone down?

I decided to check the bottom of the harbor. It was a long-shot, but after traveling six thousand miles, it seemed foolish not to have a look. I wonder now if the investigation might not have been shortened had I *been* foolish.

Father Sylvan arranged for the help of two native divers, Gregorio Magofna and Antonio Taitano. Both had been fishing and shelling around the island for years and knew most of what lay on the bottom of Tanapag. I showed them several pictures of AE's plane and asked them if they knew of the wreckage of anything that resembled it. They clucked and consulted for several minutes and then replied through Father Sylvan that they knew the locations of two two-motor aircraft. One was way out in the harbor near Maniagawa Island, a small strip of sand a hundred yards wide and long near the entrance to Tanapag; the other was about half a mile from what had been the ramps of the Japanese seaplane base.

"How old is the wreckage?" I asked.

"One very old. Other not so old," was their answer. Both locations sounded likely.

Maximo went with the divers the first day while I questioned more of the natives with Father Arnold. That evening Max and the boys returned to shore with a hundred pounds or more of the most vile-smelling wreckage imaginable. It was covered with greenish slime and growths of coral, completely unrecognizable.

"Where did this come from?" I asked.

"The area nearest the seaplane base," Max answered. "They had quite a time getting it to the surface."

I picked up a hammer and pounded until a piece of coral as

big as a doubled fist broke loose, revealing a surface of the equipment. It appeared to be a starter mechanism, but identification was impossible; salt water had consumed the marking tag and gouged into the metal beneath. One oddity appeared, though; several parts were wired together. Somewhere I had read that in the early days of aviation before the advent of shakeproof nuts, parts were wired to prevent loosening from the vibration of flight. Max and the boys had come up with aircraft gear; what vintage, anyone's guess. The next day I decided to take a look at the bottom of the harbor.

We made our way in a fair-sized outboard down a narrow channel from Tanapag Village, staying near the shore and well within the reef, until the coral fell steeply away and we reached deep water. The harbor was perfect for diving, calm on the surface with the bottom visible down to thirty or forty feet. In that part of the Pacific, the color of the water changes every few minutes as huge banks of clouds hurry across the sky, a giant kaleidoscope of grays, blues, and greens. In the center of the harbor the shattered superstructure of the *Kieyo Maru*, a Japanese supply ship sunk during the invasion, protrudes above the surface, a rotting, rusting memory of the vicious battle fought in 1944.

We churned steadily toward Maniagawa Island, the sandy apostrophe which marks one of the entrances to Tanapag, and at a point about five hundred yards from the island, Magofna fitted his face mask and slipped over the side. He began swimming in great circles, face down, scanning the bottom. Suddenly he stopped, came upright in the water and signaled he had found one of the planes. I borrowed Taitano's face mask and went over the side too. It's another world, the bottom of Tanapag Harbor. Every conceivable type of wreckage lies strewn in chaotic patterns across the sand and coral; jeeps, tanks, unexploded ammunition, landing craft, rolls of wire, all in varying states of decomposition. The aircraft was not in bad shape. Resting in sand, it had not been chewed up as much as the wreckage caught in coral. Whether it was Japanese or American, I could not tell, and it didn't matter. It was a military plane; the machine guns were still visible. Magofna and I climbed into the boat and we headed for the area outside of what had been the Japanese seaplane ramps.

The second pile of wreckage bore no resemblance to an aircraft. It was a twisted, tangled mass of junk grown over and under by coral. One mound appeared to be a motor but the prop was missing. Another heap could have represented a fuselage and tail section. It was all down in thirty to thirty-five feet of water and pulling bits of it loose proved a miserable, demanding task. I could stay down only thirty to forty-five seconds, but Magofna and Taitano would disappear for two minutes or more. They were such opposite types that it was amusing to watch them compete. Gregorio is a big, barrel-chested Carolinian in his late-twenties with a handshake that crushes. Antonio Taitano is a thin, almost emaciated Chamorran, probably over forty, and given to chewing betel nut; his smiles are all pink and orange. Both seemed intent on bringing up the most wreckage, and it was a fairly even match.

I pulled free a piece that could have been fuselage. It looked like, and was light enough to be, aluminum, but the moment I got to the surface it turned black and began to disintegrate. On my fifth or sixth dive (there had been plenty of rest between each one) I saw something that seemed to make the water turn cold. A gray fish about my size swam by within twenty-five feet of the wreckage. Something told me I had just seen a shark. I had never seen one before, but I have an excellent memory for pictures. My body resembled a Polaris Missile emerging from Tanapag Harbor. I scrambled into the boat, already occupied by Antonio and Maximo, and began shouting for Magofna to get aboard. Gregorio swam over slowly and leisurely swung over the side as I tugged and hauled at him.

"They want to know what is bothering you," said Max.

"Tell them I'm sure I just saw a shark."

Max translated, then said, "They want to know the color."

"Tell them it was gray."

When Maximo had translated, there was some laughter and then some chatter.

"They say not to worry about the gray shark; he won't bother, not inside the reef. But don't go outside the reef because the yellow one will get you."

When we got back to Chalan Kanoa, I scraped as much coral as I could from the wreckage, and on one chunk that appeared to be a generator, I found serial numbers: NK 17999. There was also a marking something like a clover leaf. They had been deeply stamped into the metal. At least we had something to check. That evening Commander Bridwell was throwing a party for me at the Officers' Bar, so I stopped by the Navy radio station and asked the operators on duty to send a message over to Guam requesting a cablegram be sent to Paul Mantz asking whether NK 17999 was a link to Amelia Earhart.

From the radio station I walked over to the party. Not too surprisingly, knowledge of my message had preceded me.

"What's NK 17999?" asked Bridwell with a smile.

"News items travel fast on Saipan," I smiled back. "NK-whatever is a serial number from some wreckage we found in the harbor. I'm trying to find out from a man who was a technical adviser for Earhart's flight whether it means anything."

Interesting things happened that evening. I had been a little late getting to the party and a few people had extra drinks in my absence. By the time we sat down to dinner, things were mellow on Saipan. The wife of one of the officers was in an especially pleasant mood. She bubbled about the number of languages spoken on the island.

"It's really difficult to be linguistic on Saipan. It was bad enough when we only had to speak Spanish, German, Japanese, and Chamorran, but now we have to learn to speak some Chinese!"

There ensued one of those silences we've all experienced, fraught with consternation and recrimination. I pretended not to have heard. From the corner of my eye, as I calmly brought soup spoon to lips, I saw the officer give his wife a look that would solve the population problem for generations. As abruptly as the silence had come, it departed on waves of double-time conversation, desperately meant to fill that tell-tale moment of truth.

The word "Chinese" was not entirely new to me on Saipan. I had heard it several times from natives we had questioned. They had talked of having seen Chinese soldiers in the jungle on the north end and east side of the island, the areas I had been told I could not visit. Other natives had seen Chinese being transported by bus from a landing field on Saipan's east coast. The letters NTTU had been frequently voiced, and finally I heard from someone what they meant: Naval Technical Training Units. I had also seen a number of Americans, not a part of the Naval Administration group, shopping in the Navy Commissary. Those people had to be living in my no-man's-land on the island. Then, too, I had climbed to the top of Mt. Tapotchau one afternoon to get a full view of the island, and Commander Bridwell had been extremely displeased. I had been able to see nothing but jungle; spying on NTTU was not the purpose of the climb, but I was suspect nonetheless. By the time I heard the word "Chinese" at the Officers' Bar, I had already been fairly well briefed, but it was useful to have another confirmation.

After dinner I told the officers and their wives what we had found out in two weeks about the possibility of Amelia Earhart's and Fred Noonan's having been on Saipan. A number of them were enthusiastic after I finished speaking and gathered around me to discuss it further. Some of them, I think, were actually beginning to believe that Amelia and Fred really were my reasons for coming to the island.

Roy Hippe, Bridwell's Executive Officer, drew me aside a few minutes later. I liked Hippe. He was a gentleman.

"Fred," he began, "I know it's been a little tough since you've been out here, but don't blame us too much; we've got a job to do."

"I don't blame anyone, Roy, and it hasn't been that bad. I have the feeling that some of the Saipanese have been told not to say anything to me. I suppose you know what the reasons are, but I don't blame anyone."

"I can't comment on that," Hippe continued, "but I will say this much. I believe you're honest and I believe you're out here for what you say you are. And, what's more, I believe you're on the right track."

"Thank you."

"No thanks due. There is one bit of help I can give you. Twenty-two tons of captured Japanese records were taken off this island by the Navy in 1944 and '45. As far as I know, most of them have never been microfilmed or even interpreted. If Earhart and Noonan were on this island—and I think there's a good chance they were—you should find some mention of them in those records. The Japanese were great at keeping records."

"Where do you think those records are now?"

"Probably in the States. Try looking around San Francisco for a starter."

The next day I finished photographing the witnesses on still and motion picture film, and was faced with a decision. Did we have enough testimony to send the "Big Hatchet" message? I decided we did and that I would take some of the aircraft wreckage back to San Francisco for appraisal.

José Matsumoto drove me up to the Navy radio station where I left the cryptic text to be cabled from Guam. José then dropped me at the mission house so I might thank and say goodbye to Monsignor and the Fathers. Less than ten minutes later Commander Bridwell's vehicle pulled up in a cloud of coral dust.

He was to the point: "Mr. Goerner, what does 'Big Hatchet Ready to Fall' mean?"

"It's just a code, Commander."

"That fact has already reached me."

"It alerts KCBS and the rest of our CBS people and the *Times.*"

"Alerts them to what?"

"That Max and I are coming back with some information."

"I hate to pin you down like this, Mr. Goerner, but I have to know what information you're talking about."

"Pin me down? Am I not free to send a cablegram from Saipan?"

"Under normal circumstances, yes, but you are asking to use Naval radio facilities to send a code."

"Commander Bridwell, I didn't really intend to give you a bad time. It sticks a bit in my throat, but I'll tell you what the phrase means. It communicates that we have come up with some information to substantiate the original story told by Mrs. Akiyama. That's all, nothing more."

Bridwell walked away a few feet and turned back.

"All right, Fred, I'll take your word for it. The cablegram will go out tonight. I'll see you off at the plane tomorrow."

In a way, I felt sorry for Commander Bridwell, having to

protect whatever was happening in the other parts of the island. Obviously the Naval Administration Unit was a front. For what exactly, I couldn't guess.

Commander York was waiting for Max and me when we arrived at Guam the next day, and he hustled us right to the admiral's office.

"Understand you've come up with some wreckage," Admiral Wendt began. "Would you mind if a couple of our aviation machinists looked at the gear?"

"No, sir, I think that would be fine," I replied. "I certainly don't want to pay the air-freight costs to the States if it doesn't represent the Earhart plane."

"Both of these men have been in Naval Aviation for about twenty-five years, so they should be able to figure out what you've got."

Admiral Wendt seemed genuinely interested in what we had learned on Saipan, so I gave him all the details while his experts went to work. I also tried to make it clear that the Earhart story and only the Earhart story had brought me to Saipan and anything else I had learned on the island would remain unpublicized.

"What did you learn?" he asked.

"Certainly not enough to break a story," I said honestly. He listened as I discussed the weighted word "Chinese," and then he appeared satisfied.

About an hour later, the two aviation machinists reported to the admiral. What they said was a surprise to both of us. There was one part of the wreckage that stood a good chance of being identified and possibly could have come from Amelia's plane. It was a generator, a heavy-duty 50-ampere generator, which appeared to be of U.S. or British manufacture, not Japanese, and it was too heavy to have been carried on a military plane. It was the type of generator that could have been used by a Lockheed Electra 10-E. It was either a Leese-Nevil or a Bendix.

"Looks as if you may have something," said Admiral Wendt.

I felt optimistic as Max and I left for San Francisco, and a maelstrom.

7

"Big Hatchet Ready to Fall" had done its work. Since the cablegram, imaginations at the San Mateo *Times* and KCBS had been soaring. Everything but a band was at San Francisco Airport to meet Max and me as we wearily climbed off the plane. Cameras clicked and eager hands took our luggage.

"We've got a press conference scheduled tomorrow," said someone from the *Times*.

"But it's going to be held at KCBS," a representative from my station retorted.

"Right. But we've got to keep this thing quiet until then," cautioned another from the rear.

Somebody finally got around to asking us what we had brought back from Saipan.

"Tape-recorded testimony from thirteen natives which supports Mrs. Akiyama's story," I replied (I wish now I had stopped right there), "and a couple of cartons of aircraft wreckage out of the harbor at Saipan."

The words "aircraft wreckage" were magic. They could not

wait to get at it, and there was great discussion as to whose car was going to carry it into the city.

The following day was July 1, 1960, by coincidence the twenty-third anniversary of Earhart and Noonan's last flight, and the all-media news conference was held in Studio E at KCBS in the Sheraton-Palace Hotel in San Francisco. If there had ever been any doubt in my mind as to how well Amelia and Fred were remembered, that conference settled it. If they had disappeared the week before, the reaction couldn't have been greater. The wire services, major magazines, newspapers, radio and television stations were all represented. Pieces of the wreckage, including the generator, had been placed on a long table, and translations of the testimony prepared.

I had attended a number of news conferences as a reporter, but never had I been the center of one; chaos best describes it. Everyone wants your attention for his deadline. After an opening statement I discussed the testimony and attempted to stress the care that had been taken in gathering it. The reporters were impressed by the translations, but even more impressed with the wreckage on the table. That was understandable; it was something one could touch and, more important, photograph.

I was in the middle of trying to make the point that Admiral Wendt's aviation technicians had indicated only that it was *possible* the generator could have come from Amelia's plane, not that it was positive, when Paul Mantz arrived from Santa Ana. A veteran of many such conferences, Paul knew how to handle the situation. To the reporters, here was authority—the technical adviser for Earhart's final flight. If the wreckage came from her plane, he should be able to recognize it.

"Hi, Fred, my boy," Mantz greeted. "Got your cablegram about that generator number. Sorry I couldn't get back to you while you were still on the island, but I've got filing cabinets full of records about AE and I haven't been able to find the exact numbers yet."

"What numbers are those, Mr. Mantz?" a reporter asked.

"That N-K-One-Seven-Niner-Niner-Niner on the generator," Paul replied, in a flier's parlance he enjoyed using.

"What about that generator?" asked several reporters in unison.

A hush pervaded the room as Mantz walked over to the table and scrutinized the wreckage. He turned the generator over, lifted it, set it down, took a small magnifying glass from his pocket, bent over and began to peer through the glass at the coral-encrusted surface.

"There it is," he murmured, "N-K-One-Seven-Niner-Niner-Niner."

"What do you think, Mr. Mantz?" asked a photographer as he struggled for position to snap the expression on the technical adviser's face.

Paul straightened up, very slowly, turned to the assembled press and enunciated, "Well . . . it looks exactly like the generator I put aboard AE's plane."

Reporters ran to telephones, photographers pleaded with Mantz to "Hold the generator up" . . . "Do that bit with the magnifying glass again" . . . "Get over by Goerner for a two-shot . . ."

We were committed, and in the way I had feared. The entire focus had gone to the generator. The testimony of the Saipanese was all but forgotten in the excitement of identifying the wreckage. Mantz explained that he couldn't be sure the Saipan find was really Amelia's until he found her records. He was going to fly right down to Santa Ana and continue looking. Amelia had, according to Mantz, two Bendix-Eclipse, 50-ampere, heavy-duty generators aboard the Electra; one was driven by one of the engines, the other had been wind-driven.

I didn't see all the newspapers in the country, but the several hundred clippings I did peruse carried the story front page with headlines: SAIPAN GENERATOR BELIEVED EARHART'S . . . GENERATOR CLUE TO MISSING AVIATRIX . . . EARHART'S GENERATOR BELIEVED FOUND. Paul and his magnifying glass had been a smash.

The following Monday I took the now famous generator to Santa Ana and Mantz's Air Service mechanics spent the day breaking it down piece by piece. It wasn't an easy job; the salt water and coral had chewed through the casing in places and the interior was badly fouled too. They finally got the bearings free, and there were more number and letter combinations: 6303 Z, 17, and NTN. One of the mechanics went to the stock room and brought out an old Bendix-Eclipse, 50-ampere generator and began to match the parts with the one from Saipan. Each part, to the last nut and bolt, matched perfectly. Mantz and I then took both generators to the West Coast representative of Bendix at Burbank Airport. He concurred; the Saipan generator appeared to be a Bendix E-5. He would send the number and letter combinations to the home office, Teterboro, New Jersey, for identification.

The next day, July 5, 1960, another story about Amelia Earhart broke across the country. Captain Paul L. Briand, Jr., assistant professor of English at the Air Force Academy in Colorado, announced in Los Angeles that two Air Force friends of his, the aforementioned Captain Joseph Gervais and Captain Robert Dinger of Naha Air Force Base, Okinawa, had in their possession photographic evidence and affidavits from seventy-two eyewitnesses to the capture and execution of Miss Earhart and Noonan. In addition, the press reported, Briand had stated the two captains had found "the original and only burial site of Amelia Earhart and Fred Noonan—on Saipan."

That afternoon I met Captain Briand. He and his wife had been vacationing in Los Angeles and had stopped by Santa Ana to see Paul Mantz to discuss Briand's revelation.

"Captain Briand," I asked, "where did Gervais and Dinger find those seventy-two witnesses?"

"A number of places," returned Briand.

"Saipan?"

"Yes, Saipan."

"Captain, are you sure? I don't mean to contradict you, but Admiral Wendt, the Commandant of the Marianas Sea Frontier, recently told me he had not permitted Dinger and Gervais to visit Saipan."

"They probably went anyway."

"Not to Saipan, Captain Briand. The island is under tight security. Without clearance, strangers on Saipan would be in for big trouble."

Briand seemed confident the information he had was correct, and I wasn't disposed to argue. It was only two days later, though, that the roof fell in on the captains. Dinger and Gervais had been summoned to Fuchu Air Base in Japan to appear before a panel of U.S. 5th Air Force senior officers and present their information regarding Amelia Earhart. Mantz, Briand, and I were at Santa Ana Airport when I received a call from Ken Dunham of KCBS News in San Francisco. He had the first wire service release from Japan on the conference. I relayed the information to Briand and Mantz.

"The U. S. Air Force today described as incomplete and inconclusive information which two Air Force officers contend proves the Japanese executed Amelia Earhart and her navigator on Saipan in 1937. Gervais and Dinger said neither had actually visited Saipan but that Gervais assembled most of their evidence during a recent trip to Guam. Gervais conceded that photographs he possessed were not really of Miss Earhart's execution. He also said the seventy-two affidavits he held—described earlier as sworn statements by eyewitnesses to Miss Earhart's execution —did not actually describe any executions. They were merely seventy-two names of people living today on Saipan and Guam who have information on the subject. The Air Force refused to divulge the complete story told by Captain Gervais, but one member of the investigating body called the story 'a bunch of garbage,' and the hearing was terminated pending word from Washington."

The last line must have been a crusher for Captain Briand. I have not seen him since that moment, although I've spoken with him by telephone several times. I felt sorry for him that day, but he might have been cheered a bit had he heard the addition to the report from Japan. "Nevertheless most of the interview with the two captains was kept secret and the Air Force clamped a security classification on the claims of Gervais and Dinger."

I should have started feeling sorry for myself; a setback was on its way. Mantz and I returned to San Francisco for another news conference. Paul had decided that now he could be more definite about the generator. At the conference he stated to the attending newsmen: "I'll give a thousand dollars to anyone who can prove the generator found at Saipan is not identical to the one I installed aboard AE's plane. It matches perfectly in every respect."

As we walked out of the conference, KCBS News Director,

Don Mozley, handed me a bulletin that had just moved on the wires from New York City:

THE BENDIX AVIATION CORPORATION SAYS A GENERATOR FOUND NEAR SAIPAN ISLAND DID NOT COME FROM THE PLANE IN WHICH AMELIA EARHART DISAPPEARED IN 1937. A BENDIX SPOKESMAN SAYS A BEARING IN THE GENERATOR THAT WAS FOUND NEAR THE PACIFIC ISLAND WAS TRACED TO THE TOYO BEARING FIRM IN OSAKA, JAPAN.

The Bendix claim was disputed by Paul, and his reply was dutifully carried by both AP and UPI, but the damage had been done. All of the evidence had become symbolized by the generator, and the testimony of the thirteen Saipanese was discarded along with the "wreckage." Mantz said he would fly to New York "with the generator in my little hot hand" for study at the Bendix plant.

He never made the flight, but KCBS did ship the generator, a starter motor, and several other pieces of the gear to Bendix for analysis. It was August 25, 1960, before we got the report. Bendix was satisfied beyond all doubt that the generator we had found was an almost exact copy of their generator, but there were enough discrepancies of detail to prove that it had not been manufactured by Bendix. There was an absence of raised cast-in numbers, and the presence of certain components such as brushes, bearings and condensers that were completely foreign to anything Bendix might have used. Any remaining element of doubt was eliminated by the presence of metric and unidentifiable screw threads. Bendix had never used metric threads in any of its manufacturing operations.

On October 3, 1960, we received the report on the starter motor; it was the same as for the generator. Two lines in both reports started me off on another trail. The bearings are definitely of Japanese origin. This, of course, does not preclude the fact that during overhaul bearings can be changed.

I remembered that Amelia had written in her notes which were mailed home before the final take-off from Lae, New Guinea, that she had been amazed to find a sister-ship to her own Lockheed Electra 10-E in service with the Guinea Airways Company at Lae. Amelia had some repairs made on the plane there. Was it possible the Lockheed's starter motor and generator had been overhauled or replaced at Lae? There must have been spare parts for the Guinea Airways' 10-E. Amelia had also had work done at Kurachi, India, and at Bandoeng and several other stops. Perhaps the gear had been exchanged at one of those points.

That possibility dimmed, too, when I learned that Japan's Nippon Kawanishi Company began construction early in 1936 of large flying boats to service their South Pacific islands. They had used Pratt & Whitney engines as their models. Also, in 1936 and '37, Nakajima Kotobuki had started construction of naval planes. The Kotobuki engines were almost exact copies of the U. S. Pratt & Whitney Wasp 550 horsepower engines, the type of engines carried by the Lockheed Electra 10-E. It now seemed certain where N-K-One-Seven-Niner-Niner-Niner had come from.

In the January 1961 issue of the Bendix Corporation's official magazine, *Flight Control*, was a note of reservation. The final report on the study was printed on page six and the last paragraph stated, "Upon completing the evaluation, it is advised that while analysis proved beyond all doubt that the parts were not of Bendix manufacture, the Earhart trail left indications that the Bendix generator and starter could have been replaced before the ill-fated flight began. Eclipse-Pioneer's disclaim to the parts therefore does not rule out the possibility that the salvage was the Earhart plane."

The plethora of reports in 1960 about Amelia Earhart and Frederick Noonan was not overlooked in Japan. The reaction in the Japanese press was strong. Some editorials even hinted that the whole issue had been raised to embarrass Japan because President Eisenhower's proposed trip to Tokyo had been aborted due to the student riots, or because James Hagerty, the President's press secretary who had preceded Mr. Eisenhower to Tokyo, had been caught in the conflict.

The accusations of the two U. S. Air Force officers, Gervais and Dinger, were the most distasteful to the Japanese. In Tokyo, a former Imperial Navy captain, Zenshiro Hoshina, denied vehemently that any executions of Americans had taken place. Hoshina, according to his own billing, had been in an unenviable position in 1937. He was chief of the section of the Naval Affairs Bureau handling executions.

"I absolutely deny it," he told the press. "No such execution could have taken place without my knowledge and approval."

There were many denials from the United States as well as Japan. The U. S. Department of State indicated that it had made a full inquiry into the matter and had even requested Japan to make a search of extant records. The results, according to the State Department, had all been negative. Both governments probably believed in 1960 that the last had been heard of Amelia Earhart and Frederick Noonan; at least some individuals must have hoped that obscurity would finally cloak the two fliers whose demise so plagued their consciences. Those hopes did not mature.

When a story breaks as widely as the one of July 1, 1960, it touches the lives of millions of people. Memories awaken; the attic of the past is sorted; bits of information, ideas, attitudes, long-endured feelings of guilt, all emerge and are sometimes drawn to a central point. I became such a point.

One example of the phenomenon involves the former soldier from Connecticut.

8

Thomas E. Devine lives in West Haven, Connecticut, and he believes that he was shown the gravesite of Earhart and Noonan. His first letter to me arrived August 15, 1960; this is the story he told at that time.

In 1945, Devine was a technical sergeant with the 244th Army Postal Unit on Saipan. One day he and a couple of friends went for a swim at a beach near what had been the Japanese city of Garapan; later they took a walk around the area and arrived at a cemetery. As they stood looking at the graves, a native woman who lived nearby began to try to tell them something. A Japanese-American interpreter was summoned, and with the interpreter's help they learned the woman was trying to show them where two whites, a man and woman, were buried. Devine had asked, through the interpreter, when and from where the two had come. "They came from the sky a long time ago," was the woman's reply. The native had then led them a short distance from the graveyard and pointed to a grass-covered spot that appeared to have received care at some time, but the location was not marked in any way. When asked about what hap-

pened to the white people, the woman replied in words punctuated by her by striking the interpreter several times. The
shaken Nisei interpreter said the woman blamed him and his
people for killing the fliers and burying them there.

Devine closed by saying he had never given Amelia Earhart
and Fred Noonan a thought at the time. He had believed, along
with most of the world, that they had perished in the ocean near
Howland Island thousands of miles away.

I answered Mr. Devine's letter and asked for more details.

His reply indicated he had learned through the interpreter
that the native woman had lived in the same area before the
invasion; therefore, he believed she might have been witness to
the burial. He was sure he could find the location again because
of nine photos he had of the general area and the fact the native
woman appeared in one of the pictures.

There was no thought in my mind in 1960 of another expedition to Saipan, so I suggested Mr. Devine give his photos and
information to the Navy for evaluation. He did, but received no
satisfaction; in fact it was almost three years before he learned
what the Navy had done with his material. Tom Devine, though,
was to play an interesting if frustrating role in our investigation
during those three years.

After the 1960 story, there were plenty of disbelievers. One of
the strongest dissenting voices belonged to Robert M. Stanley,
president of the Stanley Aviation Corporation, Denver, Colorado.
Stanley had been an aviation cadet aboard the U.S.S. *Lexington*
in 1937, and had been assigned duty formulating the plans for
the Earhart search. He decried any possibility that the flight had
ended at Saipan, and stated publicly that there wasn't the
slightest doubt in his mind that Amelia and Fred had gone
down within 150 miles of Howland. His belief he said was based
on the plane's cruising speed, fuel capacity, the known wind
conditions at the time, and other evidence in his possession
which proved the Howland Island contention. In an Associated
Press release, Stanley added, "The perversity of the fair sex led
Miss Earhart to leave a radio coil behind on New Guinea. The
coil would have permitted her to receive homing signals from
the Coast Guard ship *Itasca*, which was stationed at Howland."

Robert Stanley sent me a complete copy of the U.S.S. *Lexing-*

ton's report on the Earhart search. What I found after several weeks' study did not support Stanley's theory; it deepened the mystery and gave rise to a number of embarrassing questions that should have been asked of both the Navy and Coast Guard in 1937.

The *Lexington* had been in the Santa Barbara, California, harbor at the time of the disappearance, readying itself for Fourth of July civilian visitors. On the night of July 3 the order came from Washington for the *"Lex"* to weigh anchor and proceed to the Howland Island area to search for the missing fliers. En route the carrier was joined by three destroyers, the *Drayton, Lamson,* and *Cushing.* The battleship *Colorado* had already been dispatched from Pearl Harbor to assist with the search. At approximately 7:00 A.M. the morning of July 13, eleven days after AE and Fred vanished, sixty planes were launched from the *Lexington* to search both east and west of Howland Island. From the morning of the thirteenth to the afternoon of July 18, the carrier planes covered 151,556 square miles of South Pacific ocean. In addition, the *Colorado Swan,* which had been stationed halfway between Honolulu and Howland, and *Itasca* searched both the Phoenix and Gilbert Island groups. The effort was completely fruitless.

The *Lexington* had based its entire search on the following information which appears in the final report.

1. At 10:30 A.M. 2 July, Amelia Earhart took off from Lae, New Guinea, for Howland Island, distance 2556 miles, and gave her estimated time of flight as 18 hours. She was accompanied by Captain Noonan, who had been navigating surface craft and aircraft for the past twenty years, and had the reputation of being an excellent navigator.

2. The plane was in communication with Coast Guard cutter *Itasca* from 1418 GCT until 2025 GCT 2 July. It is therefore known to have been in the air at least twenty hours and twenty-five minutes.

3. The only complete position report from the plane stated that at 0720 GCT it was in latitude 4 degrees 33 minutes South, longitude 159 degrees 06 minutes East. This point is about 785 miles from Lae, and indicates that the plane was on course making a ground speed of 111 knots during this part of the

flight. 111×20.4 (total time) equals 2264 nautical miles. This exceeds the distance to Howland Island, 2201 nautical miles.

4. The following incomplete reports were received at times indicated:

0615 Howland Time (1745 GCT) (15 minutes before estimated time of arrival) Earhart plane reported "200 miles out and no landfall."

0646 Howland Time (1816 GCT) Earhart reported "Approximately 100 miles from *Itasca*. Position doubtful."

0742 Howland Time (1912 GCT) Earhart reported "30 minutes gas remaining no landfall, position doubtful."

0758 Howland Time (1928 GCT) Earhart reported "Circling trying to pick up island." (At this time signals were received with greatest strength from plane by *Itasca*.)

0843 Howland Time (2013 GCT) Earhart reported "Line of position 157 degrees—337 degrees."

0855 Howland Time (2025 GCT) Earhart reported "Heading north and south", and gave same position line as before. (This was the last message received from the plane.)

ASSUMPTIONS

1. That Captain Noonan navigated the plane as close as possible to the great circle course between Lae and Howland Island.

2. That he was approximately on a line passing through Howland in direction 157 degrees—337 degrees at 0843 and at 0855 (Howland time).

3. That he was not certain which side of the island he was on, since the last message stated they were running north and south.

4. That he was closest to Howland Island at 0758 (based on strength of radio signals received by *Itasca*), and that he may have been on any course at that time.

5. That 57 minutes later the fuel gave out and the plane was forced to land.

6. That during those 57 minutes the plane did not maintain course and speed since last message reported heading north and south trying to pick up the island, and 0800 message reported circling trying to pick up island.

7. That the plane landed shortly after 0855, on the water

within 120 miles from Howland Island, actual position unknown, but approximately on a line running through Howland Island in a direction 157 degrees–337 degrees.

OTHER POSSIBILITIES

1. That the plane may have landed well to the north of its intended course. This is substantiated by several radio messages supposed to have been sent out by the plane. One message stated "281 North"; another "225 NNW." Broadcast experiment of KGMB, Honolulu, indicated that the plane was north of Howland and on the water.

2. That the plane may be well to the south of Howland. This is substantiated by dubious radio bearings supposed to have been taken on the plane two or three days after it landed.

3. That the plane continued well to the eastward of Howland. This is contradicted by the bearing line reported at 0843 and 0855 as being 157 degrees–337 degrees. It is also contradicted by the fact that headwinds greater than anticipated existed over the route.

4. That the plane landed far to the westward of Howland. This does not agree with the bearing line sent from the plane. The one ground speed check available also indicates that the plane would arrive in the immediate vicinity of Howland Island at 1928 GCT, at which time *Itasca* reported strength of radio signals to be greatest.

5. Of these four possibilities, it appears that the first two are the only possible ones and that the plane landed well south or well north of Howland. The *Colorado, Itasca,* and *Swan* are investigating the area to the south, and it need not be considered by the *Lexington* group.

6. The area well to the north must be considered since it has not yet been thoroughly searched. Radio signals have been received purported to be from the plane which stated that the plane was north rather than south.

DECISION

That this force will search the vicinity of Howland Island to a distance of 120 miles, using all available aircraft on the first day. Thereafter, extending the search to the westward up to and including the Gilbert Islands. Then should this search be negative, proceed to the point 290 miles north of Howland Island and conduct such search as remaining fuel will permit.

In another part of the *Lexington's* report, I found these comments:

> The information actually available indicated that the plane arrived in the vicinity of Howland Island at about eight o'clock in the morning of 2 July. During the night run the navigator should have been able to check his position accurately and frequently by star sights, and it must be assumed that this was done, and that the navigator knew the position of his plane and the ground speed it had been making good during the night. Information available on the weather conditions do not indicate that any radical change in direction or force of the wind occurred at Howland Island during the two-and-one-half-hours preceding eight o'clock. At 0615 the plane reported that they were 200 miles out; one hour and forty-five minutes later they circled and attempted to pick up the island. This time agrees very well with the time it would take the plane to cover 200 miles at 111 knots, and it also checked with the time at which the *Itasca* reported hearing plane's radio at the greatest strength. All of the above indicates that the plane's 0615 position was reasonably accurate. This being the case, it is not reasonable to suppose that the plane was more than 60 miles off its course one hour and forty-five minutes later. Having arrived at the navigator's position of the island the plane maneuvered to make a landfall, circling first, and then running north and south indicating that they were fairly sure of their longitude. With the gasoline supply practically exhausted (½ hours gas supply remaining was reported at 0745) it is not likely the plane ventured more than 40 miles from the navigator's best position. Assuming that the gasoline gave out when the plane was at the end of one of these runs farthest from the island, the distance from Howland would be only 100 miles.

I could already see numerous contradictions in the "assumptions" of Cadet Robert Stanley and Captain Leigh Noyes, the commanding officer of the *Lexington*, but the discrepancies became ever more obvious when the report was compared with the official dispatches of the Coast Guard ship *Itasca*. There were even contradictions within that log. On July 2, 1937, immediately after the disappearance, a report supposedly containing the messages received from Amelia during the course of the flight was radioed from the *Itasca* to Coast Guard Headquarters in San Francisco and 12th Naval District Headquarters, Hawaii.

Earhart contact 0742 reported one half hour fuel and no landfall. Position doubtful. Contact 0646 reported approx one hundred miles from *Itasca* but no relative bearing. 0843 reported line of position 157 dash 337 but no reference point. Presume Howland. Estimate 1200 for maximum time aloft and if nonarrival by that time will commence search northwest quadrant from Howland as most probable area. Sea smooth ceiling unlimited. Understand she will float for limited time.

Three days later, July 5, 1937, the *Itasca* radioed another group of messages which also had been received from Amelia and Fred during the flight. Not only had the number of messages been expanded but the content of those previously forwarded had been corrected and the time and meaning altered. This dispatch was sent only to the Coast Guard Division, San Francisco; the Navy at Pearl Harbor was excluded.

Following text messages received by *Itasca* from Earhart morning of 2 July. Forwarded for Headquarters release to Associated and other presses. All messages voice on 3105 kilocycles. Any press release should clearly indicate that *Itasca* was at Howland as homing vessel only and that this with weather was sole radio duty requested by Earhart. Ship met all Earhart requests with exception inability to secure emergency radio bearing on 3105 kilocycles due brief Earhart transmissions and use voice. With exception 0803 message no *Itasca* message or request acknowledged by Earhart. Earhart apparently never received *Itasca* requests transmit on 500 kilocycles in order *Itasca* cut her in with ship direction finder. 0245 Recognized Earhart Voice message not clear except QUOTE Cloudy Weather Cloudy UNQUOTE 0345 QUOTE *Itasca* from Earhart. *Itasca* broadcast on 3105 kilocycles on hour and half hour—repeat—broadcast on 3105 kilocycles on hour and half-hour. Overcast. UNQUOTE 0453 Heard Earhart voice signals unreadable with five listening. 0512 QUOTE Want bearings on 3105 kilocycles on hour. Will whistle in microphone. UNQUOTE 0515 QUOTE About 200 miles out. UNQUOTE

Whistles briefly in microphone. 0545 QUOTE Please take bearing on us and report in half hour. I will make noise in microphone. About 100 miles out. UNQUOTE 0730 QUOTE We must be on you but cannot see you but (SIC) gas is running low. Have been unable to reach you by radio. We are flying at 1,000 feet. UN-QUOTE 0757 QUOTE We are circling but cannot see island. Cannot hear you. Go ahead on 7500 kilocycles with long count either now or on schedule time on half hour. UNQUOTE 0803 QUOTE Earhart calling *Itasca*. We received your signals but unable to get minimum. Please take bearings on us and answer on 3105 kilocycles. UNQUOTE Earhart made long dashes for brief period but emergency high frequency direction finder could not cut her in on 3105 kilocycles. 0844 Earhart called *Itasca*. QUOTE We are on the line of position 157 dash 337. Will repeat this message on 6210 kilocycles. We are now running north and south. UNQUOTE Nothing further heard from Earhart on 6210 or other frequencies. High frequency direction finder on Howland was set up as an additional emergency caution without Earhart's request or knowledge. *Itasca* had it manned throughout night but never able secure bearings. *Itasca* ship direction finder manned at 0725 and Earhart repeatedly requested to transmit on 500 kilocycles to enable ship to cut her in. Communications monitored throughout by Lieutenant Commander Baker, Lieutenant Commander Kenner, Ensign Sutter, and Lieutenant Cooper U.S. Army Air Corps.

According to the *Itasca*'s second transmission to San Francisco, nine understandable messages had been received from Amelia instead of the three previously reported. The 0646 "100 miles out" message had been changed to an hour earlier 0545. The 0742 communication reporting "one-half-hour fuel and no landfall" had been altered to 0730 "but gas is running low."

The misinterpretation of the "gas" message was important. The *Lexington* had placed considerable emphasis on the assumption the plane had run out of fuel shortly after the last message, but the *Itasca*'s commanding officer, Warner K. Thompson, had estimated the Electra could remain aloft as late as 12:00 noon. Amelia, not receiving the signals of the *Itasca*, had begun to worry about the gas situation. In such a circumstance, she would have been perfectly justified in radioing "But gas is running low." Any flier, unsure of a plane's exact position in the middle of the Pacific Ocean, would consider three, four, or even five hours of fuel to be "running low on gas."

The *Lexington* evidently had been unaware of the 0245 and 0345 messages reporting the weather as "cloudy and overcast," otherwise the planners of the search would not have presumed that "during the night run, the navigator should have been able to check his position accurately and frequently by star sights . . . and that the navigator knew the position of his plane and the ground speed it had been making good during the night."

If it had been cloudy and overcast throughout the night, Noonan could have obtained no star sights. Amelia had not given a position report with the exception of the last 157–337 and it had no reference point. It was almost painfully obvious that Noonan did not know the position of the plane, and probably had not been able to determine the effect of head and cross winds on the craft.

The Navy also assumed the Electra had been making 111 knots, judging from the 0615 message reporting "200 miles out" and the incorrect 0758 "Circling trying to pick up island." It additionally assumed "the plane's 0615 position was reasonably correct."

The *Itasca* had changed 0615 to 0515 "About 200 miles out," and added the 0545 "About 100 miles out." Not only was 0615 incorrect as to time, the 0545 message indicated the plane had flown 100 miles in thirty minutes. Amelia and Fred were apparently making 200 miles per hour instead of the 111 knots estimated by the Navy. A strong tail wind was the only explanation I could think of at that time to account for the extra speed. The Lockheed Electra's power had been publicized as twin 550-horsepower Pratt & Whitney Junior Wasp engines, giving the plane a cruising speed between 150 and 165 mph. and a top speed between 200 and 210 mph. If she were trying to conserve gasoline, Amelia certainly would not have been flying at maximum speed. It was nearly three years before I found proof of the real reason for the additional speed.

The U. S. Navy spent an estimated four million dollars searching for AE and Fred in 1937, and based its entire effort on an incomplete, incorrect group of messages. The assumptions upon which the search had been predicated could not have been otherwise but badly drawn, considering the amount of misinformation and chance of studied interpretation.

Why had the Navy been unaware of the second, corrected group of messages relayed by the *Itasca?* Why had there been so many alterations in the messages? Why had the Navy and the Coast Guard had so little communication and cooperation? Why had the Navy not been able to see the strong possibility that Amelia and Fred had gone down a considerable distance from Howland Island?

The logs of the *Itasca* and *Lexington* produced many questions and few answers. Robert Stanley had undoubtedly done the best he could with the information made available to him in 1937, but there certainly was nothing in the *Lexington's* report which proved Earhart and Noonan had been lost within 150 miles of Howland. Stanley's contention that "The perversity of the fair sex led Miss Earhart to leave a radio coil behind on New Guinea," was not supported either; nowhere in the report was this point even suggested.

The study and comparison did fairly well settle one question in my mind; whether or not Amelia and Fred had flown the Electra to Saipan. It no longer seemed "possible if not probable." Considering the content of the messages received from the plane and the times they had been broadcast, there wasn't even a million-to-one chance the plane could have been in the vicinity of Saipan. As this fact emerged, however, another theory began to appear not only possible but probable. The last message from Amelia had said, "We are 157–337, running north and south." The reciprocal of a compass heading, "157–337" could represent a northwest direction from Howland Island; indeed, that this had been the final estimation of many aboard the *Itasca* was evidenced by the fact that the vessel began its search in the northwest quadrant from Howland. The Japanese Mandated Marshall Islands lay approximately 650 miles northwest of the intended destination. Amelia could have arrived in the Marshalls while conducting a search pattern believing she had overshot Howland, or if the plane had gone into the ocean, the drift of the sea from Howland Island was from the southeast to the northwest, and could have carried a life raft or the plane itself directly into the Marshalls.

Added fuel for this theory came unexpectedly. While researching another project at San Francisco Public Library, I found an article on the back pages of the April 13, 1943, issue of the San Francisco *Chronicle* newspaper. It concerned President M. L. Brittain of Georgia Tech University and was headed AMELIA EARHART—COLLEGE HEAD THINKS FLIER IS JAP CAPTIVE. With the presidents of Northwestern University and the Universities of California and Colorado, Dr. Brittain had been a civilian guest of the Navy aboard the battleship *Colorado* on a cruise to the Hawaiian Islands in June and July of 1937. Dr. Brittain had stated, "When the *Colorado* reached Hawaii we had a radiogram from President Roosevelt telling us to proceed toward Howland Island to search for the famous American woman flier because we were some 2500 miles closer than the *Lexington*, the carrier which later joined the search. We discussed the Japanese Mandated Islands and the rumors that the U.S. government had sent person after person to take a look-see, trying to discover whether or not the Japs were illegally fortifying their possessions. We got a very definite feeling that Amelia Earhart had some sort of understanding with officials of the government that the last part of her flight around-the-world would be over those Japanese islands."

I called Atlanta, Georgia, to learn how Dr. Brittain felt about this in 1960. I couldn't; he had died.

One other bit of information had been culled from the log of the *Itasca* which indicated the trouble Amelia had experienced during the last hours of the flight. On the night of July 2, 1937, just a few hours after the disappearance, the Navy at Pearl Harbor had dispatched a long-distance reconnaissance plane piloted by Commander Warren W. Harvey. He was bound for Howland to assist in the search. This communication was sent to the *Itasca* from Admiral Murfin, commandant of the 14th Naval District, the following morning, July 3:

A message from the patrol plane enroute to Howland Island just received as follows: QUOTE About 420 miles north of Howland. Last two hours in extremely bad weather between altitude 2000 and 12000 feet. Snow sleet rain electrical storms. In daylight conditions look equally bad. Cloud tops appear to be 18000 feet or more. Am returning to Pearl Harbor. Now have 900 gallons fuel on board. UNQUOTE

Amelia and Fred had probably been facing similar weather conditions the night and day before. With clouds to 18,000 feet, Amelia would not have been able to lift the Electra above the cover to enable Noonan to get star sights. I wrote to the Navy Department in an attempt to locate Commander Harvey, hoping he could give more details. Again I was too late:

About Commander W. W. Harvey who was associated with the last flight of Amelia Earhart: I am sorry to report a research discloses that Commander Harvey died on December 12, 1940.

"Francisco Galvan," the native Saipanese Monsignor Calvo, Father Sylvan, Father Arnold and I had tried unsuccessfully to question, broke into the news November 14, 1960. An Associated Press report from Guam was headed SAIPAN OFFICER SCOFFS AT EARHART TALE.

A police inspector at Saipan when Amelia Earhart disappeared on a Pacific flight in 1937 rejected today assertions that the American aviatrix and her navigator were executed by the Japanese. The investigator, Francisco Galvan said a woman executed on Saipan as a spy was born in Los Angeles of Japanese descent. Galvan said he did not know the name of the executed woman, but recalled that she was beautiful and about 25 years of age. She appeared to be part-Caucasian and would have been mistaken for one. The former police official said the woman came to Saipan ostensibly to look for work, but was too well dressed. He said she was subsequently arrested and imprisoned two months before being hanged.

The report fascinated me. Galvan had denied to us that he had any knowledge of white persons on the island before the war. I called Guam and talked with Tony Palamo of the Guam *Daily News,* who also serves as a stringer for Associated Press; he had filed the story. About a week before, Galvan had simply appeared at the newspaper and volunteered his tale.

"Did he say why he was giving the story now?" I asked Palamo.

"No, he just said he had some information. He didn't appear to want anything else," was the reply.

I thought for a long while about Galvan's possible motives. Why hadn't he told the story to Monsignor? Was he trying to throw us off the track or had someone asked him to make the statement? What did he have to gain by telling the story?

There were plenty of questions to be asked of the pronouncement itself. How would such a woman get to Saipan? The island had been restricted from even inter-island travel in 1936. No one without clearance from Tokyo had been permitted to visit. It didn't make sense either that the United States would choose a Japanese-American who looked Caucasian to spy on Japanese territory. Someone had also elevated Galvan's position with the Japanese. He had served the Kempeitai secret police as a sergeant maintaining discipline among his fellow natives; he had not been an inspector.

Galvan had forgotten two things in making his statement. The execution of someone at that time for spying on Saipan could only mean there was something to be protected. Japan has always vehemently denied the use of the Mandates prior to the war for anything but peaceful purposes. Also, if a Japanese-American from Los Angeles had been executed, Francisco might be held responsible. The death of a U.S. citizen prior to the war still could be regarded as a capital crime.

I finally decided someone must have asked Galvan to give information to the press that would discount the possibility of Earhart and Noonan having been on Saipan. Perhaps that someone was from Japan or from the mysterious NTTU facilities. It appeared a number of persons would not be displeased if the investigation were suspended or completely dropped.

In fact, I did seriously consider abandoning the search—but there were too many unanswered questions. By May 1961 I was itching for another Saipan expedition. I wanted to have a second look at that plane on the bottom of Tanapag Harbor; there was still a chance some of the gear on Amelia's aircraft might have been changed sometime during the flight. There was more questioning of the natives to be done. I felt there must be still other Saipanese who could contribute information, and I wanted conversation with Francisco Galvan about the executed Japanese-American woman from Los Angeles. There was the gravesite, too, which had been shown to Thomas Devine in 1945. If the area could be located, it might be possible to obtain a final answer through excavation.

The regard CBS held for me as a newsman had taken a sharp dip with the 1960 Bendix generator disclosures, but another story had brought me the 1961 Sigma Delta Chi Professional Journalistic Society Distinguished Service Award for radio reporting, and the time seemed right to ask my employer to finance three more weeks on Saipan. Jules Dundes had replaced Maurie Webster as General Manager of KCBS during the year, and although he was not and is not the easiest mark in the West, he made the funds available. Late in May, we applied for permission to revisit Saipan to Admiral Daniel F. Smith, Jr., Chief of Naval Information in Washington, D.C. It was a long struggle to obtain that clearance, a struggle which finally involved both U. S. Senators from California and the Assistant Secretary of Defense.

9

"Twenty-two tons of captured Japanese records were taken off Saipan after the 1944 invasion. I think you might find what you're looking for if you can locate those records."

Those had been the words of Lieutenant Commander Leroy Hippe, Saipan's Naval Administration Executive Officer in 1960.

How tough can it be to trace twenty-two tons of records? Plenty. The chase started with a Mr. Edelsak and Captain McCoughlin at the Navy Research Center in San Francisco. Their comments led me to a Mr. Cole, director of the Federal Records Center in south San Francisco. Cole remembered something about records from Saipan, but believed they had all been moved three years before to the Clearfield Naval Supply Depot, Clearfield, Utah. A Mr. Jefferis, Chief Federal Records Center, Clearfield, suggested that I write to the Federal Records Center, Naval Supply Depot, Mechanicsburg, Pennsylvania. When reached, a Mr. Lynch, Chief Reference Service Branch, Federal Records Center, Mechanicsburg, replied, "Not here. Why don't you try the Office of Naval History in Washington, D.C.?"

Captain Loomis, Assistant Director of Naval History, answered,

"No reference has been found to the twenty-two tons of Japanese records."

At the top we got some different answers. Mr. Darter, National Archives and Records Service Director, wrote from Washington that Japanese records captured during the war had at one time been stored in Federal Records Centers but had been returned to Japan in 1958. According to Darter, the records, about 7800 cubic feet of them from Japan's War and Navy Ministries, had been closely examined before they were released.

Meanwhile I had got in touch with a Mr. Wice, Chief of the General Reference Branch, U. S. Army. He reported that in 1958 some 7000 linear feet of records had been returned to Japan, but at that point his information began to vary from Mr. Darter's. Although some of the records had been investigated while in the United States, Mr. Wice indicated the large bulk of them had remained through the years in huge mail sacks piled to the ceilings, and no one had looked at them or even had an idea where they had come from or what the contents were.

Final words on the subject came from Mr. East, Chief Archivist, World War II Records Division, Washington, D.C. He stated that records brought to the United States from the Pacific were administered by the former Office of Strategic Services in a building known as the Washington Document Center. After the war, the Washington Document Center had become the responsibility of the successor agency to OSS, the Central Intelligence Group which later became the Central Intelligence Agency. Mr. East went on to say the Washington Document Center had been liquidated in 1948, and its holdings distributed among the CIA, the Library of Congress and the National Archives. He suggested I try those organizations.

The Library of Congress answered that it couldn't answer. They had so much captured Japanese material it would take a minimum of 125 years for the present staff of the Japanese section to catalog the existing backlog. I didn't bother to reply that I couldn't wait.

The Central Intelligence Agency couldn't find what we were looking for either, but would keep trying.

Pursuit of Hippe's records was a loss, but I did make some gains where Saipan's NTTUs were concerned. Through research and several personal friends, I learned the United Nations Security Council had adopted and set up the Strategic Trust Territory of the Pacific Islands, April 2, 1947, and assigned Saipan to the United States. Administration was transferred from the Navy to the Department of the Interior July 1, 1951, but a Presidential Order retransferred responsibility for Saipan and Tinian to the Navy January 1, 1953. On March 1, 1953, the Brown-Pacific-Maxon Company, an amalgamation of three large construction companies with headquarters in San Francisco, began to erect five or more major facilities on Saipan. Travel to both Saipan and Tinian was restricted beginning in February 1953. The Navy had become the administration unit on Saipan, but strangely during all the years of NTTU, the Department of Interior representatives were also retained.

Mr. Franklin English of Inglewood, California, had been a security officer for Brown-Pacific-Maxon on Saipan for twenty months starting in 1955. Most of what had been built on the island was in permanent, concrete, typhoonproof form, and hundreds of Philippine laborers had been imported to do the job. He added one startling item: the concrete foundations went down as much as twenty-five feet.

The scope of the project on Saipan became evident when I learned from one of the top executives of the Pacific Bridge Company that the U.S. government had let the initial contract for thirty million dollars. I began to understand why so many questions were asked about the reasons I wanted to go to Saipan. I could still only guess what was happening on the island. It was possible, I thought, the concrete foundations could serve as ballistic missile launch sites. But what about the Chinese soldiers seen on the north end and east side of Saipan? How did they fit with ballistic missiles? Perhaps the Nationalist Chinese were being trained should the U.S. ever place nuclear weapons on Formosa. None of my conjectures proved to be right, but when I did finally learn Saipan's secret, it was no less important.

By the end of June 1961 there had been no answer from Admiral Smith's office about my return to Saipan. Jules Dundes, CBS Vice-President in San Francisco, called the admiral's office in Washington and spoke with the Deputy Chief of Naval Information, Captain R. W. Alexander. I was on the extension phone in Jules' office and this was the conversation I heard:

"Captain Alexander, we've been wondering how you're progressing with Mr. Goerner's permission to return to Saipan. It's been over a month since we made application."

"Just a moment, Mr. Dundes. There's a letter on Admiral Smith's desk awaiting his signature that deals with this question."

Alexander came back to the phone and said, "I'm afraid, Mr. Dundes, the permission has been denied."

"Why?" inquired Jules.

"I'm sorry. I can't tell you that."

"Well, does it concern national security?"

"It does concern security."

"Does it concern Amelia Earhart?"

"No, I don't believe it does."

"Has the Navy followed up on any of the leads produced by the CBS expedition last year?"

"I'm afraid I'm not at liberty to say, Mr. Dundes."

"Well, can you tell me if the Navy or anyone else has done any excavation on Saipan trying to locate the remains of Earhart and Noonan?"

"I still can't make a comment."

"Captain Alexander, what can we do to appeal the decision of the Navy? It seems extraordinary that a newsman cannot visit a United Nations Trust Territory, particularly when the governing authority is his own nation."

"You might try another letter and include more details as to why you feel another trip to the island would be productive."

"We do intend to appeal this matter, Captain Alexander. If our representative can't make such a trip, we'd certainly like some explanation why the permission cannot be granted."

Jules is a fighter and he went to work. First, another letter requesting clearance for Saipan was sent to Admiral Smith's office with carbon copies to Senators Clair Engle and Thomas Kuchel of California. The letter contained a six-page summary of the reasons we wished to visit the island again. Then Jules asked Ted Koop, CBS Vice-President in Washington, to approach the newly appointed Assistant Secretary of Defense, Arthur Sylvester, and determine what he could do to help us. Dundes sent a six-

1   This familiar pose of Amelia Earhart with her famous Lockheed Electra plane was used as the model for a 1963 U.S. airmail commemorative postage stamp. *Lockheed Aircraft Corporation Photo*

2   Amelia, on the right, with Neta Snook, her first flying instructor, around 1920. *Napa, California, Register Photo*

3   With her husband, George Palmer Putnam, as Amelia prepared to leave Miami, Florida, for her round-the-world flight. *Wide World Photo*

4   Interior of the Electra as it was being remodeled for larger fuel capacity. *Lockheed Aircraft Corporation Photo*

5 At Honolulu, Hawaii, in 1937, left to right: Paul Mantz, technical adviser, Amelia, Harry Manning, and Fred Noonan, the two navigators. *Wide World Photo*

6   The crash in Honolulu that ended the first attempt; Paul Mantz is in the cockpit, Amelia and Fred Noonan on the wing. *Wide World Photo*

7   Amelia and Noonan at their stop in Natal, Brazil, on the round-
the-world flight. *Wide World Photo*

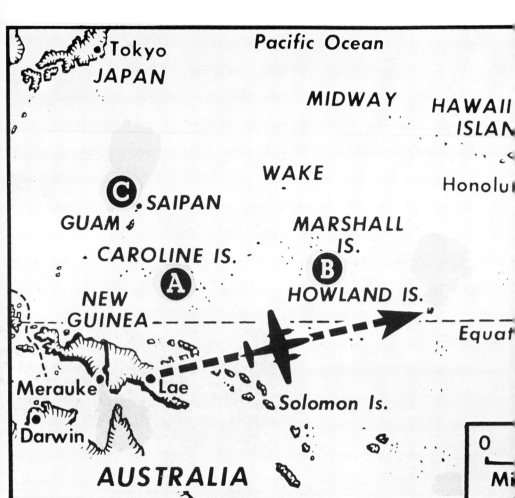

Pacific Ocean

JAPAN · Tokyo

MIDWAY HAWAII ISLAN

WAKE

Honolu

Ⓒ SAIPAN
GUAM
CAROLINE IS.
Ⓐ

MARSHALL IS.
Ⓑ
HOWLAND IS.

NEW GUINEA

Equat

Merauke Lae
Solomon Is.

Darwin

AUSTRALIA

0
Mi

8   The map shows the scheduled flight route from Lae to Howland, with A representing the Truk overflight, B the suspected Marshalls landing, and C Japanese Headquarters, Saipan. *Wide World Photo*

page letter to Koop to be hand-carried to Sylvester. Part of that letter read:

The Navy Department has stated on several occasions that it believes there is no basis for the Earhart-Saipan theory; yet, it will not divulge its methods of investigation. If the material is actually inconclusive, there seems to be no point in giving it any security classification. This does, in fact, give fresh impetus to the often heard criticism of the Military that information is sometimes improperly classified in order to prevent embarrassment.

Even those forthright words produced no immediate reaction. Arthur Sylvester checked back with Ted Koop several weeks later to report he was having great difficulty in obtaining the necessary permission or even the reasons why it could not be granted. Jules sent another letter to the Office of Naval Information with carbons to U. S. Senators Kuchel and Engle, but still the wait continued. Finally, near the end of August 1961, a letter arrived from Commander R. L. Bufkins, Assistant Director of the Navy's Media Relations Division. In accordance with the Chief of Naval Operations' message 152148Z, I was authorized to visit Guam and Saipan. I think I saw a smile on Jules' face that day.

Thomas Devine had also requested permission to visit Saipan, but the Navy refused. The fact that Devine was not a correspondent accredited to the Defense Department was one of the reasons given. I asked Tom for all the information he could furnish on the gravesite he had been shown in 1945, and the next week nine photos and several detailed maps arrived. Four of the pictures showed the Garapan jail area which I had already visited; one represented a portion of beach south of Garapan, and four others were of the native cemetery and the woman who had informed Devine of the "two white fliers, man and woman" and the location of their unmarked grave. If Devine's memory was as good as the maps indicated, there was at least a fair chance of finding a general area for excavation.

Before the second trip to Saipan, I decided to find out as much as I could about Japan's attitudes prior to Amelia's disappearance in 1937 and what support there was for the accusation that Japan had fortified her Mandated Pacific Islands in preparation for World War II. A chronicle of frustration with U.S. military intelligence developed.

World War I had scarcely begun in Europe when Japanese warships moved into Micronesia and took over from Germany the Mariana, Caroline, and Marshall Islands. The next five years were spent in reaching understandings with Great Britain, France, Russia, and Italy by which those countries would support Japan's claims to the islands at the war's end. The hopes of Japan for outright ownership, however, were not realized at the 1919 Peace Conference. A "mandate" only was delivered to Japan with ultimate control of Micronesia exercised by the League of Nations. Article 4 of the Mandate stated:

4. The military training of the natives, otherwise than for the purposes of internal police and the local defense of the territory, shall be prohibited. Furthermore, no military or naval bases shall be established, or fortifications erected in the territory.

The possible violation by Japan of Article 4 was already beginning to worry U.S. military intelligence by the early 1920s, and rumors of Japanese fortification of the Mandates enlarged. The United States, not a member of the League of Nations, had few means of gauging the authenticity of the rumors. It was suggested by Naval Intelligence in 1923 that "courtesy calls" be attempted to certain islands by U. S. Navy ships, but the U. S. State Department felt such requests might create diplomatic problems with Japan and the idea was dropped.

The U. S. Marine Corps decided also in 1923 that the Mandated Islands represented a threat to American security. Marine Lieutenant Colonel Earl Hancock "Pete" Ellis was given the task of penetrating the islands, and disguised as a German trader, made his way through the Marshalls and Carolines. Ellis had filed a report with the War Department in 1921 which predicted a Japanese attack upon the Hawaiian Islands and the United States and indicated the coming war would be fought mainly on the Pacific islands. Colonel Ellis was apparently poisoned by Japanese military police at Koror in the Western Carolines during his 1923 mission. A U. S. Navy Chief Pharmacist, who was allowed to go by Japanese ship to Koror for Ellis' remains, returned to Japan drugged into amnesia. He was never able to tell the circumstances of Ellis' death or what he had seen. The strangest aspect of the Ellis mystery is that his 1921 report remained classified in Washington until 1960.

The U. S. Army Air Corps was also deeply concerned with Japan's plans for the Pacific. In the fall of 1923, Brigadier General Billy Mitchell toured the perimeter of the Mandates, gathering any information he could. His report was filed with the War Department in 1925, and he, too, fashioned a diagram of things to come: Japan would use her Pacific islands as springboards for invasion and would attack the United States at Pearl Harbor; the strike by aircraft would come on a Sunday morning.

General Mitchell's report was classified in Washington until 1961.

The rumors of island fortification continued through the 1920s and Japan's Navy further restricted travel to the areas—thus feeding the rumors. When the Japanese Army took over partial control of the government in 1931 and launched its invasion of Manchuria, the alarm of the U. S. Navy became more evident. Admiral Frank H. Schofield, USN, then Commander-in-Chief of the U.S. fleet stationed in the Pacific, formulated plans in 1932 for Fleet Problem 14, destined to become one of the most famous fleet problems in history. Viewed with the events of December 7, 1941, in one's memory, the five elements of the problem are amazingly prophetic.

1. There is an acute situation in the Pacific. War is imminent but not declared.

2. The enemy will strike at the United States where the fleet is concentrated.

3. The enemy will use aircraft carriers as basis for its striking force.

4. The enemy will take all advantage of surprise and make raids on the Hawaiian Islands or the West Coast prior to a declaration of war.

5. Consider any enemy forces east of the 180th meridian to be hostile.

In 1933 and 1934 the Mandates Commission of the League of Nations began to ask more and more questions of Japan: Why are foreign ships not allowed in Mandate harbors? Why are the island airports not available to all nations? Why are foreigners severely restricted? In 1935, Japan grew tired of the probing, and withdrew from the League. The Mandated Islands were well under the control of the League of Nations according to international law, but the League's Mandates Commission was powerless to exercise that control. Japan occupied the islands, set its own policies, and had no intention of permitting any other nation or body of nations to dictate how its territories were to be administered.

U.S. military grew even more suspicious of Japan's use of the Marshalls, Carolines, and Marianas, and in view of Japanese demands for naval parity, her abrogation of the Washington Treaty limiting armament, her policies in Asia, and her resignation from the League, there were good reasons to be suspicious. Japan's military appropriations had risen from 27 percent of the national budget in 1930 to 46.6 percent in 1935–36.

Some Americans did manage to visit a few of the islands before the door of secrecy swung completely closed in 1936. Paul Hibbert Clyde, Professor of History, University of Kentucky, made a trip in 1934 as did Dr. W. C. Herre, curator of the zoological museum of Stanford University. The year 1935 saw adventurer-scientist Willard Price cruise through the Mandates with Japanese permission. All three reported they had seen no signs of the rumored Japanese fortifications.

U.S. military intelligence, though, was not interested in the reports of laymen. There were many ways of fortifying not involving gun emplacements and barbed wire. The deepening of harbors, building of airfields and oil storage facilities, construction of railroads and roadways, all could have military purposes.

The Japanese political situation became explosive in the winter of 1936–37. In February of 1936, Army extremists assassinated the Finance Minister, the Keeper of the Privy Seal, and the Inspector-General of Military Education. These men had been voices of moderation. With their deaths, more militant Japanese, sympathetic to the Army's dreams of aggrandizement, moved into key positions and dressed the stage for invasion.

The Japanese Army was looking northward; the Japanese Navy south and east, and the United States government began to worry seriously; at least President Roosevelt and some of his close advisers did. It was obvious now that Japan wanted control of Asia and the Western Pacific. Japan for years had suffered from a spy-fear complex and in 1936 and early 1937 the phobia grew even worse. American and British citizens by the dozens were arrested, accused of spying and imprisoned. St. Luke's International Medical Center in Tokyo was charged with being an international spy headquarters. Dr. Rudolph Bolling Teusler, director of the Center, was charged with visiting fortified zones in his sailboat and sending short-wave messages through a radio installed in the gold cross atop the medical-center building. The operating room was said to be used for broadcasting information and instructions to missionary spies scattered throughout Japan. A prominent Los Angeles businessman, Mark A. Pierce, was arrested and imprisoned in Kobe for having taken photographs on a Japanese boat of the ship's captain playing deck tennis. It was interpreted by the Japanese police as violating the Military Secrets Law. Pierce was later charged with being a naval spy when the Japanese learned he was a Commodore of the San Pedro Yacht Club. Secrecy had become a fetish with the Japanese.

By June of 1937, Japanese banners had been carried to large areas of mainland Asia (Korea, Kwantung Peninsula, Manchuria) and bayonets of the Imperial Japanese Army were being honed sharp for the next territorial extension in the names of justice, peace and partnership for all humanity.

For most Americans during this period, the thought of conflict was totally repugnant. There seemed no purpose to becoming involved in any quarrel between foreign countries. Very few believed that America could do much to settle them, and there was a danger of being caught and burned in such a conflagration. Isolationism, therefore, was a policy most American officeholders had to cope with if they were to have any political future. Certainly it was proper to speak up in defense of United States' interests where business was concerned, but no one at that time, including President Roosevelt, was going to take any action which might provoke or involve America in war. Still there were those charged with security for this country, and Japan was readying itself for invasion.

Into this atmosphere flew Amelia Earhart and Frederick Noonan in their Lockheed Electra 10-E ten-passenger airliner, bound around the world. On July 2, 1937, they disappeared in mid-Pacific. Five days later, July 7, 1937, Japan struck—at China.

It was a crucial period in Japan's history. If Amelia and Fred were taken prisoners, the Japanese could never let them go.

10

On September 7, 1961, I headed for Saipan on the second expedition. This time I made the trip alone. The cooperation of Monsignor Calvo and the Fathers had been excellent during the first effort, and there was no sense in asking Maximo Akiyama to leave his job again merely to serve as an extra interpreter.

En route I stopped at Honolulu to pick up an endorsement for my News Media Representative Certificate from Captain James S. Dowdell, director of naval information at Pearl Harbor. The same questioning I had experienced on the first trip began.

"Mr. Goerner, there has been some concern voiced about the reasons for your visit to Saipan. I'm familiar with some of your work regarding Amelia Earhart, but is a continuation of your efforts in that area the only motivation for your trip?"

I carefully explained to Dowdell the extent of the investigation to that date and also covered what I knew about NTTU on Saipan, attempting to reassure him that Amelia and Fred were the sole reasons I wished access to the island. After a half-hour's discussion, he seemed satisfied and gave me the necessary endorsement together with a direction to see Admiral Wendt at

Guam before proceeding to Saipan. Captain Dowdell was to play an interesting role two years later when we met in Washington, D.C.

At Guam, Admiral Wendt, Commandant of the Marianas Sea Frontier, was as pleasant as he had been during the first trip.

"You don't give up easily do you, Mr. Goerner?" he greeted.

"Well, there have been a number of unanswered questions, Admiral, and this second trip seemed necessary," I replied. "One thing I'd like to get straight is that I'm not out here because of NTTU. Everyone appears worried that I am."

"We're not worried," Wendt protested. "I'm sure you would never have gotten clearance from Washington if there was any doubt as to your intentions. I must ask, though, that you still observe the rules given you by Commander Bridwell at Saipan. They're really for your protection, too."

Bridwell and his executive officer, Leroy Hippe, were at Koebler Field, Saipan, to meet the flight from Guam. On approach, the island hadn't looked quite as grim as on the initial trip.

"Can't stay away from our tropic paradise, eh?" said Bridwell as he extended his hand.

"That's right, Commander," I returned. "There's something about unfinished business anywhere that gets me."

Hippe was strangely quiet when I arrived and it was a few days before I could get him to tell me the reason. Several individuals within the Navy Department had not been happy about his revelation regarding the twenty-two tons of captured Japanese records. Considering the success we had trying to locate the records, there should have been no occasion for unhappiness.

Commander Bridwell drove me to his quonset-hut home overlooking Tanapag Harbor and broke out another bottle of Canadian Club. I had the feeling, as we all do sometimes, that I had played the scene before.

"We heard the wreckage you brought up out of the harbor last year turned out to be Japanese," he said handing me a drink.

"Well, we're not completely sure of that, Commander. There's still the way-out possibility Earhart might have changed the generator and starter motor during the flight around the world."

"How could you prove that?"

"The only way is to bring more of that wreck to the surface and see if it can be identified . . . I also want to question more natives. I'm sure there must be others who can fill in some of the gaps."

"Anything else?"

"Yes. I want to check out a story that was given to me by a man from West Haven, Connecticut, who served in Saipan in 1945."

"You mean that fellow—Devine?"

I was startled. "How did you happen to find out about him, Commander?"

"Well, there was an Office of Naval Intelligence man out here a little while back checking up on some information on a grave, and he mentioned Devine's name."

"What did the ONI guy decide?"

"Darned if I know. He took off and I never did find out."

After some more general conversation I asked Bridwell his opinion now of the testimony we had obtained last year.

Bridwell filled his glass again, thought for a moment, then surprised me with his reply. "I think there's a lot to their story. There were undoubtedly a couple of Americans, a man and woman, out here before the war, and they weren't here on a friendly visit."

"Do you think they were Earhart and Noonan?"

"Could have been. The descriptions fit. But . . ."

"But what?"

"But I don't think Earhart ever flew that plane of hers to Saipan."

"Why?"

"Well, I was around an admiral's office at the time they disappeared in '37, and I heard a few things that made me think they could have possibly gone down in the Marshall Islands."

"What admiral?"

"Well, we're just talking. I'm not going to mention any names."

"Why did this admiral or why do you think they went down in the Marshalls?"

"Well, for one thing the Marshalls are pretty close to Howland Island. Second, the Japanese had a big thing about secrecy where the Marshalls were concerned, particularly Jaluit and

Kwajalein, and third, there were a couple of reports from natives during the invasion of those islands that a white woman pilot had gone down in the area before the war."

"Where in the Marshalls?"

"Well, Fred . . . I think in the vicinity of a little atoll named Ailinglapalap."

"Do you have anything to back that theory?"

"When you get back to the States, why don't you see if you can come up with the radio logs of four U.S. logistic vessels which were serving the Far East Fleet in '37 at the time of Earhart's disappearance. I think you might find some interesting reading in them."

"What are the names of the ships?"

"The *Gold Star, Blackhawk, Chaumont,* and *Henderson.*"

Bridwell was a changed man; at least that's what I thought. He altered the opinion by suggesting next that I switch the entire investigation to the Marshall Islands and forget Saipan.

"You're just wasting your time here," he said. "You need tangible evidence, and I think you can find that in the Marshalls."

"What sort of tangible evidence, Commander?

"Well, the natives have been known to talk about a two-motor plane that lies just below the surface of the water on one of the reefs down there. You could probably find it without too much trouble."

"But what about the testimony we've gotten from the natives here on Saipan?" I asked. "Couldn't Earhart and Noonan have been brought here by the Japanese?"

"Yes . . . they could. Japan had regular military seaplane flights coming in here from the Marshalls and Carolines, or they could have been brought up here by ship. I was just thinking that the tangible evidence of the plane might be easier to find than trying to dig up bones and identify them."

"Perhaps I'll go to the Marshalls another time, but right now I've plenty to check on Saipan. By the way, you aren't anguished about my remaining here because of NTTU, are you?"

I then told Bridwell what I had related to Captain Dowdell and Admiral Wendt, and once again reiterated the real purpose of my visit. He smiled and his apprehensions visibly eased.

"I still must request, Fred, that you restrict your activities to the southern part of the island. Are you going to stay at the Matsumotos' in Chalan Kanoa again? You're perfectly welcome to live up here on the hill with us."

This time I accepted the invitation, and Bridwell housed me in an ancient quonset about fifty yards above his quarters. The hut, laughingly referred to as the "Presidential Suite," had a rear exit into the jungle. Something was to happen in the "Presidential Suite" during my stay which I will remember the rest of my life; in fact, it could have cost that life.

"By the way," Bridwell said as I was taking my luggage into the quonset, "if you do get around to some excavation, I think I know a likely spot to begin."

The next morning I borrowed a Navy truck and drove into Chalan Kanoa to renew friendship with Monsignor and the Fathers. Unfortunately, Monsignor Calvo had been reassigned to the Philippines several months before, but Father Sylvan and Father Arnold were glad to see me and happy to offer more assistance; the break in routine had been welcome in 1960.

An average day for the Fathers begins about 4:00 A.M. and extends to 10:00 P.M. with each of the eighteen hours busy: Field trips to other islands; saying Mass at the main church at Chalan Kanoa, then rushing to perform the same services at San Roque and Tanapag villages, teaching several courses at the mission school; building new classrooms and repairing the old; visiting the sick, helping the old; trying to convince native mothers that their babies should be born at the hospital and not delivered by next-door neighbors or the local witch doctor. Some evenings the Fathers may appear at Matsumoto's quonset-hut motion picture theater to see part of a Japanese language film or a bad print of an American movie. The sound of the pictures is usually so garbled it's unintelligible, but the natives don't mind. As long as there's action on the screen, the Saipanese stamp, cheer, or pound on the wooden benches. Love scenes, however, are not as popular; they are generally ignored. The Fathers usually don't stay long. The main purpose in attending might be to tell several youngsters that their unexplained absence from school that day had been duly noted. It's a full and arduous life.

Our first project in 1961 was another visit to Francisco Galvan regarding the Associated Press story about "the Japanese-American appearing to be a white woman who was executed as a spy before the war." Galvan had considerably improved his existence during the year. He had gone into the scrap business, built himself a shack-office near the pier at Tanapag Harbor, and was collecting war wreckage from the jungles. A mountain of torn metal from jeeps, tanks, aircraft, and discarded combat gear had risen next to the office. Someone had advanced enough money to Galvan for a new station wagon, and he was also able to pay a number of Saipanese to locate and haul scrap to the pier.

Francisco was no more cooperative than he had been in 1960. He simply shook his head in answer to questions and even denied having knowledge of the report Tony Palamo had filed with AP from Guam. He had no information about executions under the Japanese or any persons on the island before or during the war who "appeared to be white." I produced a copy of the story as it had appeared in a San Francisco newspaper, but still the Chamorran insisted he had told Palamo nothing of the kind.

"What do you think is behind it?" I asked Father Sylvan.

"Someone may have warned him he went too far with the story," Father replied. "But where Galvan has been getting his money bothers me. A year ago penniless, and now look at him."

"To whom is he going to sell all that scrap?"

"I've heard he has a deal with a Japanese company to send a ship to pick it up, but I don't know how that's going to be done. The United States Department of State has a strict rule no Japanese vessels are permitted into the Trust Territory. Maybe Francisco knows something we don't."

I was convinced Mr. Galvan knew a lot of things we didn't; finding a way to get him to release that knowledge was the problem.

Gregorio Magofna and Antonio Taitano, my two diver friends, showed up at the mission the next morning and we headed for the harbor to raise more of the plane wreckage. The Coast Guard maintains a small Loran station on the southern end of Saipan and two young enlisted men had scuba gear, so they came along too.

It was a calm, beautiful day on the harbor and within an hour we had a hundred or more pounds of wreckage in the boat. One piece gave me the answer. On a partially corroded radio direction finder loop, an identification tag was marked with Japanese characters. The wreckage was not that of Amelia's Lockheed. I felt no disappointment, only relief that one riddle was solved. The Bendix study indicated the aircraft was probably Japanese, but it took this last evidence to assure me. I started to pick up what appeared to be a portion of a control panel to throw it back in the water when one of the coastguardsmen cried, "Get your hand off that thing! Get away from it!"

I pulled back none too quickly as a five-foot brownish-yellow moray eel lunged out of the wreckage and into the boat. Magofna calmly took his dagger from a scabbard attached to his leg and pinned the eel's head to the deck, then moved the knife around and through the head as the rest of its form thrashed violently against the sides of the boat. When he was certain the moray was dead, Greg removed the knife and dropped the creature over the side. Father Sylvan translated Magofna's remark as "One less to worry about."

During the next few days Father Sylvan, Father Arnold, and I questioned more of the Saipanese and found seven who had additional information about the "American man and woman, fliers." Several had seen them at the harbor area in Garapan and they repeated what the Japanese had said about the incident; it fit perfectly with what we already knew. Two natives, Matilde Shoda San Nicholas and José Pangelinan, gave testimony which enlarged the original findings.

It was after eight o'clock in the evening when we began to question Mrs. San Nicholas at her small frame house on one of the small, winding coral roads in Chalan Kanoa. Several Saipanese had said she could give us important information if we could overcome her fear. Matilde, now in her late thirties, was born of a Japanese father and Chamorran mother. Before and during World War II, she had lived in Garapan where her father worked as a tailor. Next to her home had been the hotel the Japanese Kempeitai secret police used to house political prisoners, and for many months in 1937 and '38, she had seen the white woman whom the Japanese referred to as "flier and

spy." Mrs. San Nicholas sat on the edge of her chair and appeared
to be nervous as Father Sylvan questioned her.

"You aren't afraid of us are you, Matilde?"

"No, but some people say I should not tell these things."

"Who said that?"

"Oh, some people," Matilde vaguely replied. "I will not say
who."

"Why not?" Father Sylvan pressed.

"It would not be good for me to say."

"You're not afraid to talk with us now?"

"No . . . I will tell you."

Father Sylvan reassured her again that she was doing the
right thing, then he asked, "Can you describe the woman?"

"Yes," Matilde replied. "She was tall and very thin and she
had not much hair for a woman; it was short."

"How was she dressed?"

"When I first saw her she was wearing a man's clothes, but
later they gave her woman's dress."

"How many times did you see her?"

"Many times. Each day she would come out into the yard
and walk around it."

"Was she guarded?"

"Yes. They watched her all the time. She could not go anywhere."

"Did you ever try to talk to her?"

"She could not speak our language, but I gave her some fruit
several times."

"Did the guards let you do that?"

"They did not bother."

"Do you know what finally happened to the woman?"

"Yes. One day she came out in the yard and she looked very
sick and sadder than usual. I gave her a piece of fruit and
she smiled. Then she gave me a ring from her finger and put
her hand on my head in friendship. The next day one of the
police came and got some black cloth from my father and had
him make some paper flowers. The man said that the lady had
died and they were going to bury her."

"Did the Japanese say what the woman died of?"

"She died of dysentery."

Matilde San Nicholas had kept the ring until some time after the war, then had given it to her sister. The sister in turn had presented it to a younger cousin, who lost the single pearl set in white gold somewhere around her house as recently as 1959. Father Sylvan and I helped the family search the house on three occasions, but the ring had disappeared. Whether or not Amelia possessed such a ring, no one seems to know. The photographs I have seen do not show it, but that does not preclude its existence. She could have purchased it at one of the stops prior to Lae, New Guinea.

Matilde provided another clue that might have produced concrete evidence, but it, too, proved a frustration. One day she had been working on a geography lesson for school when the prisoner woman took the book from her and wrote something on a map of the Pacific Ocean. Matilde had not been able to speak or read the language of the woman, and the book had been lost in the destruction of the 1944 invasion.

Was the woman Amelia Earhart? I had brought pictures of fifteen different women, including AE, clipped from various newspapers and magazines. After studying the photos only a few minutes, Matilde unhesitatingly chose the likeness of Amelia.

"This is the woman; I'm sure of it," said Mrs. San Nicholas, "but she looked older and more tired."

We reached José Pangelinan through his daughter who worked as a nurse at the native dispensary in Chalan Kanoa. She told us her father had known many of the Japanese officers before and during the war and he had spoken to his family about an American man and woman who were held and later killed by the Kempeitai. José owns a tiny grocery store alongside the road leading north from Chalan Kanoa, but the afternoon we talked with him there was no business, a situation he referred to as an average day. A small, gentle-appearing Chamorran, in his fifties, Mr. Pangelinan had an obvious dislike for discussion of the years the Japanese had occupied the island, but he, like many of the Saipanese, submitted that life had been better under Japanese rule where economics were concerned.

Father Sylvan finally overcame Pangelinan's reluctance to speak of the past, and his story was almost identical to that of Mrs. San Nicholas. He had seen the American man and woman but not together. The man had been held at the military police stockade area while the woman was kept at the hotel in Garapan. José's daughter had been wrong on one thing; only the man had been killed by the Japanese. The woman had died of dysentery. The man had been executed by Samurai sword the day after the woman's death and the pair had been buried together in an unmarked grave outside the cemetery south of Garapan City. The Japanese had said the two were fliers and spies. Father Sylvan repeatedly asked the grocer if he could show us the gravesite, but José maintained that was known only to the Japanese. He had not been an eyewitness to either the execution or the burial. The Kempeitai officers had merely spoken to him of the incident. Father Sylvan wasn't sure we had the whole story, but the old man would tell us no more. Once again I asked the familiar question: Why hadn't Pangelinan spoken before? His answer was the same as most of the witnesses: no one had asked him and it wasn't wise to talk of things that happened during the Japanese times. The Japanese had been strong on security and anyone who mentioned anything about their activities could be sure of reprisals.

As I had learned the preceding year, only one person assigned to the Catholic mission before the war had survived the invasion and the years that followed. Father Tardio had died in Spain after the war, but one of the lay brothers, Brother Gregorio, was at the church on Yap Island. During the year, Father Sylvan had talked with Gregorio at a gathering of church officials on Guam. Brother Gregorio remembered the story of the two white people, supposedly fliers, who had been held by the Japanese during 1937–38, but it was not eyewitness testimony. The Brother along with the Fathers and Sisters at the mission had been restricted to church grounds by the Japanese during that period, and then had been placed under house arrest on December 8, 1941. Two young Saipanese, the Sanchez brothers, Juan and José, had told Gregorio of the two Americans and what the Japanese said of them. The brothers had been in their teens at the time, but Gregorio was certain they had told him the truth. He felt it was extremely unlikely the boys could have invented such a story.

Father Sylvan and I traced the brothers Sanchez and found

them working as mechanics for the mysterious entity known as NTTU. They were surprised and disturbed when Father Sylvan asked them about Brother Gregorio's statement, but admitted they had some knowledge of the incident. Both felt they would like to refresh their memories before making a definite statement and promised to come to the church mission house the next day and give us the details. Only one Sanchez appeared the following morning, and his attitude had completely changed. He claimed neither he nor his brother had any information that would help us. "Brother Gregorio does not remember correctly," he said. "We know nothing of what he says."

Father Sylvan questioned hard and long but to no avail. The Sanchez brothers were obviously frightened and were not going to say a thing. Another full year passed before we learned the two Saipanese had been told by the Navy or NTTU not to cooperate with the people who were asking questions about the missing fliers. Father Sylvan and I had suspected as much in 1961.

Tom Devine's pictures, maps, and recollections of Saipan 1945 was the next chore in line.

11

Before we could get to Devine's location, Commander Bridwell advanced his ideas of the burial site, which involved a small native cemetery near Tanapag Village some distance north of what had been Garapan City. He showed us a clearing about twenty yards outside the northern perimeter of the graveyard and said it appeared a likely spot to him because Japanese military had occupied the area with the headquarters for their seaplane base just south of the cemetery. It was at least two miles from the location Devine and several witnesses had indicated, but I decided it was worth excavating on the chance Bridwell had information he had not divulged. Father Sylvan gave the Church's permission to recover any remains found outside the graveyard, and I hired a crew of ten Carolinian and Chamorran natives armed with picks and shovels. After two days sweating in the sun, we had dug a trench six feet deep through the center of the clearing and had unearthed a weird assortment of bolts, wire, and other debris which established the fact that the area had been thoroughly bulldozed either by Japanese or American forces. There was no sign of remains, human or other.

Commander Bridwell had made a bad guess. At least that is
what I thought until a young Navy ensign with the Administration Unit mentioned he had heard Bridwell joking at the Officers'
Bar about having caused the CBS newsman to dig where nothing
could possibly be found. I later learned the area the commander
had taken us to had been covered with Seabee quonset huts
erected after the 1944 invasion. If Bridwell had a motive for concocting a phony lead, the only explanation I could think of then
and now is that he was continuing to protect NTTU.

I faced him one evening with my frustration.

"Paul, why don't you let me get on with this investigation?"

"What do you mean?" he replied.

"I mean I know someone has talked to some of the witnesses
and tried to get them to change their stories, and I feel you
are doing everything you can to convince me that further search
for Earhart on Saipan is useless."

Bridwell vociferously denied it, but added, "What if you did
come up with the final evidence you need? Wouldn't every
newsman in the United States want to get on Saipan to photograph Amelia Earhart's final resting place?"

I tried to convince him that no news-gathering organization
was going to send personnel six thousand miles to shoot film I
already had in abundance, but the commander shook his head.

"Then some movie company would be wanting access to do
her life story or something."

"You guard NTTU as if it were the CIA," I probed.

The letters CIA produced an immediate response. Bridwell
fairly exploded negation of the thought.

"There's no CIA here," he blurted. Then calming a bit he
continued, "NTTU as you know is top-secret, but there is no
connection with the Central Intelligence Agency."

I left that subject but other matters continued to disturb me.
I had fostered friendships with Lieutenant Commander Hippe,
Ensign Picardi, and several other officers, and they guardedly
told me of rumors which had been circulated in the year since
my first trip to the island. I was supposed to be a drunkard
and therefore unreliable. Evidence for the character assassination
was the fact I had purchased six bottles of brandy and three

of whiskey during my time on Saipan. That part was true, but the rumor neglected to mention that I gave nine bottles of liquor to Monsignor and the Fathers at the church missions in appreciation for their help. It was a special treat as they were not permitted to purchase anything at the Navy's Ships Service. Another nasty bit of gossip had me making time with several of the young native girls, especially the teenage daughter of José Matsumoto at whose home I'd stayed in 1960. If it had not been so vicious, I would have laughed. Had I desired such relationships, which I certainly did not, the fact the Fathers were my constant companions would have frightened away the Saipanese ladies. As it was, many of the local people believed I belonged to the Church in some official capacity. The Fathers have beards, which is the custom of their Order, and when I let mine grow, the natives were doubly sure I was part of the mission.

Why, I wondered, was an effort being made to discredit me? Was it also being done in the name of NTTU? When it was suggested by one of the officers that it would be perfectly all right for me to bring any of the native girls I desired to my quarters, I was sure an attempt was being made to place me in a position of disrepute which would instill doubt about anything I claimed to have learned about Amelia and would additionally render me vulnerable to various forms of blackmail. I told the Fathers of the situation. They were irate, but there was little they could do. Their continued support, however, was enough to convince most of the Saipanese of my integrity.

The graveyard of which Devine had taken pictures in 1945 was not difficult to find. Several of the natives, including Adolpho Roppul who worked as a gardener for the church mission, immediately recognized the area and many of the gravestones shown in the photos. The cemetery, known as "Liyang" or "The Cave Graveyard" to the Saipanese, lies approximately two miles north of Chalan Kanoa and a mile or so south of what were once the outskirts of Garapan City. A narrow dirt trail penetrates about 250 yards into jungle from the beach road and terminates abruptly at the northern entrance to the cemetery. The area appeared exactly as it had to Devine in 1945 with one important exception: the jungle had grown to a height of twenty to forty feet over everything. Shafts of sunlight pierced the cover, but the graveyard had a damp, gloomy, unhealthy feel to it. Each November on All Souls' Day the natives clear the graves of debris and jungle, but within a few months their work is obliterated. The *tangen-tangen,* as the Saipanese call the jungle, never ceases in its efforts to reclaim the land from man.

Some of the graves were marked with simple wooden crosses which bore no identification. Others were covered with headstones into which had been carved names and dates. "Liyang" clearly was the cemetery depicted by Devine's photographs. The marked stones were in the same places, the legends identical. One of the pictures showed a plaster angel with arms raised; the angel still stood in the same position. Another of the snapshots showed a huge tree at the end of the cemetery, with an odd fork ten or fifteen feet from the ground. Even backgrounded by the jungle, the tree was still identifiable from a location halfway through the graveyard.

Father Sylvan and I quickly noticed, however, that Devine appeared to be wrong about the directions of the cemetery. His diagram showed the entrance facing west with the peculiarly notched tree placed at the east end of the plot. The entrance to the graveyard actually faced north with the tree located to the south. Also, the directions regarding the location of the angel appeared to be exactly opposite although the picture itself matched what we were seeing at that moment. Father Sylvan concluded as did I that the passage of sixteen years had tricked Devine's memory, but the photographs could not be disputed. There were several other things that convinced us we had found the right spot. One of the maps indicated a high rise of ground between the cemetery and the beach and a slight indenture or cove beneath the overhanging coral. A great slice of the earth had been removed after the war to level the area for the beach road, but the natives supplied the information that "Cave Cemetery" had received its name from the now-departed cove.

One map indicated that the suspected gravesite of Earhart and Noonan was outside the northern perimeter of the cemetery, just beyond a metal shed and several dozen temporary graves. The area was supposedly surrounded by trees and scrub, but took the form of a small clearing covered by grass that appeared to have been planted. Devine's photo of the shed and graves also pictured the native women who had given him the information in 1945. Adolpho Roppul and several other Saipanese recognized the woman as an Okinawan who had been repatriated to her home after the war. (Many Okinawans had been brought to Saipan by the Japanese before and during the war to work the sugar cane fields and fishing industry.) They indicated the woman had lived near the graveyard, but all believed her metal shack had been located south of the cemetery instead of north as Devine had thought. Adolpho showed us the spot where the shed had once stood, and also showed us where a small dirt road had run outside the southern end of the cemetery. Devine had drawn such a road but had located it to the north. The road had almost completely disappeared into the jungle, but another photo showed the trail with Sugar Loaf Mountain in the background. It seemed perfectly to match the conformation of the hills and the general terrain. Devine had inscribed on the photo: "Gravesite is thirty to forty feet to the left of road at this position." We aligned the photograph with the actual area and found ourselves some seventy to eighty feet outside the southern boundary of the graveyard. Pacing off thirty-five feet, we arrived in a grove of trees, outside the cemetery and just behind the notched tree which served as a landmark. The area was relatively clear but covered by a rough, coarse grass. It was there I decided to begin excavation. Father Sylvan again extended the permission of the Church and was always present as the work progressed. I first chose a fifteen by fifteen plot directly under the trees and our diggers went to work. Slowly, almost painfully, we went down nearly five feet. Some of it was topsoil, but below two or three feet the earth turned to coral in boulder form. We found absolutely nothing. I moved the effort a little to the west on the slight slope leading toward the beach. Again the excavation was fruitless. The only excitement was provided by an unexploded hand grenade one of the boys turned up with his first shovelful. The rusty bomb was taken out and dropped into the deep water of Tanapag Harbor.

Then I moved the excavation a few yards closer to the graveyard and the natives began a third series of holes. On September

21, 1961, we made a discovery. Commander Bridwell had stopped by the site to observe our activities, and it was he who first spotted the remains. About two and a half feet down, an unmarked grave had been opened. Bridwell jumped into the pit and began to pull out pieces of skull, shoulder, and leg bones. Carefully, patiently we uncovered the remainder of the find. From the amount of remains, it appeared that two persons had been buried head-to-foot in the common grave. As the natives had thrown out several shovelfuls of earth before Bridwell could stop them, I obtained a dozen two-by-fours, pieced them into squares, nailed wire screens to the bottoms, and we sifted the entire area for four days to make sure we had gotten everything. The total recovery amounted to seven pounds of bones and thirty-seven teeth. There were small teeth and large teeth and large and small bones. The remains were extremely fragile and had to be removed from the ground with great care; even then many of the bones broke apart as they were being lifted into boxes.

In 1961 we had not been able to locate dental charts for either Amelia or Fred, but I called in a Navy dentist and one of the local native dentists to examine the teeth. Both agreed we had apparently recovered the remains of a man and woman, and there was an excellent possibility the people had not been Saipanese or Oriental. Many of the teeth appeared to contain zinc oxide fillings and Japanese dentists had never been known to use that material before or during World War II.

Had we recovered the remains of Amelia Earhart and Fred Noonan? The grave had been located in the area Devine had told us to search and we had apparently unearthed what was left of two people, a man and a woman judging by the relative sizes of the bones and teeth. There was also the chance these people were Americans. But was that enough? I didn't think so. Nothing had been found in the grave save the skeletons; no boxes, no clothing, no artifacts of any kind. Without dental charts we couldn't possibly risk a guess as to the identity of the people.

One of the medical officers carefully wrapped each of the bone fragments and teeth in cotton and securely packed them in cigar boxes which were then taped together to form one large package. I asked Bridwell for permission to remove the remains from the island to Hawaii or California for study by an expert. The commander obviously didn't want the responsibility for the decision and informed me he would cable Washington for what he termed "necessary clearance." Meanwhile, I gave the package to Father Sylvan and asked him to lock it in the church vault at the Chalan Kanoa mission.

When I returned to the gravesite to be certain the natives had properly replaced the excavated earth, I found a touching scene. The Carolinian and Chamorran natives with their simple wisdom and compassion had not only neatly filled the area but had hand-fashioned a wooden cross to mark the grave and had carefully placed coral rocks around the site outlining the position in which we had found the remains.

That night brought a rather shattering experience. Early in the evening I had a sandwich and a bottle of beer at the Officers' Bar and then retired to my "Presidential Suite" quonset hut. I wrote some notes on the day's activities, cleaned the lenses of the cameras, played back several of the tapes I had recorded, and finally hit the sack at 10:00 P.M. Saipan was having one of its typical tropical storms; sheets of rain swept against the galvanized metal sides of the quonset with a rhythm highly conducive to sleep. I remember getting up once to lower slightly the canvas which covered the hut's screens. The wind was blowing harder, and a mist of water had been filtering through to my cot.

I still don't know exactly what awakened me the second time. It was about 1:30 A.M. and the storm's intensity seemed to have increased. With a start I sat upright. I couldn't see anyone, but the sense of danger in the small room was overwhelming. My eyes strained to pierce the darkness; my ears struggled to separate sounds, sense the location of the menace I felt. Suddenly a brilliant flash of lightning illuminated the quonset and I saw a man standing in the corner of the room, back toward me, apparently searching for something. I scooped a flashlight from the floor and leaped to my feet, shining the beam on him with the same movement.

"What do you want?" I shouted, desperately hoping the sound would carry down the hill to the commander's quarters.

The man whirled to face me, an ugly machete clenched in his right hand. He made one threatening half-swing with the big knife, then turned and nearly ripped the door from its hinges in his haste to get out. I remember hearing the machete's blade banging against the wall of the narrow hallway as he ran for the exit. I followed at a respectable distance, not only because I feared the man's outsized blade, but also the fact I was wearing only a T-shirt did not contribute to excessive bravery. The screened front door of the hut slammed shut in my face, but by the running light on the porch, I saw the man sprint across the road and disappear into the jungle. He was dressed in old Army or Marine Corps fatigues, wore a Seabee baseball-type cap, and I knew him! It was Francisco Galvan, whom the Fathers and I had tried so often to question, and who, we suspected, knew a great deal about the final fate of Earhart and Noonan.

I slowly walked back into the room and sat on my cot. Had it really happened, or had I been dreaming? I slapped my face a couple of times, and it hurt; I seemed to be awake. Then I noticed wet sandal marks on the floor leading in and out of the room. They removed the doubt; it was not a dream. But what was Galvan doing in my quarters at 1:30 in the morning? What did he want? Certainly it wasn't my life. With that machete he could have cut me into a dozen pieces with as many strokes. He apparently wasn't after money. There was more than two hundred dollars in cash on the dresser and it was undisturbed. Francisco also did not seem interested in motion picture or still cameras or tape-recording equipment. Expensive models of each lay untouched on the cot next to me.

Then it hit me. When I first saw Galvan, he had been searching for something in the corner of the room. The area held nothing but a small stack of cigar and packing boxes. Francisco must have been looking for the package containing the remains. Not aware that Father Sylvan had taken it to the mission house, he assumed I was keeping the find.

That led to more questions: Why would Galvan be concerned about the remains to the point of attempting to steal them? Perhaps he feared becoming involved in a matter which could result in a murder charge. If Francisco had played some role in the demise of Earhart and Noonan, there was a chance of such an implication. According to the testimony we had gathered, Amelia and Fred had died in Japanese custody before the start of World War II. If so, their deaths could justifiably be labeled murder. But to risk being caught in the act of trying to remove the evidence would then be the most stupid action Galvan could take. Discovery would be almost an admission of guilt. There had to be some other motivation.

One question required an immediate answer. Should I report the incident to Bridwell? I decided simply to tell him a prowler had entered the quonset during the night and the man had fled when I awakened. If Galvan was determined to get the package, perhaps he would make another attempt and I might be able to take him at a disadvantage which would force him to talk. The next afternoon I borrowed a revolver from one of the coastguardsmen at the Loran station, and tucked it in my travel bag under the cot. It really wasn't a smart thing to do, but if Mr. Galvan returned, I was determined his reception was going to be hostile. Father Sylvan was more than a little upset with my plan and threatened to move into the "Presidential Suite" with me until the madness passed. However, his fears and my preparations were entirely wasted. When Francisco Galvan disappeared across the road and into the jungle, he must have kept moving with no intention of coming back. The Fathers were not to see him for many weeks, long after I had left the island.

Before my departure, though, there were still more surprises to be experienced. I was about to meet with the Central Intelligence Agency and discover one of the best kept U.S. military secrets since the end of World War II.

12

The invitation came by telephone from a man whom I shall call Johnson.

"Mr. Goerner, how would you like to come up to the northern end of the island tonight and be our guest for cocktails and a chat?"

"Certainly would, Mr. Johnson," I replied, "but how do I get there? I understand you have some formidable restrictions."

"Don't worry about that. I'll have a driver stop by your quonset and pick you up about six-thirty."

"I hope this isn't a dress affair," I continued. "I'm afraid my wardrobe is now limited to khaki pants and a clean shirt."

"That's formal on Saipan," returned Johnson. "We're just folks up here. I think you'll find everyone very congenial. By the way, would you mind saying a few words to the folks about your Amelia Earhart investigation? We've all been interested in what you're doing and speculation is running high."

I had a strong hunch the "just folks" of NTTU knew more about my investigation than I did, but I resisted the urge to say so.

Within seconds of 6:30 that evening, a new black Chevrolet sedan driven by an American civilian pulled up before the "Presidential Suite." The man hopped out, jogged around the car and opened the door for me. Whatever color one might call the Saipan carpet, it was being rolled out. We drove north for a mile or so from the Naval Administration area until we reached the high fences topped with barbed wire which stretched across the road and disappeared into the jungle. One of two Saipanese guards came over to the car and checked the driver's identification. They obviously knew each other, but the process of perusing credentials was still more than perfunctory. The Chamorran, whom I recognized from a chance meeting in Chalan Kanoa, was thorough to the point of looking in the back seat and trunk to make sure no one was being smuggled into NTTU land.

My chauffeur, a well-manicured fellow in his early thirties, dressed in slacks, white shirt and tie, was pleasant but completely noninformative. I marveled at his skill to parry my not too subtle leads: "How long have you been on the island?" "Where is your home in the States?" "What's your job with NTTU?" "How many of you folks are there on Saipan?" All questions were smoothly redirected to less sensitive subjects. For instance, the query regarding his tenure on Saipan received this reply:

"Long enough to go through several tropical storms like the one we had the other night. Boy, it really came down, didn't it? How have you been adjusting to the weather here?"

As a newsman-broadcaster, I've had some difficult times obtaining direct answers from interviewees, but NTTU's emissary would head my list of ten top dodgers.

From the guard post at the fence, the road wound through the jungle and began to climb a large landmass the driver referred to as Denni Hill. (I later learned the area had been called Army Hill for several years after the U.S. 1944 invasion.) We hadn't passed anything of interest; the scenes were identical to the rest of Saipan, jungle in varying density. The gentle rise of the hill became a sharp incline and my dissembling guide shifted the Chev into second and finally low gear. Pulling hard, the car topped the grade and I stared ahead, incredulous. There, in the middle of the jungle on a tiny island six thousand miles from San

Francisco, was a modern town which could shame many better-class U.S. suburbs. Spread over the terraced hillsides were more than a hundred two- and three-bedroom homes with concrete, typhoonproof roofs. Up-to-date in every respect, they lined lighted, landscaped streets with wide, park-like areas separating each cluster of buildings. Near the town's center we passed a complex which included a library, soda fountain-snack bar, barber shop and theater-auditorium. The permanent concrete structures surrounded a large parking lot simulating contemporary shopping districts to the extent of marked exits, entrances, and parking stalls. As we cruised through the avenues, my amazement heightened. Carefully tended lawns circled each home with precisely spaced palm trees bordering connecting sidewalks. Through louvered windows of the houses I could see attractively decorated living rooms and kitchens with the latest appliances. New automobiles were parked in carports and driveways. Women's, children's, along with men's clothing hung on lines behind garages. The obvious family situation added to my puzzlement.

"You look a little flabbergasted," chortled my guide. "Bit of a shock to come out of jungle into this, isn't it?"

"So this is where the thirty million went," I murmured.

"Not all of it," said my companion. "There's still a lot you haven't seen."

At that moment we passed a huge, two-story edifice which extended almost a block.

"Is that the administration building?" I asked.

"No . . . No . . ." chuckled the driver with a slight overtone of condescension, "Headquarters is much larger. No, that's just an apartment house for the single members of the group."

"Sorry," I said. "Silly of me . . . By the way, and I hope this isn't out of line, I have a modicum of curiosity as to where the hell we're going."

"I'm sure you do," he replied. "We'll be there in a minute. A lot of folks are waiting for you at the club."

The car climbed another hill from a side which prevented a clear view of its summit. Only a corner of a building was visible initially. My fey chauffeur drove slowly along the crest of the hill giving me time to absorb the spectacular panorama: to the east the Pacific Ocean; the Philippine Sea to the west. With dusk approaching, the scene reminded me of closing footage from an old Burton Holmes' travelogue: "As the sun sinks slowly into the vast Western Pacific . . ."

". . . We arrive at the recreational heart of NTTU," my Saipan-tour guide unwittingly finished the cliché for me as with a flourish he curbed the car before the club. The portion I had first seen actually represented less than a quarter of the structure. It was immense. It was a night club and restaurant belonging on the outskirts of Las Vegas, Nevada. A sixty-foot canopy decorated with colored lights stretched from street to entrance. Large glass and steel double doors opened into a spacious lounge. Two cocktail bars, stocked with every brand and kind of liquor, were at either end of a commodious dance floor which also featured a bandstand equipped with microphone and spotlights. To the left of the main entrance was a huge dining room with sliding partitions which could be used to divide the area for meetings and other activities. A good part of the sprawling complex was provided with picture windows and sliding glass doors which looked upon a beautifully landscaped patio and afforded a fabulous view of the island's western shore and the sea beyond. The club obviously was designed to remove most of the pain from even a prolonged stay on Saipan.

Several hundred NTTU "folks" were waiting for me. The estimate is modest; men and nearly an equal number of women were seated at the bars, throughout the lounge, in the dining room and around the edge of the dance floor. As I entered, every head turned, conversation quieted and recorded music on a speaker system was silenced. For a moment, I felt a strong urge to check my fly. The mood of attention was somewhere between a long-anticipated arrival of Queen Elizabeth and the entrance of an accused killer-rapist into a crowded courtroom. Suspicion, admiration, and curiosity were evenly mixed, and I almost expected to hear applause punctuated by a few boos and a hiss.

A gentleman who identified himself only as the "manager of the club," met me at the door and I was escorted through the throng toward the bandstand.

"Mr. Johnson asked me to welcome you, Mr. Goerner," the

man began. "Our folks are most anxious to hear your speech."

"I didn't know you wanted a formal address."

"Well, we canceled the movie this evening, and Mr. Johnson said you would be willing to discuss your investigation with us."

"Where is Mr. Johnson?"

"He's out at one of the units right now, but he'll be along in a few minutes. Is anything wrong?"

The weird scene was beginning to irritate. The prospect of speaking before a strange, probably hostile group of people didn't bother me, but the manner in which I'd been brought into the situation did. During two trips to Saipan I'd been denied access to NTTU despite complete Defense Department accreditation as a foreign correspondent. In how many ways my efforts had been impeded, I could only guess. Absolutely no information about the secret project had been given to me; yet, here I was, being shoved into a spotlight and asked to divulge results of the investigation to an audience which undoubtedly had little sympathy for any newsman, especially one probing their home grounds. I decided to give the "manager" a small hard time and have at least a couple of laughs from my predicament.

"I'm afraid there's a lot wrong," I replied with a worried look. "For one thing, I don't have my teleprompter with me. Had I known I was to deliver a formal speech I would have brought my teleprompter."

"We'll send someone right over to the Navy area and pick it up, Mr. Goerner."

"You'll have to go a lot farther than that; I left it in San Francisco."

"Couldn't you possibly go ahead without it? Be as informal as you like."

"Oh, I could make a grand effort and do without my teleprompter, but there's also the matter of AFTRA. As manager of this club you should know of the American Federation of Radio and Television Artists. When Mr. Johnson called this morning, I didn't know I would be performing in Las Vegas tonight. My fee will have to be adjusted to match the demand of circumstances and audience."

"Fee? Did Mr. Johnson promise you something for your appearance this evening?"

"Well, I understood we would discuss it when I got here. When did Mr. Johnson say he might show up?"

"He didn't say for sure. Soon, I hope, but I can't be certain. The folks are going to be awfully disappointed if they don't get to hear you speak. Ah . . . a small fund does exist at the club for parties and the like. How much were you thinking of for a fee? Perhaps we could meet it from that."

The man was sincerely distressed, and I began to feel a little ashamed of my attemps at humor. It was difficult to believe he had swallowed the teleprompter bit, but in his eagerness to please me and the crowd, he really had not comprehended.

"That won't be necessary. Let's consider this performance a public service; I'm sure I can convince AFTRA it's not a violation of the talent code."

His face shone with gratitude. I had made at least one NTTU friend. Climbing onto the bandstand, he blew loudly into the microphone and firmly thumped it with a finger to check its awareness. Then, after much throat-clearing, he proceeded with a five minute puff and introduction which included a personal biography of me in far greater depth than anything CBS ever turned out. Someone had done considerable research.

Finally, to warm applause not punctuated by boos and a hiss, I ascended the podium, adjusted myself atop a bar stool before the microphone and began to speak.

"Good evening, folks of NTTU. It's a delight to be with you here in Las Vegas . . ."

It was a good audience; quiet, attentive, and it laughed in the right places. Any speaker would have been pleased by the response. The first communications of hostility rapidly faded and were replaced by a sense of genuine interest in Amelia Earhart and the reasons for my two visits to Saipan. For forty-five minutes I revealed what we had learned, omitting a number of items which seemed best left unmentioned. In conclusion, I offered this observation:

"It appears now that Amelia Earhart and Fred Noonan may have played a prominent role in relationships between Japan and the United States in the four years preceding World War II. The difficulties our investigative efforts have encountered indicate, I believe, the extent and importance of that role. It's strange that this twelve-by-five-mile island should have been witness to so much history. NTTU will surely add more fascinating pages."

The four magic letters froze the folks into complete concentration. The only sound from any part of the club was the deep throbbing hum of the huge air-conditioning system. Everyone was straining to hear what was going to be said about Saipan's secret.

"Nearly a quarter of a century has passed since Earhart and Noonan disappeared, and only now are facts beginning to emerge. It may be another twenty-five years before the story of NTTU can be told. But when that time arrives, America and the free world will be grateful for your contributions in this decade since President Truman committed U. S. Forces in Korea . . . It's been nice talking with you this evening. Thank you for your attention."

I must have said the right thing; the applause was strong and solid and burst forth as it does from people who have been collectively affected. Actually, it was the only approach I could have taken without revealing I didn't know exactly what NTTU was about. Within seconds they surrounded me. Many volunteered bits of information learned from various natives about "the man and woman fliers before the war." Others had questions about the investigation, about me, about CBS and broadcasting in general. All seemed hungry for a celebrity even if they had to create him.

Gradually the crowd diminished and I became aware of a man who had been standing in the background observing the scene with a slightly derisive smile. He was my size, six feet, two inches, and wore a sweat-stained sport shirt, open at the throat with sleeves rolled high to disclose well-developed biceps. His age was difficult to judge; probably late-forties.

A hard, calculating face gave him the appearance of a middle-aged commando, used to giving orders and receiving total obedience. His gaze penetrated, challenged, exuded confidence.

He was not exuding friendship as he moved forward to greet me.

"That's a good act you have, Mr. Goerner."

"Thank you, Mr. Johnson," I replied. "It is Johnson, isn't it?"

"That's right," he said, smiling without humor. "Let's have a drink at the bar."

The rest of the people kept clear. Johnson obviously was the boss of NTTU and no one was going to interrupt his conversation. A bartender delivered two beers, then maintained respectful distance, too.

Johnson took a swig of cold brew and asked, "CBS . . . what's that—the Conman's Benevolent Society?"

The affront was unpleasantly voiced; provocation seemed to be the purpose. I decided to counter the challenge momentarily by issuing one of my own.

"What are you, Mr. Johnson? A GS 16 or 17?"

(Most CIA personnel are classified by General Services Administration numbers. GS 16 and 17 are among the highest and both correspond to the rank of admiral in the Navy.)

Johnson showed no reaction at first. Calmly he appraised the bottles behind the bar, stared at himself in the mirror for a few seconds, then turned to me and said, "Just how much do you know about NTTU?"

The classification numbers had struck a sensitive nerve; however, the ill-natured jab at CBS tempted me to less than a civil answer.

"Why ask that of a Conman's Benevolent Society member? Certainly you couldn't believe my observations."

Johnson leveled his eyes at mine but when after a moment it became evident that the stare technique profited little, the rugged face broke with a grin, and he said, "Okay, Goerner, let's stop jousting. How much do you know and what have you guessed? There'll be no pressure, but I'm responsible for this operation and your information might help me."

With that attitude, Johnson won my cooperation.

"Know some, guessed some," I replied. "I know President Truman took control of Saipan from the Department of Interior and gave it to the Navy . . . but the Navy is a front for you people. Thirty million or more dollars were spent on your facilities; I believe you're training Nationalist Chinese. And from what I've seen and heard, the endeavor is Central Intelligence Agency sponsored and staffed. I guessed about your rank, and conned the club manager tonight because I'm fed up with the jazz that's been fed me and the obstacles which have been shoved in my way during both visits to this island. I don't know NTTU's mission and don't give a damn; whatever you're doing with Chiang's boys is your business. Amelia Earhart, regardless of what anyone says, thinks or suspects, is my sole reason for being here."

Johnson's grin grew wider.

"I believe you," he said. "Washington was fairly sure of that when they let you come here a second time. But what's your beef about obstacles? I haven't given any orders to block your investigation; in fact, I've encouraged cooperation."

I told him about the Fathers' feeling that someone was interfering with witnesses, attempting to get them to alter or abrogate their testimony.

"I'll look into it," Johnson promised, "but you have to help us in return."

"How?"

"By keeping quiet about NTTU. I can't confirm or deny your comments about us; I only say you could seriously jeopardize U.S. security by spilling any of it. It's been a battle from the beginning to keep Saipan out of the news."

"Why? What's the big deal? The UN Charter allows for defense of the peoples of Trust Territories. As far as research goes, we have the Nike-Zeus test project at Kwajalein in the Marshalls. Everyone, including Russia, knows about that."

"You've answered your own question," Johnson continued. "We're obviously something else and we can't afford to have Russia challenge the United Nations about a Trust Territory whether our position is defensible or not."

"Are the Russians curious about Saipan?"

"Plenty. In the last few years, we've monitored several Russian submarines cruising around the island, undoubtedly photographing us through their periscopes. Fortunately, our facilities are constructed so none is visible from the sea. The purpose of the mission would not be definable even from overflight aerial photographs."

"How do you get past the UN inspection team?" I asked. "It checks these islands every couple of years, doesn't it?"

"Yes," said Johnson, "but it's a pro-Western team. The Navy

guys handle them and there's never been a request or a reason for them to visit the north end or east side."

"You mean they don't know about NTTU."

"That's possible. Let's say they don't make a problem."

"Don't the natives complain?"

"A few aren't too happy, but living conditions are better than some other Trust Territory islands because NTTU brings money into the economy. The Saipanese know this, and while like anyone else they want more, they're not about to kill their provider."

"I'm not going to knock you off either, Mr. Johnson. I don't know any more about your project than the Russians."

"You know a lot more, and if you broadcast or wrote about it, there could be trouble. When you return to the States, I'm sure you'll be contacted by one of our people. He'll probably give details on us and more reasons why we need and expect your cooperation. And forget the crack I made about CBS."

"Forgive. Not forget. I like you owing me. I may need a favor."

"It was just a small thrust . . . to check your guts."

"And?"

"They're O.K."

When I left the club that night, Mr. Johnson and I were using first names. That was the last time I saw him. The Central Intelligence Agency recently informed me that he is now serving in another part of the world, and I was requested to withhold his real name from publication to protect a necessary anonymity. This I have done, but the next chapter discloses Saipan's secret. Johnson was right about the contact to be made on my return. It was almost as bizarre as meeting the headmaster of NTTU.

Three days passed without word from Washington regarding permission to take the remains from Saipan to an anthropologist. It was impossible to wait longer, so I booked on the next Navy flight. As Father Sylvan drove me to the field, I outlined a plan: if and when clearance was given, the package was to be plainly wrapped and addressed only to the anthropologist whose name I would send. One of the Fathers would then hand-carry the box to Guam and turn it over to Pan American for transport in the gem-cargo hold of a jet liner. Nothing would be said to anyone about contents. If it took considerable time to obtain permission, the remains would stay in the church mission vault. Should the Navy or NTTU ask for or demand custody of the package, Father Sylvan was to insist notification be sent to me.

Goodbyes were said, and I climbed aboard the old DC-4 which promptly taxied to the end of the strip where engine checks were begun. Instead of taking off, the big plane rolled back toward the quonset hut station. I assumed one of the engines was rough, but the co-pilot opened the cockpit door and hollered back that the Navy Administration radio was receiving a coded message from Washington which concerned me. We were to be detained until contents of the communication were known.

Father Sylvan hurried back to the mission to get the package. Everyone seemed certain Washington's response would be positive. Commander Bridwell appeared relieved; the decision, whichever way it went, was no longer his. It took twenty or more minutes for the decoding center to relay the text of the message; evidently they wanted to be sure there was no mistake. I could tell from Bridwell's expression as he walked across the concourse that the words had been strong and negative.

"I'm sure sorry, Fred," he began, "but Washington says nothing is to be removed from Saipan."

"Any reasons?"

"No."

"What else?"

"You're to turn your film over to a Commander Gorski on Guam."

"Why?"

"I don't know. That's all it said."

As the DC-4 broke ground and climbed from Koebler Field, I saw Father Sylvan's Volkswagen pull up to the terminal. At last glimpse, he was standing beside the car, holding a seven-pound box which was destined to become famous.

At Guam, I learned Admiral Wendt had been replaced by Admiral John S. Coye, Jr., who could not at the moment be available to discuss disposition of film situations. His Public Information Officer, Commander John Gorski, informed me that any still or motion picture film in my possession was to be given to the Marianas Sea Frontier Command for screening and evaluation. At some time in the future, the film would be forwarded to me in San Francisco; there was no estimation how long clearance would take.

That was that. I went home.

13

An unknown number of people, including at least one U. S. Senator and one admiral, had concerned themselves with the investigation. Senator Leverett Saltonstall of Massachusetts was anxious for reports as he had received a letter from a West Medford, Massachusetts, constituent, Mrs. Albert Morrissey, asking him to block further attempts to determine the fate of Amelia Earhart. Mrs. Morrissey had a special interest in the case; she was Amelia's sister.

Admiral Daniel F. Smith, Jr., the Navy's Chief of Information, also wanted enlightenment, although his office made it clear our efforts were considered a near cabal.

I say "an unknown number" were interested because word of Saipan's unmarked grave and its possible contents had been circulated through several departments of U.S. government and military, resulting in a steady flow of official and unofficial requests to Smith's staff for additional facts. The queries were embarrassing to the Navy for two reasons: no one was certain what we had found or how much we knew. And whatever answers were issued, Saipan would have to be mentioned and thereby become a subject for discussion—a distressing development for NTTU.

I reported the situation to Jules Dundes at KCBS in San Francisco. He was not happy with the Navy's decision precluding study of the remains and even less pleased by the confiscation of film.

"It's unbelievable," he said. "What's going on over there that has to be kept secret?"

I gave him an oral sketch of Johnson and NTTU, but it didn't ease his reaction.

"That shouldn't have a bearing on Amelia Earhart," he countered. "We have to press for release of the package and the films. Someone has a lot of explaining to do . . . and soon."

Jules was living up to his reputation as a fighter, but he was also being too optimistic.

Ted Koop, CBS Vice-President in Washington, was asked to intercede again at the Defense Department. Within a few days, he learned from Assistant Secretary of Defense Sylvester that we were in for a struggle; the Navy had no intention of making it easy. Before clearance could be gained, CBS would have to obtain permission from the nearest relative of both Earhart and Noonan.

The stipulation was more than just premature. There was no positive indication the remains represented Amelia and Fred, yet their next of kin had to be consulted! The requirement would have been valid only if identification had been established and final disposition were the question.

Koop was also informed that CBS would have to provide indemnification for the Navy, holding it blameless should litigation result from removal and study of the remains. Arthur Hull Hayes, president of CBS Radio, reluctantly presented the network's New York Legal Department with one of its most unique cases: indemnifying the Navy for a case not yet ascertained but for which the Navy should have borne responsibility in any instance.

Even CBS' Big Daddy took a personal interest. Dr. Frank Stanton, president of all CBS surveys, flew from New York to San Francisco to discuss the situation. It was my first meeting with the man who is the image and spokesman of the broadcasting industry. I expected Madison Avenue: a glib, advertising-oriented pragmatist. In some respects, the preconception was correct. Stanton, however, is much more: competitive, dedicated, yet controlled—mellowed by responsibility. Physical appearance does not reflect his astuteness. Sandy hair, freckles, and a somewhat boyish face give the impression of an easy-goer at least ten years younger than fifty-eight. It was one of the rare times I have instinctively liked and trusted an individual. He was wearing a jazzy sport coat and slacks combination when I met him in Jules' office, and his greeting was equally relaxed.

"Understand you have things gyrating a bit at the upper echelons in Washington."

"They would like us to go away, Dr. Stanton."

"Forget the Doctor business. Make it Frank, please."

"All right, Frank, but I think they would prefer in Washington that we were all academicians rather than reporters."

Stanton smiled. "A Ph.D. hasn't and won't prevent news gathering or even newsmaking. Give me the details."

With a chance to star for the boss, I presented a thirty-minute ad-lib capsule. There were no interruptions. When my dissertation ended, Dr. Stanton asked four penetrating questions:

"What makes you think we can come up with an answer to the Earhart mystery when the government apparently failed?"

"I suspect the Navy and several other Departments are holding classified information," I replied. "It's also possible a thorough investigation has never been undertaken. The protection of NTTU would be one reason for a lack of interest."

"Why weren't the remains of Earhart and Noonan reclaimed a long time ago? You say the U.S. has controlled Saipan since 1944."

"That has puzzled me, too. Lack of interest or top-secret classification are the only answers which make sense."

"If we do get the package released, what are the chances of identifying the remains?"

"They're good. A capable anthropologist should be able to determine age, sex, approximate height and weight, and how long buried. There's a chance, too, we may be able to locate dental charts. That would clinch it one way or the other."

His fourth question was the big one.

"Are you convinced you've found Earhart?"

"No, but I think indications are strong enough to demand expert opinion. I'm only sure of one thing: an American man and woman, supposed to be fliers and spies, were held by the Japanese on Saipan before the war. It's hard to believe they were other than Earhart and Noonan."

Stanton thought for a moment, then decided. We would fight for an answer. Jules and I were to choose an anthropologist from one of the local universities. When that was arranged, I was to visit the relatives and get written permission for the study, explaining the entire situation and guaranteeing there would be no publicity unless positive identification was established. If the bones could not be identified as those of Earhart and Noonan (or anyone else), the box would be shipped back to Saipan. It was unanimously agreed that a premature break in the story could have unpleasant results. The relatives certainly would be subjected to press harassment and CBS might be accused of sensationalism; therefore, all contacts were to be kept confidential and as few persons as possible given details.

The search for an anthropologist was simple. Dr. Joseph Lohman, dean of the School of Criminology at the University of California, Berkeley, recommended another U. of C. professor, Dr. Theodore D. McCown, who had recently identified the remains of Junípero Serra, the pioneer California Catholic missionary, after the bones of the famed Franciscan priest had lain in a lost vault for more than 150 years. McCown was familiar with the latest verification techniques, and additionally was qualified by several years' experience with U. S. Army Graves Registration during World War II. The project interested him and he agreed, after some persuasion, to do the study if and when the Navy relented. There was another reason for choosing McCown: he was a quiet man who disliked publicity.

The problem of locating members of Fred Noonan's family appeared difficult. I checked all the beauty salons in Oakland, California, hoping Mary Bea had continued in that business after Fred's disappearance: no Noonans or Martinellis.

It was time for some good luck, and a coincidence. Dr. Ted Hatlen, my old boss at the University of California at Santa Barbara, sent Mary Bea's current address. His thoughtfulness saved me many months of tracing and checking.

Hatlen was head of the Speech Department at UCSB when I was an undergraduate student there from 1948 to '52, and it was he who arranged for me to receive a graduate fellowship to the University of Utah. My debt to him deepened on Sunday morning, October 1, 1961. He read an article in the Santa Barbara *News Press* about a Mrs. Harry B. Ireland, one of the world's leading experts on cymbidium orchids. According to the newspaper, Mrs. Ireland had previously been "married to Frederick Noonan, navigator for Amelia Earhart in her tragic flight around the world."

"A year later, on a boat returning from Hawaii," the story continued, "she met Mr. Ireland of Philadelphia, who had lost his wife the previous year. They subsequently were married and came to Santa Barbara to live." The article also told of Mrs. Ireland's more than two thousand orchid plants in greenhouses on the grounds of her home and gave her address.

The address added the coincidence. I had driven past the Ireland mansion almost every day during my years as a student, and even had dated a girl who lived several doors away at a sorority house. There had been some talk of a lovely, but strangely sad lady, who spent all of her time raising orchids.

Mrs. Ireland is a charming, dignified, warm-hearted woman. Her gray hair was carefully groomed and the dark eyes flashed with anticipation and curiosity the afternoon I arrived in Santa Barbara. She made it clear, however, there was no hurry to begin a discussion of Fred Noonan. First we strolled through the greenhouses and talked of her experiments with orchids. Using a toothpick, she showed me how pollen is taken from a standard cymbidium stud plant and placed in a tiny cavity in the column of a dwarf plant from which its own pollen has been removed. The purpose is to control and enhance the colors of the blooms.

Finally, Mary Bea led me into the great house. We sat on a sun porch next to the living room. With deliberation she poured cups of tea.

"I think I'm settled to talk now," she said. "Thank you for not pressing the issue right away."

"I know it's difficult. As I said on the phone, Mrs. Ireland, I wish there were a better way."

"Don't worry about me," she replied. "It's only that I got quite a start when you walked up the drive. For a few seconds, I thought you were he. People have probably mentioned that you bear a striking resemblance to Fred Noonan."

Her reaction surprised me. Paul Mantz was the only other person I had met who knew Noonan and he had not suggested a likeness.

"It's the way you move," Mary Bea continued. "Purposefully —as a man should. Fred was always full of energy, too. Couldn't wait to go and do."

"I hope I haven't appeared impatient."

"I didn't mean that. There are many other ways you resemble Fred. He was tall and good-looking. Not that he was a beautiful or even handsome man; it was simply a pleasant experience to see him."

We talked about her Fred for a while, then Mary Bea searched my eyes and said, "I want you to know how it was for us. Many people have wondered about Fred's and my relationship. It's natural, I suppose. We were married such a short time before the disappearance. Some people have even speculated that Fred and Amelia were having an affair and decided to land at some uninhabited island where they could spend the rest of their lives together."

She left the room for a minute and returned with a large leather-bound scrapbook. Spaced between yellowed newspaper clippings were dozens of letters from Fred, some addressed to "Miss Mary B. Martinelli," others to "Mrs. Fred Noonan." The latter group included a number written from various stops during the around-the-world flight.

I read all of them—twice—but a few words would have been enough. The letters were from a man completely in love with his wife. There could be no misinterpretation of Noonan's remarks about Amelia. They were casual and innocuous. The flight obviously was business, and he had been anxious to complete it.

The last letter, mailed from Bandoeng, Java, spoke of navigational and mechanical troubles which had delayed the Electra. There was no mention, however, of apprehension of what lay ahead; only reiteration of Fred's love for and desire to be with his bride.

The correspondence gave me a better understanding of Noonan but nothing to help solve his disappearance. Mary Bea could not add anything in that respect, either. She felt there were things Fred had not told her about the flight. An aura of secrecy had surrounded it. When she had questioned him about the venture, in particular the Pacific route, he had become evasive.

Then, following the disappearance, the official attitude in Washington had distressed her.

"It was as if no one wanted ever again to hear the names Noonan and Earhart," she said. "No one was supposed to dispute the decision they were lost at sea."

It was dark on the porch when I finished telling of the investigation, the finding of the remains, and what we wanted her to do. For a moment, Mary Bea looked at me without seeing; the reverie was deep and she was loath to leave it. Finally, with obvious effort, she shook herself and smiled in a tired, distant way.

"All right, Mr. Goerner, whatever is necessary. To whom do I write?"

"Secretary of the Navy John Connally would be best."

"I don't understand it," she puzzled. "Why is the Navy involving itself now? Over the years they have continually said Amelia and Fred were a civilian concern."

"I'm not sure. It may be a guilty conscience. The stronger possibility is a high-level classification dealing with something else but somehow connected to the disappearance."

Mary Bea nodded vaguely at my double-talk. I was grateful for her acceptance; it relieved me of discussing NTTU.

Mary Bea walked down the drive with me.

"Don't worry about it," she said. "I know you must pursue this thing; you can count on my help."

"I don't want to cause trouble for you."

"Let me handle that. By the way, if anyone ever writes the biography of Fred Noonan, I'd like it to be you."

"That's nice, Mrs. Ireland. Thank you."

"Why don't you call me Mary Bea. That's the way you think of me, isn't it?"

Three days later in San Francisco, I received Mary Bea's letter of permission to be forwarded to Secretary Connally.

H. B. Ireland got himself quite a woman when Fred Noonan disappeared.

It's about forty-five minutes by cab from Boston Airport to the Morrissey home in West Medford, Massachusetts. During the drive, I wondered what Amelia's sister would be like. She had already written to Senator Saltonstall, with a carbon copy to Dr. Stanton, asking that further investigation be stopped. Obtaining her permission could be difficult.

In preparation, I had researched Mrs. Morrissey; the results were impressive. As a teacher of high school English, she was successful and well-liked. The position had not been easily achieved. Her undergraduate work had been completed at Smith College and Radcliffe, but the Ed.M. degree from Harvard Graduate School of Education was delayed by marriage, two children, and several years of teaching. That, seemingly, represented a parallel to Amelia's tenacity; however, biographical likeness ended there. While her older sister roamed the world in search of tall headlines, Muriel Earhart settled down with Albert Morrissey, a Cambridge, Massachusetts, manufacturer. They had now been married thirty years and belonged to more than the usual number of civic betterment and service organizations. In brief, they typified the proverbial solid citizens.

My fears were not realized. Muriel was kind, gentle, understanding. While careers had differed, physical traits had not. It might have been Amelia who opened the door. The sixty-year-old, gray-haired woman had the same rangy figure and gaunt sweetness of face, the same introspection and curious reserve.

Albert was as pleasant. "Chief," as Muriel called him, stayed interestedly in the background, entering the conversation only when he had something positive to contribute.

Their attitudes toward my nearly memorized account of the investigation were encouraging and sympathetic. But as it had been with Mary Bea, recounting discovery of the remains was difficult. At first mention, the Morrisseys winced, so I withheld the most distasteful aspects. When the tale was finished, Albert moved to his wife's side and placed a comforting arm around her shoulders. Muriel, however, showed no great emotion; her silence only indicated consideration of facts.

"There have been so many stories," she began, "but for the first time, one sounds right."

"You've done a remarkable job of research," Albert added.

"No compliments are due," I replied. "I'm not sure I'm right."

"About what?" Muriel asked. "From what you've said there's no other conclusion."

"The question of the remains," I answered. "I'm satisfied there were two Americans of the description of Amelia and Fred on Saipan in 1937, but whether or not we've found the right grave is another matter. That's why your permission for the study is essential."

Muriel nodded, and said, "I suppose you know that I've been trying to block your efforts."

"Yes, Senator Saltonstall has been militant on your behalf. That's one of the reasons Dr. Stanton insists we proceed only with your permission."

"Well, let me rest your mind. You may have the permission for what it's worth. I'm sorry if our reticence has hindered you, but we had no way of knowing your effort was legitimate. After that generator business last year, I was afraid there would be more sensation seeking. Each new surge of publicity over the years has been a torture; not only for Chief and myself, but for Mother, too."

It was a moment before her last words registered, and then they were hard to believe. Amy Otis Earhart, mother of Amelia and Muriel, was still living!

Muriel noticed my surprise, and added. "She's upstairs now."

I didn't see Mrs. Earhart. She was ninety-four years old and beyond receiving visitors. The Morrisseys had provided a home for her since 1946 when the old lady finally gave up hope Amelia would be found alive, and closed her own house in Berkeley, California.

"I'm not going to tell Mother of our discussion," Muriel said. "It would only disturb her."

"What does she believe about the disappearance?" I asked.

"She feels there were things about the flight Amelia couldn't tell her. For many years she was sure my sister was a prisoner of the Japanese, but now she's resigned there will never be a final answer."

"What's your conclusion?"

"Until this evening, Chief and I believed Amelia and Noonan were lost at sea. That's what most people have accepted. Perhaps it was convenient and less painful to think so, but also there was some logic. The radio messages received at Howland from the plane seemed to indicate it had been close to the island at one point. A crash-landing on the ocean was more likely than capture by the Japanese."

"How do you feel now?"

Muriel looked at Chief and he nodded in return.

"I can answer that by asking you a question. To whom else must I write to accomplish the clearance you need?"

We decided on Navy Secretary Connally, Senator Saltonstall, Assistant Secretary of Defense Sylvester, and I asked Mrs. Morrissey to send an additional letter to Dr. Stanton stipulating her willingness to cooperate.

A week later Frank sent to me in San Francisco a copy of Muriel's communication. It expressed thanks for our efforts and granted permission to study the remains. It was a kind, gentle letter.

Albert Morrissey had been fortunate in his choice of a woman, too.

My introduction to interesting people continued, although I was not able to learn the names of all of them. A few days after my return to San Francisco, I began to suspect I was being followed. My first reaction was to wonder if this were paranoia, but some careful observations convinced me that imagination was not the cause of my apprehension. I was in truth under surveillance.

At least three men, working in shifts, were trailing me wherever I went. One watched my apartment at night from a car parked down the street, and followed me to work in the morning. Another picked me up during the day at the KCBS elevator, staying well in the background as I went about San Francisco to various news conferences and returned to the station for my broadcasts. The third had the early evening hours, and from cocktail time to my return home, made every scene I did. After four or five days, I had their techniques figured, but not their purpose. There was no feeling of danger, and I almost became amused.

One afternoon I told a friend, George Gallup, who headed CBS Radio Spot Sales on the Pacific Coast, about my ubiquitous chums, and we cooked up a small game of counterspy. At 5:00 P.M. we walked through the Palace Hotel lobby with Number Three in modest pursuit, and stopped in the Happy Valley Bar, ostensibly for beverages. Number Three promptly took a lobby chair opposite the entrance to the bar. We, meantime, departed the rear exit, circled the lobby, then stationed ourselves on opposite sides of Number Three's chair. His reaction was one of those marvelous moments: a slow-take followed by a quick double-take. Number Three, however, was noncommunicative. He denied following me, would not give his name, and explained his presence as "waiting for a friend." He waited and waited. We sat across from him and watched him wait. Finally, he feigned disgust, and strode from the lobby. I believe, though, I detected a small smile of appreciation on his face for our ludicrous situation.

That ended surveillance; at least my three regulars disappeared. Perhaps the first string went to work. If so, they were so smooth I wasn't aware of them. The whole thing may have been explained by a provocative telephone call I received the next day.

Lola Bizarri, my secretary, initially took it and reported, "There's a man on here who won't give his name, but says he wants to talk to you about Saipan."

"I have to go on the air in ten minutes," I replied. "Tell him to call back or write a letter."

Lola is usually good at putting off those who try to reach me at a bad time, but she had no success with this one.

"He says to tell you this is official U.S. government business, and he'd like to talk to you for a minute right now."

The voice was pleasant and casual and identified itself as

belonging to "Frederick Winter of the Central Intelligence Agency office here in San Francisco." I remembered Johnson's comment about my being contacted upon return to the States.

"What can I do for you, Mr. Winter?"

"Would it be possible for me to chat with you some time this afternoon?"

"I'm clear between two and three. Can you drop by the studio then?"

"Well, I'd rather it was somewhere else."

"Name it."

"Well, why don't I meet you on the main floor of the Palace Hotel next to the elevator entrance to KCBS."

"It sounds as if you have an aversion to studios with recording facilities."

"It's a normal precaution in our business," laughed Winter. "We'll go somewhere for a bite to eat."

"There's a convention in the Palace today. How will I know you?"

"Don't worry about that, Mr. Goerner. I'll know you."

He did. A tall, friendly faced fellow in black suit and matching Homburg came directly to me as I left the elevator.

"I'm Fred Winter," he warmly greeted.

"I'm Fred Goerner," I replied. "Oh, sorry. You already know that."

"Yes, I know quite a bit about you."

"I'll bet you do. Say, that's quite an outfit. One would never expect a CIA man to be so elegantly attired."

"Most of us don't change our dress when we join the intelligence community. I've always been fond of Homburgs."

I liked Winter. He was bright, and charming, with a sense of humor—I had thought of trenchcoat types as always effecting programed omniscience.

The next hour was, in understatement, incongruous. At Blum's, San Francisco's chic milk-shake parlor, Winter ordered a dish of strawberry ice cream for himself, coffee for me, and we discussed one of the best kept U.S. military secrets since the end of World War II: NTTU. This is the story:

When responsibility for administration of Saipan and the other Trust Territory of the Pacific Islands was transferred from the

Navy to the Department of the Interior on July 1, 1951, the interests of the United States in the Far East were being badly damaged.

China had already fallen and Chiang Kai-shek was in semi-exile on Formosa. Communists, using techniques from propaganda and internal dissension to the full-scale invasion of Korea, were achieving frightening successes.

North Korea, aided by Russian equipment and Red Chinese soldiers, was determined to push United Nations' forces into the sea.

Where would the Communists stop? What would be their next target? What could be done to harass and deter them? How rapidly was Red China developing a nuclear capability?

Those were only a few of the questions which plagued President Truman through 1951 and '52. The U.S. was fully committed to the war in Korea, and it was obviously essential that we know the designs and activities of the enemy.

The Central Intelligence Agency needed a new kind of guerrilla-spy: a man who could penetrate all parts of Communist-occupied territory in Asia, speak the language fluently, survive every menace and accomplish any of a thousand assignments.

He might slip through the barbed wire to North Korea, reach mainland China by air drop, infiltrate secretly from Hong Kong and Macao, or sail the tricky currents of the 100-mile-wide Formosa Strait in a junk. His most important mission would be establishment of a communications and espionage network for disseminating propaganda and discontent and relaying intelligence information.

As the 1952 U.S. presidential election neared, Red China had clearly emerged as the greatest danger in Asia. The CIA decided, with President Truman's knowledge and permission, to concentrate its efforts there, using the pick of Generalissimo Chiang's forces as the new secret agents. The U. S. Military Assistance Advisory Group (MAAG) was already teaching guerrilla warfare to Nationalist troops at training areas on Formosa. The problem was how and where to give the best of those troops a post-graduate course in espionage.

It couldn't be done on Formosa. The island was too large and well populated. The Reds had their own agents who reported regularly from Chiang's retreat, and the nature of such special training would soon come to their attention. Also, it would be embarrassing for the U.S. should the rest of the world become aware of the CIA plan. We were fighting the Red Chinese in Korea under the banner of the United Nations, but we were not officially at war with China; therefore it would not profit America to be found supplying Nationalist Chinese with the knowledge and tools to spy upon and harass a regime with whom we were ostensibly at peace. Such a revelation would not surprise or shock the Reds, though they would say so in their propaganda, but it would damage the U.S. with many uncommitted nations, who might believe the Communist cry that "the agents are the hirelings of American imperialism."

Of all the islands in the Western Pacific, Saipan most closely matched CIA requirements. Within reasonable flight range of both Formosa and Okinawa, its World War II bomber strips were repairable and well placed. The island's size, twelve by five miles, and population, 7500, were nearly ideal. At least half the land could be restricted without seriously displacing or overcrowding the natives. Saipan's topography was another plus. The mountains, plains, heavy jungles, and beaches would provide every training challenge.

The deciding factor was Saipan's proximity to Guam. The 115 miles allowed for isolation, yet provided the logistic accessibility to the building materials, equipment and labor needed for major construction.

There was one bureaucratic fly in CIA's ointment. The Department of the Interior had been given control of Saipan and had no intention of relinquishing its administration. Saipan was being planned as headquarters for the entire Trust Territory of the Pacific Islands—"The Capital of Micronesia."

When it learned the CIA request also included Tinian Island, three miles south of Saipan, the Interior Department was even less enthusiastic. CIA maintained that the closeness of Tinian to Saipan demanded equal restriction. There could be no security for Saipan without control of its southern neighbor.

It took the President to settle the dispute. Truman decreed CIA should have Saipan and Tinian, and Interior should be headquartered on Guam, a U. S. Possession outside the Trust Territory. Interior gained a single concession: one representative of the Department would be maintained on each of the islands. He would have no authority, but would be a constant reminder that Interior did not approve of CIA's power-play and intended someday to have the islands returned to its jurisdiction.

Then came the strangest switch. Truman obviously could not publicly announce that Saipan and Tinian had been turned over to CIA. The Russians and Red Chinese would immediately know what was happening, and the United Nations, too, would take a dim view of a Trust Territory being used as a training ground for spies. The transfer had to be made within the terms of the Strategic Trust Territory Agreement; that meant a return to Navy control. The Navy was not pleased with the role as front for CIA, but it was given no choice.

On January 1, 1953, as one of his last acts as President of the United States, Harry Truman signed a special order which secretly presented Saipan and Tinian and their Chamorran inhabitants to CIA. The Navy went into its act as administrator with hardly a nod to the Interior Department assistant.

The next month travel was so restricted that only those with Defense Department security clearance could reach the island. Travel by natives was thoroughly discouraged.

In March 1953 the first contract for thirty million dollars was let and the NTTU, Naval Technical Training Units, were born. The name was the only connection with the Navy.

In addition to the ultramodern town for CIA faculty which I had visited, there were eleven training sites. At each of the locations was a trio of permanent, concrete buildings for the student spies. A comfortable barracks accommodated fifteen or twenty men. A washhouse and large dayroom building with offices for the instructors completed the arrangement.

The tightest possible security was maintained throughout. The men selected for Saipan never knew where they were trained. If captured, they would not be able to divulge the island's secret to the Communists. The spy-school candidates were flown into Kagman Field on Saipan's eastern shore at night. They were then blindfolded and driven in curtained buses to their assigned unit. All sites were of course buried in the jungle and invisible from offshore. The instructors never addressed each other by name while in presence of the students. The worst torture the Reds could conceive could not force a man to tell facts he did not know.

The closely guarded fence I had encountered actually closed off Kagman Field and the training areas from the rest of the island. The students could not leave and no one but CIA personnel could enter. Only when the espionage tutoring was completed did the graduates depart as they had arrived. The units then were readied to receive the next class.

Saipan's production was small at first, but improved with each month. Between six and seven thousand guerrilla-spies had been trained by mid-1961, and sent forth to accomplish their delicate and dangerous work. How well they did could be judged by loud and lengthy Communist reaction. The U.S. was accused of sponsoring "paid mercenaries who commit unpardonable sins against the people of China." The Reds could not prove, however, that the Nationalists were American supported.

Chiang Kai-shek played along, insisting that every agent he sent to the mainland was trained in secret by his own people and received no U.S. military assistance. He was also reticent to comment about the fate of the agents, although at one point he did admit that some had been killed.

Others undoubtedly surrendered and were reindoctrinated. And there certainly were those who safely returned to Formosa with information which altered U.S. foreign and military policies in the Far East.

Fred Winter would not give an evaluation of the guerrilla-spy program. He limited himself to saying the CIA operation had been well planned and well carried out. But then I hardly expected him to be disloyal to his employer.

"We very much want your cooperation," Winter continued as he scooped up the last of his strawberry ice cream.

"The petard under NTTU's gate has a short fuse. If you light it by disclosing what you know, the explosion could affect our country's security."

"That's appreciated," I said, "but lately I've been concerned with a petard that's attached to me. Has the CIA had me under surveillance?"

"What do you mean?"

"I mean the three guys who have been tailing me for at least a week."

Winter did not smile when I told him the story.

"I don't think they are our men," he said. "In any case, I didn't assign them. A security check has already been run on you by the FBI."

"What's my rating?"

"We know you to be a good American."

"Then tell me why I'm being followed and why we're having to fight for every bit of information regarding Earhart?"

"As I said, there's no one from our intelligence community reporting on you now; at least as I'm informed. It might be another group noting your habits and contacts, hoping for some untoward act on your part which could be used for blackmail."

"That's a happy thought. Communists?"

"Possibly. But I don't think so. They would go about it differently."

"Who then?" I asked with agitation.

Winter smiled at that point and shook his head. "I have no answers, but don't worry about it."

His calm made me see some of the humor so I joined it.

"If they are Communists, aren't you afraid I'll commit an 'untoward act,' fall into their clutches and spill about NTTU?"

"Not very. Your record is excellent. We have faith in you."

"Thanks, but I'd rather have some protection."

"Let me know if they continue to bother you, and I'll see what can be done."

"All right. But you haven't explained Earhart."

Winter thought for a moment and said, "That is somewhat puzzling. I don't believe the intelligence community is intentionally withholding the material you want."

"Then why are we having such a hassle getting permission to study those remains? Why does the Navy act as if I'm the ghoul of the year for mentioning the matter when everything we've learned points to Earhart and Noonan having been on Saipan?"

"There's no doubt there," Winter replied. "The Navy is protecting NTTU the best way it can. It wouldn't be advantageous at this time to have more newsmen attempting to get permission to visit Saipan."

"As I told your man Johnson, there's almost no chance anyone will demand a twelve-thousand-mile trip to get a story and pictures we already have. There's a much greater possibility if the thing is left in limbo."

"That may be true."

"Let's be direct. Does the CIA have information or evidence concerning Earhart which has not been made public?"

"I don't know."

"Okay," I said rising from the table, "that's indefinite enough. Thanks for the coffee."

Winter picked up the check and walked with me toward the cashier. "I'd like to have your promise you'll protect our friends on Saipan."

"You have it," I replied. "But I've already told Jules Dundes, Art Hayes, and Frank Stanton of CBS. You'll have to get them to go along, too."

"We're familiar with the gentlemen. There should be no problem."

"I'd like a promise in return. If the story of NTTU ever can be told, an exclusive rightfully belongs to CBS. Will you give us the beat?"

"You can depend on it, but I wouldn't be too optimistic about an early release date."

Winter paid the check. I had been easy on his expense account, and I remember wondering how a CIA man filed for reimbursement when his organization had a completely hidden budget in Washington. Our ice cream and coffee probably showed up as part of a Navy requisition for lead pencils.

As I returned to KCBS that November afternoon in 1961, there were several disturbing questions in my mind.

When and to what extent in a free society should a newsman cooperate with his government? Was the United States justified in using a United Nations Trust Territory for the training of spies? Did we not accuse Japan of using the same island for her own purposes before World War II in violation of the League of Nations' Mandate? If it was wrong for the Japanese, why was it right for us? Were we substituting pragmatism for honor? Or were those just words when the real question was one of survival? This set of facts produced my answer:

The creation of NTTU had been a decision of Democratic President Truman. The project had grown and flourished during the administration of Republican President Eisenhower. It now continued to operate with the sanction of Democratic President Kennedy.

If these three men, with their superior knowledge of what we faced in the world, had decided NTTU was necessary to the security of the United States, then I should trust their wisdom.

What about Mr. Winter? Was he really with the CIA? He had only mentioned the letters in his initial telephone call; the rest of the time he referred to the "intelligence community." To be certain of his identity, I sent a letter to CIA headquarters, and received a confirming reply from E. D. Echols, director of personnel for that organization. My host for coffee and conversation was what he represented himself to be.

I have not seen Fred Winter since the 1961 meeting, although there have been two subsequent telephone conversations.

I kept my promise about NTTU; he was not able to keep his about the story rights.

He was completely correct about one thing; that I should not worry about the men who had been following me. They never reappeared. Whether they were CIA men, or represented as Winter hinted, "another intelligence community," I have never learned.

14

DISCOVERY REVIVES EARHART MYSTERY
NEW EARHART CLUE FOUND IN ISLE GRAVE
BODY FLOWN HERE . . . AMELIA EARHART'S?
AMELIA EARHART BONES FOUND IN ISLE GRAVE?
MYSTERY BONES RENEW AMELIA EARHART CASE

Those headlines and hundreds more blossomed on the afternoon of Friday, November 24, 1961, and the following morning, Saturday, November 25. Amelia was the lead story for the newspapers and wire services and almost every radio and television station in the country. It was an amazing tribute to the vitality of the Earhart image. The interest was greater than it had been in 1960. That fact, however, was not pleasing to me or CBS. Our careful planning was wasted, and I could not keep my promise to Mrs. Ireland and the Morrisseys. The news break caught us by surprise when it should not have. The signs were there had we the sense to read them. Chronologically, this is how it went.

The still and motion picture film, which the Navy impounded

at Guam, had been released to me several weeks before. Not too curiously, a number of photos taken in the general area of NTTU were missing, and several shots showing U.S. naval officers inspecting the excavation were so poorly developed they were useless. Accompanying the film was a letter from Admiral Coye, the new Commander of Naval Forces Marianas. His staff had reviewed the film and decided it was safe from a "security aspect," but he added a warning.

"Any legal consequences resulting from the use of this film for any purpose whatsoever must be the full responsibility of yourself and the Columbia Broadcasting System."

He concluded, "a copy of all photography which has been reviewed has been retained for record purposes."

I immediately sent a letter to Coye complaining about the missing films and asking for clarification. I also requested co-operation from his Command in shipping the remains should Washington permit.

On November 10, we received a visit in San Francisco from Admiral Daniel F. Smith, Jr., Chief of Naval Information. He came to KCBS with Commander John Pillsbury, Public Information Officer for the 12th Naval District, and met with Jules Dundes, Fred Ruegg, CBS Vice-President in charge of station administration, and me.

We liked Smith. He was not particularly impressed with his position or authority; in fact, the admiral had obvious distaste for his role as Official Voice of the Navy. Smith was a pilot during World War II, and carrier duty is still his great love.

I first stipulated our awareness of NTTU and the task of the Naval Administration Unit in protecting the Central Intelligence Agency on Saipan.

I gave Smith the Earhart investigation without reservation. He listened patiently, even to our conclusions.

"That's a hell of a story," he mused. "I don't think anyone in Washington knows how much work you've done on this thing."

"Is the Navy holding back any information?" Ruegg asked.

"Naval Intelligence says 'no,'" the admiral shrugged. "But Intelligence frequently says that regardless of how much they may have on the subject. You can't blame them. That's what intelligence work is about."

"Can you offer us any help?" Dundes asked.

"I'll do my best. I'll put one of my men to work locating the logs of those four ships Bridwell told you about."

"The *Gold Star, Blackhawk, Chaumont,* and *Henderson,*" I reminded.

Smith wrote the names in a notebook, and said, "I can't promise anything, but we'll give it a try."

"What was the situation in 1937 when Earhart disappeared?" I asked. "Were we close to war with Japan at that time?"

"We were very close, and this is something most people don't know. I believe any incident of real significance might have precipitated it. The war would have come a lot sooner, too, if Japan hadn't decided to chew off a piece of China first."

"Did the Japanese fortify the Mandated Islands before Pearl Harbor?"

"There's no question on that," the admiral answered. "Japan began preparations for war with the United States long before Pearl Harbor and long before Earhart and her navigator decided to fly around the world. The Mandates, with the exception of Truk and a few islands in the Marshalls, were not fortified as we usually think of the word. Instead of bomb shelters and coastal defense guns, the Japs concentrated on deepening harbors and building piers, airfields, fuel storage tanks, roads, ammunition dumps, barracks and latrines, all of which are important to war. They were getting ready for offense, not defense."

"Did the Japanese violate the League of Nations Mandate?"

"Of course they did. Don't get me wrong. The Japs built some defenses, too, but they figured they weren't going to have to use them. Hell, I flew low-level strafing missions over some of those islands during the war, and they were fortified. I remember one pass over Yap Island in the Carolines. I started pumping 50-calibers into what appeared to be native grass-roofed huts where we suspected the Japs were holed up. The slugs just bounced off the roofs. There was armor-plate under the grass. Those defenses had been there for a long time."

Fred Ruegg showed his comprehension of the subject by asking, "Do you mean that if the U. S. Navy had gone ahead and searched the Marshall Islands for Earhart in 1937, it might have started a war with Japan?"

"Right," said Smith. "Japan made it clear we were to stay out of there. I've always wondered what would have happened if we'd have moved into the Marshalls then. It sure would have changed what happened four years later. With Japan committed to the China invasion in '37, she would have played hell trying to handle us."

"Were we ready though?"

"That's the other side of it. We weren't ready to fight anybody in '37. Military appropriations were miserably low, and we didn't get the draft until a couple of years later. No one wanted war either. 'No foreign entanglements,' people were saying. 'Let the rest of the world fight it out.' President Roosevelt would have had a hell of a time convincing the country that war with Japan was inevitable. If he'd started anything with the Japs in '37, a lot of people would've wanted to impeach him."

If his dialogue reads gutsy, I have quoted Smith properly; he is that kind of man.

Before the admiral left, he guaranteed cooperation from his office, and said he believed permission to study the remains would be coming from the Chief of Naval Operations within the month. He also suggested we might profit from discussions with Japanese military or Okinawan civilians who had lived or served on Saipan during the years 1937 to '44. There apparently were two intelligence files, labeled Four and Fourteen, housed on Guam. They contained names and photographs of the Japanese and Okinawans who survived the invasion of Saipan and were repatriated at war's end. Information obtained from the enemy via interrogation was also ostensibly a part of the files.

On November 17, an airmail letter arrived from Admiral Coye on Guam reassuring us of the cooperation of his command and explaining that a considerable part of my film had been improperly exposed. That fact, therefore, accounted for any photographs I had found to be missing.

Having explained that small embarrassment, Coye added that

every effort would be made to expedite shipment of the package to Dr. McCown as soon as proper authorization was received from high authority.

I mailed a return note that afternoon, thanking the admiral for clarifying the film situation, and indicating that there had been several rolls in my bags which I had forgotten to give Commander Gorski and which were much better exposed. I hastened to add they were portraits of individuals, so there was no security factor involved. I also mentioned Intelligence Files Four and Fourteen, and requested knowledge of their whereabouts and availability. In conclusion, I gave Coye our plan for transporting the remains: "Father Sylvan Conover or Father Arnold Bendowske will carry the package from Saipan to Guam for inspection by Customs. The carton will then be placed in the hands of the Pan American Airways representative for a registered, special-handling, air-freight shipment to Dr. McCown in San Francisco."

I had taken Robin Kinkead, Pacific Coast Public Relations Director for Pan Am, into confidence on his promise to reveal nothing. It was essential that delivery of the package be handled carefully and quietly. Robin, who has helped CBS people many times, cabled Willis Snyder, the Pan Am station manager at Guam, and instructed him to facilitate shipment without attracting attention.

Wednesday morning, November 22, Ted Koop phoned from Washington that he was hopeful of gaining clearance within a few days. By evening, the Navy still had not notified CBS that permission had been granted. The next day was Thanksgiving, beginning the long holiday weekend, and we assumed nothing would be done before the following Monday. We were wrong.

At 5:00 A.M. Friday morning, Ken Ackerman, KCBS' *Music 'Til Dawn* announcer, called me at my apartment. Through a haze of sleep, I could hear his excitement.

"For God's sake, Fred, wake up," he pleaded. "Can you hear me?

"They are dropping the bomb on you. On you, my friend, do you understand?"

"At this hour they're welcome. All right, what have you got? Who the hell are they?"

"It just moved on the wire. It's got an emergency bulletin heading, and it's exclusive to Associated Press. The origin is Guam. You ready—this is all over the country right now.

"'THE REMAINS OF TWO HUMAN BODIES—POSSIBLY THOSE OF AMELIA EARHART, FAMED AMERICAN FLIER, AND HER NAVIGA-TOR—ARE BEING FLOWN TODAY TO UNIVERSITY OF CALIFORNIA AT BERKELEY, CALIFORNIA, FOR ANTHROPOLOGICAL STUDY. A PAN AMERICAN AIRWAYS OFFICIAL AT GUAM SAID THE RE-MAINS INCLUDE DENTAL PLATES AND OTHER BONES.'"

All I could think of was the last sentence "The remains in-clude dental plates and other bones." If the remains were the ones we recovered, there were no dental plates. It was a good example of how news stories can be distorted even in their first transmission.

"Do you have any more?" I asked. I was now wide awake, and I more or less kept the phone at my ear as I pulled on my clothes.

"Here's a followup on AP," he thundered. "Nothing on UPI yet.

"'THE SKELETAL REMAINS OF 2 BODIES—POSSIBLY THOSE OF FAMED AVIATRIX AMELIA EARHART AND HER NAVIGATOR, FRED NOONAN—ARE BEING FLOWN TO THE UNIVERSITY OF CALIFORNIA FOR STUDY. THE 2 FLIERS VANISHED IN 1937 WHILE FLYING ACROSS THE PACIFIC ON A ROUND-THE-WORLD TRIP. THE RE-MAINS WERE DISCOVERED RECENTLY IN A GRAVE ON SAIPAN ISLAND.'

"Okay, here's the guy who tipped on us. 'Willis Snyder, Pan American Airways District Manager at Guam, reported that those who recovered the remains on Saipan said they included dental plates.'"

"Don't blame Snyder yet," I said. "Someone else could have broken it. Snyder is wrong about the dental plates. Either he's mistaken or whoever filed the story is misquoting him. I'm sure Father Sylvan or Father Arnold never mentioned dental plates."

Ken exploded again. "United Press International has a big bulletin moving now out of Medford, Massachusetts!

" 'MRS. MURIEL MORRISSEY SAYS THAT UNOFFICIAL SOURCES HAVE NOTIFIED HER THAT TWO BODIES FOUND IN THE FAR PACIFIC ARE BEING FLOWN TO CALIFORNIA AND MIGHT BE THOSE OF HER LONG-MISSING SISTER AMELIA EARHART AND AMELIA'S NAVI-GATOR. THEY DISAPPEARED ON A ROUND-THE-WORLD FLIGHT 24 YEARS AGO. MRS. MORRISSEY SAID THE BODIES HAD BEEN UN-COVERED THROUGH THE EFFORTS OF A NEWSMAN . . .'

That's you, Frederick."

"Unfortunately. Is there anything else in the news?"

"Not much. The Defense Department says Russia made about fifty nuclear tests in its recent series, so the U.S. is going to start a new round of them. And the Dominican Ambassador has denied that the United States is interfering with the internal affairs of the Dominican Republic. Whoever blew the whistle on us sure chose the right news day. We're going to get all the play. Do you think those remains really are Earhart and Noonan?"

"I don't know, Ken. Could be. Either way, we should know soon."

It took nearly a half-hour to reach the Morrisseys. Newsmen all over the country were trying to get a statement from Muriel. When I explained the break was a complete surprise, she was gracious and understanding.

"It's all right," she said. "Don't feel badly. I know you did your best."

"There were too many people involved," I replied. "I should have known from the way things were happening that it couldn't be held."

"We'll survive. I'm not going to tell my mother, though. There's no sense in getting her hopes up. By the way, I haven't given your name to any of the people who have called here. I've simply stated that we were informed that remains believed pos-sibly to be my sister's had been found. They've been trying every way to get me to tell them your name. Should I continue to withhold it?"

"Tell them the truth, Mrs. Morrissey. Maybe I can take some of the burden from you. It'll only be a matter of a few hours before they trace it to me anyway. Most of the San Francisco news people know my interest and the fact that I was on Saipan again last September. I can only tell you that we'll do our best to keep it out of the mud."

"I know you will," Muriel said. "Whatever happens, know that Chief and I are glad you're handling it. We believe in you."

At the station, Jules Dundes had decided to hold an all-media news conference at noon and broadcast it live. Reporters would have a chance to question me on the air. A hundred things which should have been done, had we been expecting the story to break, were not done. The promotion department did not have even a rudimentary biography on Earhart or Noonan or their flight, and there was no written compilation of the facts of the investigation to date. Only contact prints had been made from the Saipan negatives. Eight-by-ten-inch prints by the dozens were needed. The tapes I had recorded on Saipan with Commander Bridwell, Father Sylvan, and the witnesses had not been dubbed or edited.

New York was almost as unprepared. The motion picture film, sent there after Navy release, was developed but not edited. Walter Cronkite wanted at least two minutes of film and commentary for his evening television news. The problem was to cull two minutes from nearly five thousand feet when no one but I knew anything about the film and I was three thousand miles away with problems of my own. Don Hewitt, Cronkite's producer, settled it by selecting a couple of aerial shots of Saipan and the rest from footage I had shot at the excavation scene. I then wrote a two-minute script, memorized it, and went to KPIX-TV in San Francisco where their cameramen and engineers fed my voice and image on closed circuit to New York to be video-taped for replay later.

While I spent my time with the television side, instead of radio, where I belonged, Don Webster, my office partner at KCBS, prepared two-page biographies on Amelia and Fred and started a press release detailing the last year and a half of investigation. He had also conned a local photographer into promising one hundred eight by tens by noon.

Robin Kinkead called with defense for his Pan Am agent at Guam. He had talked with him via radio-telephone, and Snyder denied breaking faith. According to Snyder, someone, probably the Customs Officer, tipped the Guam *Daily News*, who in turn fed the story to AP.

"Forget it, Robin," I said. "I know you did your best. But damn it, if you talk to Snyder again tell him to stop giving quotes about 'dental plates' being a part of the shipment. There aren't any, but I'll have a hell of a time clarifying that now."

Thomas Devine was overjoyed when I called him. He had been slowly losing his mind because I would not tell the results of the September Saipan trip. Reluctantly we had withheld the findings because Thomas had been free with the press before and might have been tempted again. It was a pleasure to tell him to stick to the facts but to be as talkative as he liked.

Dr. McCown was perfectly in character. He was pleased the package was on its way, but not impressed. He planned to spend the weekend at Yosemite Park with his family and saw no reason for a change. He would pick up the package at the airport Sunday night, and did not want to be bothered with newsmen until then; in fact, if the reporters could be avoided, he would prefer not to speak to them at all.

A few minutes before I went into the conference, I placed a call to Mary Bea Ireland. She was understanding, too, and added what seemed to be valuable information. She had located a canceled check for dental work performed on Fred Noonan by a Dr. James Scott of Oakland, California.

"I believe Dr. Scott moved to Palm Springs," said Mary Bea. "Perhaps he's still practicing there."

Studio E overflowed. Many of the newsmen who had attended the 1960 conference were there, along with more than fifty photographers and reporters I had never seen before. They came from every part of northern California, and several had flown up from Los Angeles to try to get an exclusive. Don Mozley, KCBS' News Director, tried to calm them and explain the conference was to be broadcast live, but there were too many deadlines to be met. When we hit the air at noon, the background was a low roar composed of newsreel and still cameras and shouted directions and questions.

Mozley finally got attention and we opened with a five-minute statement, giving the background to and the results of the second expedition. I explained in detail how the remains were found, recovered, stored, and now shipped. Bridwell's testimony and that of the other witnesses was sketched, and I discussed our reasons for selecting Dr. McCown to study the bones and teeth. Several times I stressed that the remains had *not* been identified and it was only a possibility they might represent Amelia and Fred.

At that point, we began to take questions. The next fifty-five minutes were a trial I would not care to repeat. Most of the reporters were after a story and interested in facts. A few, representing San Francisco newspapers and television, were out for blood. A radio station which competed for the attention of the same public they served, had an exclusive, and that rankled.

"The theory seems to have changed. Last year they crashed at Saipan, and now it's the Marshalls. That's a convenient alteration, isn't it?"

"There's no convenience to it. The possibility of the Marshalls was suggested by Saipan's Naval Administration Commandant, Commander Paul W. Bridwell. He volunteered the information, and it meets with considerable acceptance on the part of many in the military. I also have come to regard the Marshalls as a probable landing place. After studying the logs of the U.S.S. *Itasca* and U.S.S. *Lexington,* we reached the conclusion it would have been impossible for them to fly their plane to Saipan, at least as part of the flight during which they disappeared. The Marshall Islands, however, appear to be a definite possibility."

"You mean that Earhart and Noonan were taken to Saipan by the Japanese from the Marshalls?"

"I mean that would have been logical. The area headquarters for the Marshalls was at Kwajalein Atoll, but the over-all military headquarters for the Japanese in the Pacific before and during World War II was Saipan Island."

"You're saying then that Earhart was on a spy mission."

"No, I'm not saying that. It is possible, but there is no evidence or testimony in our possession which would support such a conjecture."

"What were the names of those four ships again that . . . what's his name . . . Birdwell . . . gave you?"

"Bridwell said we should seek out the radio logs of the *Gold Star, Blackhawk, Chaumont,* and *Henderson.*"

"What have you done about them?"

"Admiral Daniel Smith, the Chief of Naval Information in Washington, offered full cooperation, and has a search under way for the logs."

"Mr. Goerner, you seem to have conveniently forgotten the fact that one of the last messages received from the Earhart plane said they were down to one-half-hour of gas, and they were pretty close to their destination at that time. How could they have ended up in the Marshalls which is six or seven hundred miles from Howland Island?"

"I'm not forgetting, and there is no convenience connected with any of this. Serious discrepancies have been found in the official logs of both the *Itasca,* the homing vessel provided by the Coast Guard at Howland Island, and the *Lexington,* the search carrier provided by the Navy. The 'one-half-hour of gas' message was later changed to read 'running low on gas.' There are many interpretations which can be given each version."

"That's all very well, but have you talked with the *Itasca's* radio operator?"

I recognized the antagonist who asked the last two questions. He was George Draper of the San Francisco *Chronicle.*

"Which one?" I asked.

"The chief radioman of the *Itasca.* Surely you know the one I mean. The *Chronicle* did an exclusive story on him last year at the time of your first revelations. His name is William Galten, and he lives on the peninsula in Brisbane. He says Earhart radioed that she had only a half-hour of gas and couldn't find Howland. In addition, he says her radio could not be heard more than fifty miles, so she must have been very close to the island when she went in. Howland is a long way from the Marshalls."

My voice began to rise as I said, "Your 'chief radioman' doesn't know what he's talking about. I've never met him, but there is proof that what he's supposed to have told you isn't true. The photostatic copies of the *Itasca*'s log clearly indicate the changes in messages. As far as radio range is concerned, Amelia checked in with Lae, New Guinea, 795 miles out en route to Howland Island. There are duplicates of that message, too. If her radio was good only for fifty miles, what did she use to contact Lae, mental telepathy? If you're really interested, I'll be glad to show you all the photostats right after this broadcast."

Draper retired momentarily. The rest of the reporters, however, allowed no respite. They seemed to have an inexhaustible supply of questions. I stuck with the truth, except for one instance. Yancey Smith of the San Francisco *News-Call Bulletin* asked if the Central Intelligence Agency had somehow been involved with the investigation. I had not expected that challenge. A dozen half-answers darted through my mind, but with great originality I chose, "I don't believe I care to comment on that at this time." Sheer genius; Frederick Winter would have taken my ray gun away had he heard how I stumbled. Fortunately, another reporter broke in with a question and Smith did not have a chance to press. The only solace was I did not have to lie to protect NTTU. Simply omit.

As we neared the end of the conference, I tried again to make it completely clear there was *no* positive identification of the remains as yet, and that we had wished to keep the study secret to protect the Morrisseys and Irelands from the ordeal of more publicity.

"Oh, come now," one of them said. "You don't mean to tell us you've been doing all this from the goodness of your heart for the sake of Earhart's and Noonan's families?"

"I don't like your implication," I replied. "Admittedly, there is a great news story involved, but if we were after that alone, we would have broken it a long time ago. I don't know how anyone who calls himself a newsman can fail to recognize that fact. Why did we sit around and take the chance of having the story stolen, as it was this morning by Associated Press? Because we wanted to protect the relatives by avoiding a conference like this."

When the broadcast ended at 1:00 P.M., there was the emotion a man feels when he leaves a battlefield and finds to his surprise that he is still alive. My colleagues, save one, praised the way

9   The last known photo of Amelia and Fred Noonan, taken at Lae, New Guinea, July 2, 1937. The man in the center is identified only as "Jacobs of New Guinea Gold Company." *Wide World Photo*

10 Copy of a photo found by U.S. forces in a Japanese officer's house on Saipan in June 1944. The bracelet on Amelia's wrist was mistaken for handcuffs and the photo was taken as proof that she had been held captive by the Japanese. The photo was later identified as having originated in Honolulu in 1935 (see next photo). *Napa, California, Register Photo*

11   Amelia in Honolulu before her 1935 Hawaii-California flight.
Note that Amelia's outfit, including bracelet, matches that in photo
opposite. *Napa, California,* Register *Photo*

12   On Saipan during the author's 1960 expedition, left to right:
native witnesses William Guerrero Reyes and Joseppa Reyes Sablan,
Fred Goerner, Monsignor Oscar Calvo, and Rev. Father Arnold
Bendowske of Saipan Catholic mission. *Author's Photo*

13　Cell block of old Garapan prison, Saipan, where "white woman flier" was reportedly held. *Author's Photo*

14　Interior of cell in which Amelia Earhart was said to be held, in old Garapan prison, Saipan. *Author's Photo*

15 Fred Goerner with Lieutenant Commander Leroy Hippe, Executive Officer of Naval Administration Unit on Saipan, 1960, who gave the author a lead on captured Japanese records that were removed from Saipan after the 1944 invasion. *Author's Photo*

16 The author recovering a piece of aircraft wreckage in Tanapag Harbor, Saipan, 1960. *Author's Photo*

17 Corroded airplane parts recovered from Tanapag Harbor, Saipan, during author's 1960 expedition. The controversial generator is at left. *U.S. Navy Photo*

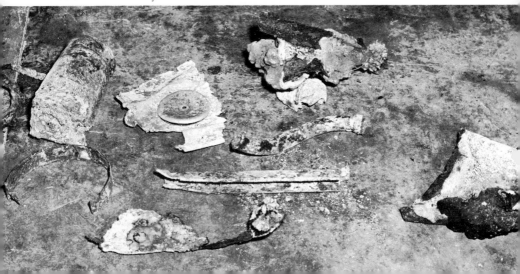

18 Examining the generator at a news conference in San Francisco in July 1960 are, left to right: Moe Raiser, Associated Press reporter, Paul Mantz, and the author. *Wide World Photo*

the conference had been handled. The one was Jules Dundes, and his criticism made a valid point.

"You lost objectivity," he said. "For a minute I thought you were going to punch somebody."

"It would have felt good," I replied.

"There's your problem. If you were merely reporting the facts of a not yet substantiated story, you would have evidenced a certain amount of skepticism yourself. Instead, your attitude convinced every reporter in that studio that you believe Earhart and Noonan were prisoners of the Japanese and died on Saipan."

"Until someone explains who those 'two white fliers' were, that's exactly what I believe."

"But do you as strongly believe the remains being flown here are theirs?"

"No. Of course I don't."

"It's going to be hard for those who attended today's conference to separate the two opinions."

Jules' prophecy was accurate. Most of the reporters intimated in their stories that I believed there was little doubt the remains of Amelia and Fred were on their way home.

Strand of UPI and Raiser of AP were impartial and wrote fair pieces closely quoting the conference. All of the out-of-town newsmen did the same, but the local papers entertained no struggle against their bias. A few barbs and digs, though, are part of the competition of gathering news.

The only story which pushed me out of shape was the one printed by the *Chronicle*, based on the report filed by George Draper. Thirty-seven lines of the article were devoted to the comments of Bill Galten, the man Draper had asked me about. Galten was quoted as saying the Earhart radio under favorable conditions in daylight hours could broadcast only fifty to seventy-five miles, so the plane must have gone down close to Howland because the *Itasca* had heard Amelia's voice. Galten also emphatically stated he had heard Earhart say, "thirty minutes of fuel left"; therefore, she would not have had enough time to fly to the Marshalls. It was difficult for us to believe Draper sat through the conference, asked the questions he did, then went back to his paper and wrote such a story. He had even been offered the official logs of the *Itasca* and *Lexington*, which proved Galten's remarks were unfounded, but George chose to ignore the evidence. I listened several times to the tape recordings of the conference, and there was no mistake about the answers given his questions.

Things were happening too quickly for me to go to work on Galten then, but he later provided some interesting insights regarding the morning Amelia and Fred disappeared.

It did not take long for the press to locate Dr. Scott. He still practiced in Palm Springs, and he remembered the work he had done for Noonan. There had been dental charts at one time, but they were lost or misplaced; however, the doctor felt he might recognize his own work. He had placed several fillings in Noonan's teeth; although, as he recalled, they had been gold or silver, not zinc oxide. If his help was needed, he would be glad to come to San Francisco.

Our old friend Paul Mantz reacted quickly. Two hours after the conference, an Associated Press story from Los Angeles quoted him as saying: "I plan to fly immediately to San Francisco to see if I can identify the remains brought from Saipan as those of Amelia. I think I could tell by looking at the teeth. Amelia's teeth were quite unusual."

I hastened to send Paul a telegram advising him to save the trip. IF DR. MCCOWN NEEDS YOUR HELP, it read, HE WILL CONTACT YOU. A similar message was sent to Dr. Scott.

The package was scheduled to arrive that night at 1:00 A.M. by jet clipper from Honolulu. Pan Am notified me that someone would have to receipt for the box if it was to be stored in a safe at the field rather than being delivered directly to McCown. It was raining heavily as I arrived at the San Francisco International Airport a few minutes after midnight, and I blamed the rain for the unusually large amount of traffic around the terminal. Drivers frantically sought parking spaces close to the main building to avoid a long walk from auxiliary lots. The press parking places were crowded, too.

What was happening did not reach me until I saw the concourse area and overheard some of the conversation. Hundreds of people of all ages were gathered around the arrival gate for Pan Am's inbound Honolulu flight, and the numbers increased every minute. Radio, television, and newspapers had headlined

Amelia's story all day and mentioned frequently the flight number and arrival time of the plane.

These people had come with the hope of witnessing a moment of history. Some wanted to see "the bones" they had read and heard so much about. For them, titillation was the evening's order. Many others were there because Amelia had somehow been a symbol in their lives, and they wanted to pay their respects and feel once more the force of her personality. The scene was macabre, but dignity was present, too. I spoke briefly with one older gentleman and his wife who witnessed Amelia's departure in 1937, and had driven across the Bay to watch her come home in 1961.

A Pan American official took me into an office next to the concourse and explained I would be required to identify the package when it came off the airliner, sign a statement that it arrived in good condition, and then watch as it was placed in Pan Am's precious cargo safe to await Dr. McCown. I would also have to be present when McCown claimed the package to certify that he was receiving the item I had previously identified. It sounded as if the rules had been made for the specific occasion, which they probably were.

The huge jet arrived ten minutes early, and the crowd, now over a thousand, pushed forward, each person trying to get a glimpse of the plane from one of the waiting-room windows. Twenty or more reporters and cameramen, who had clustered outside the gate, moved through the rain toward the craft the moment its engines shut down.

The script played as written. An airline representative carried the package by hand across the concourse for my inspection. We then walked across the field to Pan Am's cargo office where I signed the statement and watched the box locked in a safe. Each action was recorded on film.

Suddenly I felt a strong depression. Part of it was emotional and physical exhaustion; the rest came from the realization we were now appealing to the public's morbid interests, and there was no way to avoid what was to come.

"How do you feel now about all this, Mr. Goerner?" one of the reporters called after me as I headed for my car.

"A little sick," I replied. "Probably catching cold from standing around in this rain."

"You sure have started something. Do you have any idea where it's going to end?"

"Not the slightest," I answered.

15

"Amelia Earhart crash-landed somewhere between Majuro, Jaluit, and Ailinglapalap in the Marshalls. We knew it back in 1944."

That was the beginning of a telephone conversation with John Mahan, a Berkeley, California, real estate man the morning after the package of remains arrived. He said he had been a Navy yeoman working with the senior U.S. military government officer at Majuro Atoll after the invasion, and they had learned of Amelia from several Marshallese natives who spoke English and served as interpreters.

"There were two brothers," said Mahan, "Joe and Rudolph Muller. They told us the Japs picked up two American fliers, a man and woman, and brought them for a while into either Jaluit or Majuro, then took them to another island. They said it was 1937, and the Japs thought they were spies. According to Joe and Rudy, the Japs captured some of their equipment, too."

Mahan also remembered that the senior MGO, a Lieutenant Eugene Bogan, had prepared a report on the information. Bogan had been a Washington, D.C., attorney before joining the Navy.

Why was Mahan so tardy in telling his story?

"If I'd known somebody wanted it, I would have," he said. "I was just an enlisted man during the war. A lot of officers must have known about it."

Finding Eugene Bogan required one telephone call to Washington, D.C., information.

He was at home Saturday afternoon, and my queries were welcome.

"My God, this is strange," he began. "I saw you on the Walter Cronkite news last night, and I was sitting here trying to decide whether I should contact you or not."

"What about?"

"I wanted to tell you that you're right. There is no doubt in my mind that Earhart and Noonan came down in the Marshalls."

"Do you remember a John Mahan?"

"Yes, I think I do . . . Mahan . . . I connect him with Majuro. He was our yeoman as I recall."

"That's right. He says he typed a report for you that gave details on Earhart."

"I never filed that report; I wasn't permitted to. The captain who was Majuro commandant said it was hearsay and might raise false hopes that Earhart was alive."

"What's the captain's name?"

"I think it was Jasper Grow. Captain H. B. Grow."

"What was your duty at Majuro?"

"We were responsible for the welfare of the Marshallese natives at Majuro. It really wasn't an invasion because the Japanese had pulled their forces out of Majuro several months before. I became the senior U.S. military government officer for the Navy and served as the Summary Courts-Martial officer for the area, too. We tried to get the Marshallese back on their feet and take care of their medical, educational, and economic needs."

"From whom did you get the lead on Earhart?"

"A native named Elieu. He was the most trusted and respected of the Marshallese. His father had been principal of the school and Elieu was a teacher himself. He helped inoculate the rest of the natives against yaws and other diseases. I depended on Elieu to do almost everything, and he always came through."

"How did Elieu happen to tell you about the fliers?"

"It was only a week or so after we arrived. We were talking about the Japanese and how they had administered the Marshalls and what a big thing they had about secrecy. Elieu got in the conversation and asked if we knew of the white woman flier who ran out of gas and landed between Jaluit and Ailinglapalap. I nearly flipped."

"Did he actually see the woman?"

"No. He made that clear. The story had been told to him before the war by a Japanese friend named Ajima who was a trader with Nanyo Boeki Kaisha, a trading company the Japanese used as a front to cover certain military activities in the Marshalls and other Mandated Islands."

"What happened to the woman?"

"A Japanese fishing boat picked her up and brought her into either Jaluit or Majuro. Then she was taken presumably to Kwajalein or Saipan."

"Why there?"

"Kwajalein was area naval headquarters for the Japanese, and Saipan was over-all headquarters. Jaluit and Majuro were just tin-pot administrative centers. No Japanese military or civil administrator would have taken responsibility for such a hot potato."

"Did this Elieu mention a man accompanying the woman?"

"No. He confined himself to what he had been told by Ajima. It's logical the Japanese would have been greatly impressed by a woman pilot. Females are so inferior in Japan that it would be unheard of for a woman to learn to fly. The man wouldn't have mattered at all."

"Did you believe his story?"

"I believed it then and I believe it now. Elieu was honest and intelligent and could not have invented a story like that. He's probably still living. You ought to take a trip down there and talk to him yourself."

"Couldn't someone have fed him the information?"

"Who? We were the first ones in there. The Japanese completely cut those people off from the rest of the world. Elieu had never heard of Amelia Earhart."

"Your ex-yeoman, Mahan, says he got his information from two brothers named Muller."

"I remember their name. Both were interpreters. They could have known, too, but I found out from Elieu."

"Is there anyone else I might be able to reach who could substantiate this?"

"Sure. I can give you the names of at least two men who heard the same things I did. Where they are today is the problem. I've lost track of almost all the guys from the war. Lieutenant Bill Bauer knew Elieu quite well. I think Bill came from somewhere in California. Jimmy Toole heard the story, too. Before the war, I handled legal matters for his mother, and it was a complete surprise when I bumped into Jimmy on Majuro in 1944. He was all grown up and skipper of a little LCT we used for shuttle purposes on the lagoon. I think Jim lives in Bethesda, Maryland, now and has something to do with the Navy."

"You have a good memory, Mr. Bogan."

"Well, as I said, I've been thinking about this thing since I saw you on TV last night. I have the clippings in front of me right now."

"What clippings?"

"From the New York *Daily News,* the New York *Sun,* and the Oakland *Tribune.* Friends sent them to me during the war. They're dated March 22, 1944, but they were actually written by the AP man around March first because that's the time he was at Majuro."

"What do they say?"

"Just about what I've been telling you. This correspondent, Eugene Burns was his name, heard us talking about Elieu and what might have happened to Earhart. He latched right on and wrote a story mentioning Elieu, me, Bill Bauer, and Jimmy Toole. The higher brass didn't want Burns to send the story out, but he got it through anyway. I'll send you photo-copies of the clippings if you'd like."

The development did not amaze me; I was by then inured to the unusual. A call to a friend in Washington produced Mr. Bogan's credits: one of the most talented tax attorneys in the country with a reputation beyond question.

Bogan's memory was as good as his reputation. Jimmy Toole

lived in Bethesda. He worked for the Navy as a Manpower Division analyst in the office of the Under Secretary of the Navy, and he remembered Elieu. Charles James Toole said, "I don't know why someone hasn't put these facts together before. Elieu was undoubtedly telling the truth. I think there's a lot more to this Earhart business than anyone has let on."

I was too late trying to reach Burns, the AP correspondent. The local Associated Press Bureau told me he had been killed some years before while covering a riot in Tehran. However, his widow lived in Sausalito across the Golden Gate Bridge from San Francisco. She said her husband spoke many times of Amelia Earhart; in fact, he talked of returning to the Marshall Islands to follow Amelia's trail. He had been convinced the Japanese captured her.

Dr. McCown called late Sunday afternoon, and Don Webster and I met him at the airport to claim the package. A crowd of photographers recorded the taking of the package from the safe, the signing of release forms, the carrying of the package to McCown's vehicle. In answer to persistent questioning, Ted coolly replied, "When I've had a chance to make a preliminary study, I'll have a brief statement. There will be no other comment until that time."

In his University of California laboratory, McCown carefully unwrapped the outer package, placed the cigar boxes in a row on a long table, opened the first in line and began sorting pieces of bone into compartmented trays. Nothing was said. Don and I watched the professor gently scrape bits of earth from various fragments and begin to fit a few pieces together. The box containing the teeth provided the greatest interest. Each was held to a bright light for close inspection, and then replaced in the cotton nest. Finally he turned, cleared his throat and said, "It's not going to be easy. The bones are heavily fragmented and by no means are all of the skeletons present. I say 'skeletons' because you have apparently recovered parts of at least two persons. I'm not ready to give an opinion on sex yet, but from the size of teeth there is a possibility that at least one man and one woman are represented. The problem is not impossible, but it's going to take some time. How long I can't say."

"Do you want help from this Dr. James Scott who was Noonan's dentist?" I asked.

"I don't want any advice or assistance at this point," McCown answered. "I have purposely avoided reading the newspaper releases, and I have not looked at photos or heard any physical descriptions of either Miss Earhart or her navigator. I don't want to know how much they weighed or how tall they were. That way I will not be in danger of trying to twist the facts to fit a preconception. I'll go just as far as I possibly can with identification, and if that is not sufficient to determine whether these remains represent your two friends, then I will ask for any help that is available. There is already special-delivery mail in my office which deals with the case. I will turn this over to you for evaluation, and should it pertain to identification, you can give it to me when needed."

With difficulty I persuaded McCown that it would be necessary for him to repeat his remarks to the press the next morning.

"If you want them to leave you alone, Ted," I said, "you'll have to give them something to chew on; otherwise, they'll be camping in the hall."

We set the conference for ten the next morning in a seminar room of Kroeber Hall, the anthropology building.

Among the letters sent to McCown were two from dentists who had done work for Amelia and Fred. Horace L. Cartee, D.D.S., of Miami, Florida, wrote that on the day before the flight began he had removed an upper-right third molar for AE hoping to cure some severe headaches she had been having. Cartee listed his credits which included a term as president of the American Society of Oral Surgeons, and referred to a Dr. Collins Swords, who had been Amelia's general dentist in Miami. Swords had died several years before and Cartee had never gotten a complete dental chart of AE from him, but he did remember that Amelia had a full complement of teeth from the upper-left cuspid to upper-right third molar, and a full complement from lower-left cuspid to lower-right second molar. The third molar was missing.

Almost as interesting was a letter from F. Clifford Phillips, D.D.S. of Exeter, California. Dr. Phillips believed he was the last dentist to have done work for Fred Noonan in 1937. He said Fred had fractured four of his upper anterior teeth in a fall in a hotel bathroom in Hawaii, and had come to his office, which then was in Oakland, California, for help. Phillips had made an upper metal cast removable bridge for Noonan, and was to have made a lower one upon his return from the around-the-world flight.

The accident probably happened after the aborted take-off when Amelia and Fred were waiting to bring the Electra back to California for repair.

Dr. Phillips saved his most provocative news for conclusion. He had retained the models of Noonan's teeth and jaws for many years, and believed they were still stored, though, after several moves, he was not sure. He did not have a dental chart, but recalled Noonan had only two bicuspids and cuspids on each side of the upper jaw plus the bicuspids and anterior teeth of the lower jaw.

I sent letters of thanks to both and asked Dr. Phillips please to look for the models.

A third letter contained different evidence. Wilmore B. Finerman, M.D., of Los Angeles wrote that Amelia had been a patient at his office in 1934, and he knew her skull should show evidence in the right maxillary sinus of an Caldwell-Luc type of operation.

If Dr. McCown asked for help, there was going to be some available.

GIs FIND ON SAIPAN: FOTO OF AMELIA . . . read the headline of the Sunday, November 26, early edition of the New York *Daily News*. Unfortunately, it had to be changed in the next edition.

Harry Weiser, a foreman for Kollsman Instrument Corporation on Long Island, had given the *News* a photograph of Amelia. He had found the picture on the wall of a Japanese house during the invasion of Saipan in 1944. Weiser served as a corporal in the Army's 805th Engineers and said he had been sent with eleven other GIs to clean out a nest of Japanese snipers on Saipan. About two miles in from the shoreline, he stumbled into a damaged, one-story frame building so comfortably appointed he felt it must have belonged to an officer. Tacked to one wall with ribbon and nails was the small snapshot of Amelia. Weiser grabbed the photo and some larger publicity prints of Deanna Durbin, Shirley

Temple, Jack Benny, and Mary Livingstone, and stuffed them in his pocket.

In the picture a cheerless Amelia was seated on the running board of an old black sedan which had the words STANDARD OIL PRODUCTS emblazoned across the door. Dressed in light slacks, dark leather jacket, with a scarf knotted Ascot-fashion around her throat, she appeared tired and dispirited. The jacket was dirty and torn at one sleeve, and in the background, on Oriental, wearing an officer's or chauffeur's hat, peered over the car's hood.

"I never learned who occupied the house, how the picture got there, or where it was originally taken," said Weiser. "I just kept it and put it in my album when I got home. When I read about the remains being found on Saipan, I remembered it."

EARHART MYSTERY FOTO WAS TAKEN IN HONOLULU, SAYS GI . . . headlined the next edition of the *News*.

Francis Rapkiewicz, it said, a Brooklyn truck driver, blinked when he saw Weiser's Saipan snapshot of Earhart; he had one exactly like it. Rapkiewicz immediately telephoned the newspaper to reveal that the picture had been taken in Honolulu in 1937 after the crash which ended the first flight. The photographer, a member of the Signal Corps, had given Rapkiewicz a copy of the photo in 1938. He could not recall the man's name.

There was no reason to doubt either Rapkiewicz or Weiser. The question is: Why did the snapshot receive a place of honor on the wall of a house occupied by Japanese military on Saipan? There could be many answers.

The only other information I turned up through telephone calls was that Weiser's photo had "⁂751" marked in black on its back; Rapkiewicz's bore "⁂456." The photographer has never made himself known.

Before McCown's conference Monday morning, some bizarre and interesting contributions arrived by letter and telephone from widely separated points.

Ernest E. Wiles, a Honolulu attorney, served on Tinian Island in 1946, helping repatriate Japanese and Korean civilians from the Marianas. An enlisted man told him that one of the internees from Saipan had talked about an American woman who crashed or landed in an airplane at Saipan before the war. It was not clear as to whether she had been executed or had died of other causes.

Wiles added, "He did not remember the name of the Japanese internee and the person had already been returned to Japan when I heard about it, so there was no way to followup. Whether the identity of these remains is that of Amelia Earhart is a question, but I think there is no doubt some woman of Caucasian ancestry who came in a plane perished on Saipan a few years before the war."

Another dead end, but Wiles had reached a conclusion with which I had some sympathy.

Betty Elizabeth George telephoned from San Lorenzo, California. Her late father, Harry S. George, who had served in the Navy as a chief pharmacist mate, had stated that complete physical examinations were given to Amelia and Fred at Alameda Naval Air Station before the start of the 1937 flight. The check-ups were conducted by Navy doctors and included dental charts. Betty's father also had said the Navy swore Noonan into active service prior to the flight.

I sent a letter to Admiral Smith asking the Navy to make available the reports from any physical examinations of AE and Fred.

Associated Press picked up a weird story in San Diego, California. Floyd Kilts, identified as "a former U. S. Coast Guardsman now on leave from a State Department of Veterans Affairs job," said he went to Gardner Island on a Coast Guard mission during World War II. (Gardner, one of the Phoenix Islands along with Canton and Enderbury, constituted part of the British Mandate.) Kilts reportedly said a native had told him that the skeleton of a woman and the skull of a man were found on the shore of Gardner in the latter part of 1938. A white planter believed the skeleton might be Amelia's and started to Suva with it. The planter, however, died of pneumonia on the way and the superstitious native boatmen threw the skeleton *and* the planter overboard.

An intriguing story, but a look at a map shows why the planter should have been thrown overboard before the voyage began. Suva, capital of the Fiji Islands, is more than eleven hundred miles from Gardner. The Gilbert, Ellice and Samoa Islands, including American Samoa, are all much closer, and more accessible.

Two letters were challenging.

Frederick Chapman of West Coxsackie, New York, wrote, "I was with the 27th Division on Saipan during the 1944 battle, and I remember seeing snapshots of Miss Earhart at that time. Perhaps some of our former buddies might still have some snapshots."

Ralph R. Kanna of Johnson City, New York, won the letter-of-the-day award. He had been Platoon Sergeant of the I&R Platoon, Headquarters Company, 106th Infantry, 27th Division, during the assault on Saipan. It was his duty to take prisoners for interrogation purposes.

"On Saipan we captured one particular prisoner near an area designated as 'Tank Valley' at the time. This prisoner had in his possession a picture which showed the late Amelia Earhart standing near Japanese aircraft on an airfield. Assuming the picture of the aircraft to be of value, it was forwarded through channels to the G-2 [Intelligence Officer]."

Kanna had a still more provocative disclosure.

"Upon questioning this prisoner through one of our Japanese-American interpreters, he stated that the woman in the picture was taken prisoner along with a male companion and subsequently he felt that both of them had been executed. From time to time I have told these facts to associates, and they finally have convinced me to write."

Roy Higashi, William Nuno, and Richard Moritsugu were the three Japanese-American interpreters who had soldiered with Kanna on Saipan, but he couldn't remember which one had been with him on the day the captured Japanese was questioned.

"This picture I spoke of must be somewhere in government files. How it can be obtained, I wouldn't even try to imagine."

Ralph listed his profession as "test deskman with the New York Telephone Company." I called NYTC's director of personnel in Endicott, New York, for verification. Ralph Kanna had been with the company for sixteen years and was regarded as a trusted and earnest employee.

A phone conversation with Kanna produced additional details. He believed Moritsugu was the interpreter, although it was possible the man had been Nuno. Higashi rated as a long-shot. Ralph remembered Hawaii or California as the home of Nuno and Moritsugu. Higashi could have come from Chicago. The interrogation had taken place July 5 or 6, 1944, in an area northeast of Garapan City on Saipan, and the enemy soldier had belonged to the 118th Japanese Infantry, Code ※11933. He was certain the photo showed Earhart before aircraft, and it was a snapshot, not a magazine clipping.

Frederick Chapman's story was not as promising. He served with the Medical Detachment, 249th Field Artillery Battalion, 27th Division, and covered most of Saipan during the fighting. He could not remember where he had seen the pictures or what they depicted, simply that someone at a medical aid station had shown them and he recognized Amelia Earhart.

With no hesitation, I chose to follow the Kanna trail. A Honolulu telephone directory gave me Richard Moritsugu, a very startled man. His voice quavered and broke as he recalled Saipan and Sergeant Kanna. He gained control, and with it, reticence.

"I read about the woman in today's newspaper," he said, "but I have no desire to discuss the war. It is over, and there can be no good for Japanese-Americans in remembering it."

Nothing I said moved him. Finally I asked about Higashi and Nuno, but he had not seen them since the war and did not know their home towns.

At his news conference, Ted McCown was as I thought he would be: calm, precise, aloof, with a dash of testiness.

"No," he said. "I don't want any help at this point, and I don't want telephone calls. When I reach a conclusion or call for assistance, CBS will be notified. It is they who have requested me to conduct this study."

"May we view the remains?" asked a reporter.

"Absolutely not," McCown retorted. "Until they have been identified, they are my responsibility. There will be no sensationalism."

"How long do you think it will take you?"

"The study could be long and difficult. I cannot set a time limit."

"Could those bones represent Earhart and her navigator?" another newsman demanded.

"They could, but there is no clear indication of that. There are at least two people represented, but I have no judgment yet as to sex, height, or weight."

The conference lasted half an hour, but Dr. McCown would not be cajoled into guesses.

Stories were filed and Page Two double-columns with McCown's picture appeared that afternoon and the next morning in nearly every newspaper. The saga of the remains was becoming a serial to millions of people.

The first Japanese reaction came from Hitoshi Tsunoda, representing the war history department of the Japanese defense agency. "It is impossible and nothing more than nonsense," quoted a Tokyo UPI dispatch, "to think the fliers wandered far enough off course to land at Saipan."

As a Japanese Navy pilot, Tsunoda said he had flown to Saipan in 1937 a few days after the disappearance, and had heard nothing of an execution. "It's a small island," he added. "Even if a dog were killed the population there would immediately know about it." As for Amelia being on a spy flight, Tsunoda said it was "hard to believe because natives of American-controlled Guam were permitted to visit Saipan and thus spying was not necessary."

The Japanese war history expert concluded, "If Miss Earhart was picked up by a Japanese fishing boat or a ship, she and her co-pilot would have been taken to Palau Island where the Japanese Southseas Islands Government office was. The small Saipan branch office could not have conducted such interrogation."

I disregarded this account entirely, for several reasons. For one thing, Nanyo Kohatsu Kaisha, the Japanese Southseas Development Company, was a front for the Imperial Navy in the 1930s. Saipan was not "a small branch office" of NKK as Tsunoda stated. Saipan was Japanese military headquarters for the Mandated Islands before and during World War II, and it was precisely the place Earhart and Noonan or anyone else would have been taken for questioning.

Palau, which Tsunoda mentioned, was the only area Japan had left open to foreigners in the Mandates at the time Amelia and

Fred disappeared. It served as a paper-passing center for the phony civil government which had no power and no purpose other than to disguise Japanese military design in the Pacific and let Japan thumb its nose at the League of Nations.

Natives of Guam were not "permitted to visit Saipan" in 1937. Hundreds of Guamanians testify that 1935 was the last year any outsider could land at Saipan. Pan American Airways representatives recall that Japanese passengers arriving at Guam from Hong Kong, the Philippines, or the United States and bound for Japan via Saipan, could only be taken halfway to Saipan by boat and then transferred to Japanese vessel.

And Saipan was not a "small island" where "the population would immediately know about even the killing of a dog." The Saipanese people feared Japanese military. They speak of Chico Base at Tanapag Harbor and the fences and secrecy which surrounded it. A severe beating was the least a native could expect if he approached Tanapag without permission. "It was not wise," the natives say, "to know too much about the Japanese Navy or Kempeitai secret police. They were on Saipan many years before the war and they were hard people."

There were two other things wrong with this statement. It discussed what would have been done with Amelia had she been "picked up by a Japanese fishing boat or a ship." The only other person who had suggested that possibility was Elieu, and his testimony had not been revealed. And Tsunoda stated that as a Japanese Navy pilot he had flown to Saipan in 1937. If the island was but a civilian outpost, what was a Navy flier doing there?

Reaction from the *New Japanese American News* in Los Angeles was noncommittal. A small article mentioned the remains and the hope for solution to the mystery. It avoided any illusion to involvement with Japan. In appropriate juxtaposition, an item on the same page revealed that "The Association for the Return of Okinawa to Japan in Tokyo" had petitioned UN Secretary-General U Thant for transfer of the Ryukyu Islands from U.S. to Japanese rule within the next year.

In July 1960, U. S. Congressman J. Arthur Younger from San Mateo, California, had asked the State Department to make available all information on Earhart and Noonan and to request an official statement from Japan. In early August 1960 the

Japanese Foreign Office advised that it had completed an exhaustive investigation "which revealed no basis whatsoever for the rumor the Japanese had executed Amelia Earhart at Saipan in 1937." It added that all available Japanese records had been searched and all former officers and officials were reached during the investigation. The report was transmitted to the State Department by the U. S. Embassy in Tokyo.

The Japanese response was what we expected in 1960. The incident of the generator had generally discounted the Saipan theory; however, the Japanese even then were careful to state Amelia had not been "executed at Saipan in 1937." Other possibilities were not discussed.

Hitoshi Tsunoda's statements were the only Japanese reaction in 1961, and they were unofficial. We, therefore, were dumfounded when Congressman John F. Shelley stated in an interview on KGO Television in San Francisco that he had received a telegram from the State Department saying a Japanese report, obtained from Japan at his request, gave no evidence that Amelia Earhart was ever on Saipan. The State Department also denied that it possessed any classified information on the matter.

The fact was the State Department did not ask Japan for a further statement in 1961. Shelley received the same report given Congressman Younger in 1960. Confirmation of this fact came December 7, 1961, from Edwin O. Reischauer, U. S. Ambassador to Japan. The only statement officially attributable to Japan was contained in the August 1960 report of Captain J. R. Bromley, Naval Attaché at the Embassy in Tokyo.

Shelley was embarrassed when I reached him through his administrative assistant. He explained that he had no idea of what was involved and sent the telegram to the State Department at the television station's insistence.

His assistant said, "I thought it was funny the State Department could get an answer from Japan that quickly."

However, Shelley's statement made the wire services coast to coast and further confused an already perplexed public. The friendliness Admiral Smith showed before AP broke the story was not continued afterward by his Washington staff. The danger to NTTU disquieted the Office of Naval Information, and Captain

R. W. Alexander told the press: "The Navy is not involved. Amelia Earhart is a civilian concern."

As days passed, we became tense waiting for McCown's decision. Dr. Scott, the dentist from Palm Springs, flew to San Francisco with his wife again to offer his help. It was difficult to explain to him that he would not be needed unless McCown called for assistance. I did not further disappoint Scott by telling him he had competition for the "Last Dentist to Do Work for Noonan" title.

"Could you and Mr. Dundes come over to the laboratory in an hour or so? I'd rather give you the details in person."

"Are they negative?" I asked.

"I'm afraid so," he replied.

It was a gloomy drive to Berkeley.

What McCown determined in one week was amazing. Sections of his report follow:

"The bone fragments comprise between 500–600 pieces. There are 6 or 7 fair-sized pieces, the largest of which is a fragment of the shaft of the tibia, about 90 mm long. Generally the numerous pieces are quite small. Some of this is due to the recent recovery operations, but the stained and soil-encrusted edges of many fragments show that prior to recovery, the bones were already heavily fragmented.

"The teeth consist of 37 adult teeth, 12 molars, 7 pre-molars, 18 canines and incisors. None of these have any adhering fragments of alveolar bone.

"All the teeth are moderately-to-heavily worn. X-ray examination confirms visual macroscopic examination that *no* metallic fillings are present. Clearly developed carious lesions are minimal, although in most small-to-large areas the dentine is exposed by wear. Some considerable decalcification is present, and the dentine is worn moderately soft. Low power examination with binocular microscope reveals no traces of wear on the crowns which would argue for the former presence of bridges or partial plates.

"The teeth suggest a minimum of four individuals. The extreme wear which is present on well over half of the teeth, suggests conditions that would be rarely met with in the diets of most

Americans. Such conditions of wear are met with in some individuals of our population, but among those in the seventh or later decades of life. The conditions present, however, would be not at all uncommon in many middle-aged individuals of Pacific Islands or Asiatic populations. The characteristic of the crowns of the incisive teeth described above would be uncommon to the point of virtual absence in white Americans.

"The front part of a lower jaw has been reconstructed from two fragments. It is thick from back to front in the chin region, but with a low height of body, a median and not prominent chin eminence. There is nothing to disassociate it from the skull.

"The right mandibular condyle and neck are present. Two fragments came from the left side at the angle where the descending front margin of the wing of the jaw joins the body. These two fragments overlap and indicate two jaws and two individuals. The larger mandible fragment is so broken along the tooth bearing border that none of the teeth present can be fitted to the partially preserved sockets with any degree of confidence.

"The general conclusion, relevant to the hypothesis that the remains are those of a white American male and female buried not more than twenty-five years ago in the Saipan location, is not supported. The implications are more strongly in favor of a supposition that a secondary interment of the fragments of several individuals was made, but how anciently cannot be determined with precision."

When distilled, it meant we had found the remains of four or more Chamorrans instead of "two white fliers, a man and woman."

"Why did the dentists on Saipan say there were fillings in the teeth?" I asked.

"Their mistake is understandable," said McCown. "They thought the calcified dentine in the teeth was zinc oxide. In appearance, it is almost identical."

"Couldn't they tell there were at least four people?"

"It took me a week, and I'm supposed to be an expert," replied McCown.

"What did you mean about the bones being from 'a secondary interment'?"

"I think you opened a common grave filled with refuse from

previous burials. The remains might have been of one family, and when the family vault or plot was moved, someone was lazy. Instead of digging a deep hole inside the new cemetery, whoever was responsible simply marked the designated gravesite and then dug a shallow grave outside the cemetery and threw in the remains. Such things are not uncommon."

There was a long silence as we stared at the pathetic display on the laboratory tables. Deep disappointment mixed with frustration filled my mind. I thought of the work, patience, planning, and fighting that had been necessary to produce this moment. And what did we have? A pitiful pile of unidentifiable bones that a grave digger more callous than Shakespeare's had tossed into a hole in order to avoid work.

McCown sensed my distress. "I hope you won't give up the investigation," he said. "You may have missed the actual gravesite by six inches, six feet, or sixty feet. That's the way it is with archaeology."

"Thanks, Ted," I replied, "but I'm afraid this does it. We've struck out twice in public, and according to the rules of this game, that ends it. The newspaper and television guys will eat us alive."

"You're wrong about that," said McCown. "I've watched you, and they couldn't miss the integrity you've shown. I think some of the reporters will be nearly as disappointed as you."

"I hope you're right," interjected Jules.

"Besides that," continued McCown, "I think you may be right about this business. I've never known a story with as much fact and testimony behind it as this one has not to have a basis in truth."

It was a balm to hear those words from someone I respected, but there were two immediate problems to be faced before I could return to optimism. Mrs. Morrissey and Mrs. Ireland would have to be notified, and another conference would have to be called to inform the news media. McCown needed more time to put his report in finished form and have copies of the X-rays made, so we settled on Monday, December 4, at 1:00 P.M., as the time for public announcement.

As we walked toward the door, Jules casually said, "You'll send your bill, or course, Dr. McCown, to KCBS."

"There is no bill," said McCown. "I'm glad I could help."

Dundes protested strongly, but Ted would not change his mind. They finally compromised. KCBS would establish a scholarship fund for the Department of Anthropology.

On the way back to San Francisco, Jules tried to cheer my spirits by discussing a new assignment. Beginning the first of the year, I would be one of two hosts for a challenging departure in radio, a four-hour all-talk program, 1:00 to 5:00 P.M. Monday through Friday. The format would include interviews and dozens of news related features.

"You've had it on the Earhart investigation, haven't you?" he asked.

"There doesn't seem any choice," I replied. "The decision has been made for us."

I telephoned the Morrisseys on Sunday, and they were grateful to have the news before the official announcement.

"Is this going to end your search?" Mrs. Morrissey asked.

"Someone else will have to provide a final answer," I said. "There still is no doubt in my mind that Amelia and Fred, or two other American fliers who looked like them, were on Saipan coincident with the months that followed the disappearance, but it could take many more years to find all the answers and piece them together."

"Whatever you decide," she said, "Chief and I want you to know we appreciate your thoughtfulness and your efforts."

Monday, at 1:00 P.M., I tried for the tenth time without success to reach Mary Bea. She was out of town. Then I went into Studio E at KCBS to face what we thought was going to be a hostile press. We broadcast the conference live as we had the first one. Jules figured if I was going to be drawn and quartered, the station might as well have a top audience rating.

Ted McCown could double as an oracle. With few exceptions, the newsmen were understanding and sympathetic. Most of them decided we were honest, and some had begun to hope the story would be proved. Even the San Francisco *Chronicle* took it easy with a page-three, three-column straight report of McCown's findings.

There were no editorial judgments save Roger Grimsby's at

KGO-ABC Television. "It may be quite a while," he said, "before Mr. Goerner makes another unfounded claim about something he's dug from a sandy beach on a Pacific isle."

I smiled as I watched Roger's newscast. And it almost didn't hurt.

16

"Fred, there's a big South Seas island native in the lobby to see you. He has a war canoe and a bunch of other natives with him, and he says they've come for the bones of their chief!"

This dialogue, written by Bob Kirmer, a KCBS engineer, was relayed to me one morning by Winnie, our switchboard operator. Thus was my life after McCown's announcement. The jibes and kidding tested my sense of humor and sometimes found it spent. I felt the fool many people thought me. For nearly two years, my personal hangup had been an old mystery, and as far as the public knew, I had twice tried and failed to solve it.

We boxed the now famous remains and ruefully shipped them back to Saipan where Father Sylvan interred the unknowns in consecrated ground within the boundaries of the cemetery. If there was a "chief" among them, he had returned to his people.

At that point, I quit. The Navy Department gave me no reason to hope a solution would ever be possible. Official letters closed every potential source of information. Commander Merle Mac-Bain, representing Admiral Smith, took care of the four vessels Commander Bridwell had mentioned. His search had failed to find any radio logs, and the available deck logs of the four ships contained no indication of any contact or communication with Japanese vessels. MacBain explained that current Navy directives provide for destruction of radio logs after six months except those relating to distress or disaster which become eligible for destruction after three years. Logs deemed of special historical interest may be retained longer but provision is made for the elimination of all logs whenever a ship is decommissioned or deactivated. MacBain appeared thorough although it seemed odd that deck logs of the old ships existed as all logs supposedly were destroyed at decommissioning or deactivation.

On December 13, 1961, Admiral Coye answered my request for access to Intelligence Files Four and Fourteen with regrets. The files could not be found, and additional research had failed to reveal any information concerning surviving Japanese military or civilian personnel who served or lived in the Caroline or Marshall Islands during the years 1937 to 1941.

It echoed our 1960 efforts to locate the twenty-two tons of records which Commander Hippe had said were removed to the United States from Saipan after the invasion.

A few days later, another letter from MacBain contained the crowning frustration. He reported that substantive intelligence records for the period 1937 to 1941 had for the most part been destroyed.

I shook my head in disbelief. That intelligence documents for one of the most critical periods in U. S. Military Intelligence history had been eliminated was incomprehensible, especially when unanswered questions abound regarding United States-Japan relations in the years preceding World War II.

The information from Betty George about Amelia and Fred receiving physical examinations at Alameda, California, also produced nothing. MacBain said the information officer for the Navy's Bureau of Medicine Record Retirement Center in St. Louis, Missouri, was not optimistic. He pointed out that since neither Earhart or Noonan was connected with the Navy, and physical examination would have been merely a courtesy, any records or charts would normally have been given to them in person or destroyed. Betty's father had either been mistaken about Amelia and Fred being sworn into the service, or the fact had been withheld from other departments of government.

MacBain's letter might have been filed with all the rest if he had not tacked on a paragraph about some conversations he had had with the Department of Naval Intelligence. The official position was that Navy Intelligence never had any connection with the Earhart flight nor any interest in it. It was further believed, according to MacBain, that the Japanese would have dealt openly with any case of spying, and that the Japanese did not have anything to conceal in connection with the Mandated Islands at that time.

The last point was contradictory to every piece of evidence I had gathered and to the opinions of dozens of Navy officers, including Admiral Smith. Naval Intelligence apparently wanted to end any discussions of Japan's pre-war use of the Mandated Islands and any efforts of the Navy and other branches of the military to obtain knowledge of the islands before the Japanese bombing of Pearl Harbor.

Enigmas persisted, and no amount of diversion could make me dismiss them. Why were so many people anxious to forget about two white fliers who had been on Saipan? Why had no one been able to refute the testimony of the Saipanese? Why had the United States chosen at the war crimes trials not to press the issue of Japan's misuse of the Mandated Islands? Japan's negative position was understandable, but the U.S. should have sought complete explanation. Were Amelia and Fred keys to events which led to Pearl Harbor? Did a government service involve itself in the final flight for espionage purposes?

Was that service forced to abandon Amelia and Fred after their capture rather than chance an international incident and possible war in 1937? Perhaps that was the reason Japan had not been required to discuss the years preceding Pearl Harbor. Japan, forced to reveal the extent of her pre-war violation of international law, might also have disclosed the Earhart-Noonan episode. Such an exposé might have been politically embarrassing.

Those and a hundred more unanswered questions intrigued and plagued me.

The letters and telephone calls continued. For instance, Robert

Kinley of Norfolk, Virginia, wrote that he had served with the 2nd Marine Division on Saipan in 1944 and had found a photograph which showed Amelia with a Japanese officer. The picture, which appeared to have been taken on Saipan, had been lost in July 1944, when he was wounded. Kinley added that his Marine comrades had opened a grave by a small graveyard near a Japanese radio tower, and had recovered the remains of an American naval aviator who had been shot down a few days before the invasion. He had discovered the photo in a house close to the graveyard.

The former Marine saved his most provocative information for the last paragraph of the letter. Near the house, his squad had dynamited the entrance to a tunnel leading to a Japanese command post, and he believed the man shown in the photograph with Amelia was probably trapped in the explosion. He also felt that Amelia might have been buried in or around the cemetery where the Navy pilot had been found.

Kinley enclosed a hand-drawn map depicting a portion of Saipan's western shoreline on which he located the radio tower, graveyard, the house where the photo had been found, and the approximate position of the entrance to the Japanese command post. He also noted the area had been a sector of Red Beach One designation during the invasion.

The letter and map left no doubt in my mind that Kinley had been in the same area as Thomas Devine, probably as much as a year before Devine had been shown a gravesite. Father Sylvan spoke of the Japanese radio tower south of the cemetery, and Bridwell mentioned the Navy fliers who had been killed by the Japanese before the invasion and whose remains were recovered on the edge of the graveyard.

I requested details from Kinley; however, he had little to add. He had been clearing the house of booby traps when the picture was found. It had been tacked to a wall along with a piece of ribbon. A short time later a Japanese mortar shell exploded near Kinley and tore away part of his chest. The photo was lost at that moment, and Kinley's life nearly went with it. After emergency treatment, he was taken from Saipan, placed aboard the hospital ship U.S.S. *Solace*, and eventually returned to the States. Whether the shrapnel destroyed the photo or it was taken by one

of the medics, Kinley cannot remember. He recalls that it showed
Amelia standing in an open field with a Japanese soldier, and he
believes the man wore some kind of combat or fatigue cap with
a single star in its center.

At the time Kinley wrote his first letter, Lore Thieben, who had
been my secretary at KCBS when the investigation began, lived
within two blocks of him in Norfolk, Virginia. She had gone to
Virginia to work for Human Sciences Research, Inc., and was delighted to have coincidence bring her again into the quest for
Amelia. Lore met several times with Robert Kinley and tape-recorded his recollections of 1944 Saipan. The concluding statement on the tape started me thinking about a third expedition.
He said: "Mr. Goerner, if you go back to Saipan again, I'd like
you to do me a favor. Go south from where the native graveyard
is, down by where they buried the 2nd Marines who got it there.
I want you to take a bottle of Jim Beam and salute those guys.
Salute 'em to the north, the east, the south, and the west and
say, 'Here's to the greatest bunch of bastards in the world. You
gotta be free to fight the way you did, and we're still free because of the way you fought.'"

Not a bad toast.

Alex Rico of Torrance, California, made the next contribution.
He had been with a Seabee outfit on Saipan in 1944 and '45, and
often served as an interpreter with the Saipanese because he
spoke Spanish. Several natives told him the Japanese had been
bragging before the war of capturing "some white people" and of
bringing them to Saipan where they were "buried near a native
cemetery." Rico sent two photos of his Seabee encampment on
Saipan which had been located north of Tanapag Harbor and
the Japanese naval seaplane base, and he added that a small
native cemetery had been located within the area. He also indicated there had been a native graveyard south of Garapan
City. In closing, he suggested we search in both places as he felt
the natives had been telling the truth.

Rico's pictures fitted the area where Bridwell had indicated we
should excavate. I assumed the other cemetery was the one
Devine and Kinley had encountered.

Mrs. William Irwin Southern of Los Gatos, California, sent no
startling information but informed me that she had given Amelia

her initial flight instruction in the early 1920s. Mrs. Southern's maiden name had been Neta Snook. She spoke of her own training at Curtiss Aviation School, Newport News, Virginia, in 1918, and of her association with Amelia. She had felt sad, she said, when she read of the possibility of AE being imprisoned by the Japanese in "dirty quarters." It was unthinkable to her because Amelia had been such a fastidious person. Mrs. Southern recalled that Amelia would not eat the cone part of an ice cream cone because of unclean handling.

The insight to Amelia, when connected with the woman held as a political prisoner on Saipan in 1937–38, was distressing. Having tasted Saipan's fare, I knew what AE's reaction would have been.

Navy Chief Petty Officer J. F. Kelleher of the U.S.S. *Fulton* added fuel to the landing in the Marshalls theory. In 1946, he had worked for the U.S. military government in the Marshalls and had lived in close contact with the natives. "Several trustworthy natives" had told him of a plane going down in the vicinity of Likiep Atoll before World War II, and that the Japanese had taken a white man and woman to Kwajalein. According to the natives, the crash had taken place near enough to an island off Likiep so that the man and woman had been able to get ashore. The natives then said the man and woman were later picked up by a Japanese ship. Chief Kelleher said he had never filed an official report because he assumed the U.S. government already knew about it. He named four natives of Likiep, Edward and Bonjo Capelli and two individuals known simply as Jajock and Biki, as those who had told him the story.

The possibility that Amelia and Fred conducted reconnaissance for a military or civilian department of our government broadened with a letter from John F. Day who had recently resigned as Vice-President of CBS News. At the Democratic National Convention in Los Angeles in 1960, Day had met a man who taught technical writing at UCLA, who told Day in turn of an individual who had audited one of his classes and had spoken of having worked on Amelia's plane in Burbank, California, at the time the Electra had been brought back from Honolulu for repair. According to this individual, the engines installed were not those described in publicity releases, but were nearly twice as powerful. The plane's fuel capacity was also increased and the consequent range and cruising speed was much longer and higher than the figures released to the public. He was quoted as adding, "Aerial cameras were then placed in the Electra and equipped for automatic operation from the cockpit. We signed an oath we would not reveal any details of the preparations and I feel I am still at least partially bound to that oath."

I got in touch with Day's informant. "I've been researching this thing myself," he said, "but following a different tack from yours. My theory is based primarily on the distress messages reportedly received along the West Coast several days after the plane disappeared. While the messages were dismissed as a hoax at the time, better understanding of ionospheric-skip characteristics in high-frequency communication leads me to believe that these messages might have been genuine. I'm trying now to gather accurate radio-propagation data for the dates in question in an effort to backtrack the messages to a possible origin point."

He gave me the mechanic's address. In return, I wished him luck with his specialized pursuit.

The former mechanic was cautious on the phone. He acknowledged saying the things attributed to him, but would not amplify them.

"I can't talk about this business," he said.

"I'm told you have indicated aerial cameras were installed aboard the plane."

"That's right."

"Who installed them?"

"I can't say."

"Why?"

"I gave my word."

"But you've already talked to some people."

"I know, and I shouldn't have."

"What harm can there be in it now?"

"I don't know."

"Was it the Navy or Army Air Force?"

"That what?"

"Equipped Earhart's plane with aerial cameras."

"Neither one."

"Who was it then?"

"Civilian technicians."

"The military didn't have any part in it?"

"I didn't say that."

"Can you give me the names of any of the other men who worked on the plane?"

"No."

"You can't or you won't?"

"I won't."

"Will you give me any lead?"

"You might talk to some of the people who were stationed at Hamilton Army Air Force Base in northern California at that time."

"You mean the Army Air Force was involved?"

"I mean only what I've said."

"Please answer this," I said, "and I'll let you go for now. After the special work was done on the Electra, was it capable of flying over the Caroline and Marshall Islands en route Howland?"

"Yes."

A strange postcard, canceled in Denver, Colorado, arrived a few days later. There was no return address, and it was simply signed with an initial and last name. The writer said that he had spent over a year, 1943–44, working toward a solution to the Earhart mystery, and that all the military services had been looking for information regarding her. He believed that the true fate was known and U.S. government archives contained the secret, but it would require access to those archives and the records of other countries before a final answer could be made public. He added that he had last seen Amelia in Berkeley, California, and learned of her mission a few years later. He closed by saying it was too bad Major Wales of Berkeley was dead because the major could have shed some light.

Again the sound of truth, but the sender could not be found. I called every name in the Denver phone book that matched his. I reasoned then that the card could have been dropped in a Denver mailbox as the writer passed through or visited the area, or he might not have used his real name.

"Major Wales" seemed a better lead. At least I knew he had once lived in Berkeley. The first call produced results. A woman listed as Mrs. Sidney M. Wales knew of a James Wales who had held the rank of major in Army Air Force Intelligence before World War II. James Wales had also been the editor of the Berkeley *Gazette* and Mrs. Wales' husband. He had died in 1944. All Mrs. Wales knew was that the major had considered himself a close friend of Amelia's and had been deeply interested in the around-the-world flight.

I later learned from Brigadier General Robert L. Ashworth, Acting Deputy Assistant Chief of Staff for Intelligence, Department of the Army, and "a Major James E. Wales, editor of the Berkeley (California) *Gazette,* was a Military Intelligence Reserve Officer from 23 July 1926 until 13 September 1941. His only active duty during the entire time was for two-week periods with the 40th Division, California National Guard."

Army Intelligence files contained no record of any official military involvement between Wales and Amelia.

The idea of a possible reconnaissance mission widened further with the appearance of Mrs. Vivian Maatta of Oakland, California.

"I've wondered for a long time whether or not I should talk about this," she began. "There were some strange things about the disappearance of Miss Earhart, and I just can't keep quiet any more."

Mrs. Maatta received an interview assignment from her employment agency one day early in 1937. She was to meet a man named William Miller at the Leamington Hotel in Oakland and discuss the possibility of becoming personal secretary to someone of importance. The girl at the agency cautioned her not to mention the meeting to anyone.

Miller introduced himself as an executive with the Civil Aeronautics Authority in Washington, D.C., and questioned Vivian at length about her ability to maintain secrecy should she become privy to confidential material. Apparently satisfied with the responses, Miller informed the young secretary that her employer for the next few months would be Amelia Earhart, who was planning an around-the-world flight and who would spend considerable time in Oakland and Berkeley preparing for the effort.

Vivian ecstatically accepted what she considered good fortune. Amelia had always been her idol, and the chance to be the flier's companion was more than she could have dreamed.

"It didn't go that way, though," said Mrs. Maatta. "They established a small office in Oakland, and I ended up doing more work for Mr. Miller and Mr. Putnam than I did for Miss Earhart. George Putnam, Miss Earhart's husband, paid my salary, but I had the feeling Bill Miller was footing some or all of the bills. Mr. Putnam always paid in cash; never by check."

"What was Miller's role in the flight plans?" I asked.

"I'm not sure. It wasn't discussed openly. He had long meetings with Miss Earhart, and they pored over maps. I think he was responsible for setting her itinerary."

"What was wrong with that?"

"The fact that they kept it all so secret. I'm sure it didn't have anything to do with what they were telling the public."

"Did they make you responsible for any classified information?"

"Only one time and that was an accident."

"What was it?"

"Well, I came back to the office from lunch one day, and Mr. Miller was on the telephone. He apparently was talking to someone very important who was giving him orders. Well, Bill had had me listen to several of his conversations and make notes, so I listened to that one and jotted a few things down. He was being ordered to go to Port Darwin, Australia, on some sort of special mission which had to do with Miss Earhart."

"What happened then?"

"Well, after he hung up the phone, I asked him if he wanted me to type up my notes for a permanent reference on the call. When I said that, he became very excited and wanted to know how much I had heard. Then he said for me to forget the whole thing, and not to mention it to anyone. He impressed on me that his trip was top-secret government business."

Mrs. Maatta went on to describe Miller as a "confident, kind man" who had been about forty years old in 1937. He had gone on his mission to Australia sometime after Amelia and Fred and their Electra had returned to California after the Honolulu crackup, and she had never seen him again. There had been an exchange of Christmas cards for several years, but the cards had stopped in the early 1940s, and she presumed William Miller was dead.

Miller—man of mystery—never existed as far as the Department of Commerce knew. Bureau of Air Commerce charts for 1937–38 made no mention of him. It took me more than two years to get some answers, and then they provided only basic facts in Miller's story.

Born August 8, 1899, William Thomas Miller was educated at the University of Michigan, learned to fly with the Navy, and held a reserve commission as lieutenant commander. In 1935, he became Superintendent of Airways of the Bureau of Air Commerce—and an agent of American interests in the Pacific Ocean area. Pan American Airways had surveyed possible commercial routes in the Pacific and was preparing to commence regular clipper service between San Francisco and the Philippines. Commercially the U.S. was racing Japan and air travel symbolized the competition. Military overtones of that competition were unavoidable. With the exception of Midway, Wake, and Guam, Japan controlled the Pacific islands north of the equator. The land fields and seaplane bases surreptitiously constructed and being constructed on those islands could be used for military aircraft and provided a formidable challenge to the United States. We needed bases of our own, but the only islands available within practical commercial and military range of Japan's Mandate efforts were Baker, Howland, and Jarvis. Among our oldest possessions, they had not been inhabited for years, and although U.S. claims were not presently being challenged, fear existed that succeeding tours of inspection by Coast Guard or Naval vessels might find a Japanese population busily bulldozing airstrips, claiming possession by the proverbial nine-tenths. The main problem was disguising the obvious military purpose of building land fields on the islands when Pan American, the only U.S. airline active in the Pacific, used nothing but flying boats. Also, none of the islands afforded harbors or anchorages; therefore, seaplane bases were out of the question. Japan had hidden her military preparations in the Marshall, Caroline, and Mariana Islands by discouraging visitors and creating the supposedly civilian Nanyo Kohatsu Kaisha, South Seas Development Company, to front for the Imperial Japanese Navy. U. S. State Department policy would not tolerate possible offense to Japan through overt military construction on Howland, Baker, and Jarvis, so Japanese tactics were copied, and the Bureau of Air Commerce was assigned the task of colonizing the three islands and constructing the necessary landing fields. The U. S. Army Air Corps was testing a new long-range bomber designated B-17 and war with Japan seemed inevitable to those who envisioned the islands as bases for the new weapon.

Early in 1935, Bill Miller sailed to Jarvis aboard the U. S. Coast Guard cutter *Itasca*, and landed March 26 with a small party. He raised the American flag, created a community, named Millersville, for himself, and populated it with colonists who would build and maintain the airfield. He repeated the ceremony shortly thereafter on both Howland and Baker Islands. The coup did not go unnoticed by Japan, but the United States was back on the equator within range of the Marshalls and top-secret Truk.

Except for Washington bureaucracy, the plan might have worked. The Interior Department bitterly complained that colonizing activities belonged within its purview. When the challenge to the Commerce Department began to reach the public, President Franklin D. Roosevelt ordered the colonists withdrawn pending a change of administration. The year 1936 was an election year, and the hassle embarrassed Roosevelt. In the midst of his efforts to pull America from depression, he was being forced to defend expenditure of federal funds for construction of airfields on South Seas islands by civilian departments of government. When a reporter suggested the incongruity of building land fields for seaplanes, the President acted. May 13, 1936, he issued an executive order placing Howland, Baker, and Jarvis under Interior's jurisdiction to be administered by Dr. Ernest Gruening and the Division of Territories and Island Possessions. Gruening (now U. S. Senator from Alaska) selected Richard Blackburn Black, a civil engineer who had been to Antarctica with Admiral Byrd (1933–35) to continue the re-establishment of American interest on Jarvis, Baker, and Howland.

The Commerce Department was out, the Interior Department in, and Dr. Gruening, an M.D.-journalist-turned-politician, evidently saw no advantage in spending taxpayers' dollars on airfields which could only serve military purposes. Then, as to-day, the Interior Department jousted the military services for control of any and all territories; the question of national de-fense notwithstanding. Control meant larger budgets and more personnel, and that consideration superseded all warnings of future hostilities with Japan. Gruening stipulated that light-houses and weather stations were to be maintained on the three islands, but no airfields. Richard Black, later a rear admiral, USN, began to execute this order in July 1936. He organized a series of cruises to the islands, and arranged for the facilities on each to be manned by students from the Kamehameha Boys School of Honolulu. The Hawaiians were rotated regularly be-cause of the loneliness of the posts.

Gruening's decision did not please President Roosevelt, the Army Air Corps, the Navy, or William Miller. As Japan became increasingly militant, the United States would need air bases from which to neutralize Japanese strength, particularly in the Marshall Islands. An excuse with emotional impact was needed to justify construction of a landing field on Howland, the nearest U.S. controlled island to the Marshalls. Into this establishment need came Amelia Earhart, asking for assistance for her around-the-world flight.

President Roosevelt had requested the Navy, in November 1936, to cooperate with AE by making arrangements for in-flight refueling near Midway Island, but Miller and intelligent-minded Air Corps officers, who believed in strategic, long-range bombers, then discovered their emotion-laden reason for build-ing Howland's airfield. Appealed to on the grounds of national security and service to her country, Amelia consented to reroute her flight to include Howland Island. On January 8, 1937, AE informed President Roosevelt by letter that although arrange-ments for refueling in flight had been made with the Navy, she had changed her plans. If an emergency landing field on How-land Island could be completed in time, she would land there to refuel. She asked FDR if he could expedite the allocation of funds.

Roosevelt happily obliged. Marvin H. McIntyre, assistant secretary to the President, replied on January 11, 1937, that an allocation of federal funds had been made by the President to the Works Progress Administration to enable the Bureau of Air Commerce to carry out the construction of such a field.

Within two months, work was under way. The priority project, directed by Robert Leslie Campbell, Divisional Airport Inspector for the Department of Commerce, received assistance from the WPA and grudging support from the Interior Department. The Navy and Army Air Corps also helped, but their efforts were veiled because of possible repercussions from Japan. The work had to appear to be civilian motivated and sponsored.

Some experts told Amelia she was crazy to attempt a Howland landing, but William Thomas Miller and the Army Air Corps were confident. If AE proved the feasibility of land planes for ocean flight, Congress might be persuaded to vote more funds for airport development in the Pacific and for purchase of long-range aircraft. The Air Corps assigned a lieutenant and two enlisted assistants the duty of surveying the field and placing the required markers and flags. The lieutenant and his men proceeded to Howland aboard the U.S.S. *Itasca* at the time of the flight. The lieutenant was also to be available for any technical assistance that Amelia might require after landing on Howland.

The Navy lost much of its enthusiasm when Amelia canceled the Midway refueling arrangement and announced her new itinerary, but the need to know of Japan's Pacific military preparations was sufficient in many Navy groups to arouse more than casual interest in the flight.

Embellishments to the original plan were inevitable. AE soon found herself in a mission within a mission within a mission. Bill Miller stayed in the background. He had a new assignment as Chief of Aeronautical Surveys of the South Pacific Ocean, and his presence was not calculated to stimulate unstinting cooperation from the Interior Department. He worked long hours with Amelia, detailing each leg of the flight. All information she could bring back about airfields in any part of the world would immeasurably help the U.S. in the event of war.

William Miller, President Roosevelt, Henry Morgenthau, Jr., and many officers in Navy, Army Air Corps, and Marine Corps Intelligence desperately wished success for Amelia and Fred. If the Pacific could be traversed by a land plane, the construction and maintenance of island airfields would become acceptable.

There was also the matter of military information that perhaps only a civilian such as Amelia could obtain.

When the Electra failed to arrive at Howland that July morning in 1937, hope that the three islands could be used for retaliatory or reconnaissance purposes vanished, too, and the crisscrossing Howland runways again became a refuge for birds. The abandonment of the islands as possible air bases was only one of the prices military aviation paid prior to the war for the loss of Amelia and Fred. When the Army attempted to demonstrate that land planes could fly over great stretches of ocean to bomb a target or accomplish photo reconnaissance missions, skeptics pointed to the Howland failure. Whether or not Jarvis, Baker, and Howland could have provided a striking force sufficient seriously to hamper the Japanese will never be known. If the three islands had hangared even a few light bombers at the time of Pearl Harbor, 1941, great damage might have been in turn visited upon the Japanese bases at Kwajalein, Mille, and Wotje in the Marshalls. It is known the Japanese feared the islands, especially Howland. After the attack on Pearl Harbor, Japanese land-based bombers struck at the tiny field which four years before had waited for Amelia Earhart. They bombed the runways and strafed the lighthouse, killing or wounding several of the Hawaiian cadre. Symbolically, a plaque honoring Amelia, which had been placed on the lighthouse after her disappearance, was shattered by Japanese machine-gun bullets.

The "aeronautical survey of the South Pacific Ocean" phase of William Miller's career ended with the *Lexington*'s 1937 abortive search. He became Chief of the Civil Aeronautics Administration's International Section that year, and later was named Chief, Air Carrier Division, of the CAA, a post he held until his death from a heart attack in Washington, D.C., in 1943. The Commerce Department, however, cannot find any report filed by Miller which deals with his Amelia Earhart association. He appears to have disappeared for considerable periods of time, and there is no record of his accomplishments or lack of them. Unless Miller kept a diary or notes regarding his involvement with AE and Fred and those documents are extant in the possession of someone I have not yet contacted, the complete story may never be known. There is, of course, the possibility the Commerce Department is withholding information or has given the files to a department of the Military.

Vivian Maatta served only as AE's replacement secretary while Amelia was in Oakland. I finally found the woman who was the secretary in 1935–36–37. She worked then and lives now in North Hollywood, California.

"I promised secrecy," she said to me when I spoke with her on the telephone, "but I'll tell you this. If Eugene Vidal is still living, he can tell you all you'll ever want to know. I used to pick him up and drive him around when he came to Burbank from Washington. He made several trips during the period when the plane was being rebuilt."

"What was unusual about that?" I asked.

"I'll ask you a couple of questions," she replied, "and you can draw your own conclusions. First, do you really think Purdue University bought that plane for Amelia, and do you think that it was intended for some kind of vague experimentation? Second, if the whole thing was a publicity stunt as a lot of people seem to think, why did the government assign some of its top experts to the flight, and why did President Roosevelt have an airfield built for her? Last, do you believe the President ordered the Navy to spend four million dollars on a search for a couple of stunt fliers?"

"Won't you tell me what *you* think?" I asked.

"Only this. President Roosevelt knew about everything. He knew the price Amelia paid."

"Don't you feel it's about time Amelia received some justice?" I continued.

"When one does the things Amelia was doing, one can't expect to receive justice. She knew that. She talked to me about it."

"Do you think there's any possibility Amelia is still alive?"

"She's dead. She died a long time ago. If she had survived the war, she would have come home even if she had to swim."

"Do you think the Japanese captured her?"

"Of course they did."

"Where?"

"All I can tell you is that it was within moderate range of Howland Island."

"Did she intend to land at Howland?"

"In the beginning, she did."

"Beginning of what?"

"I mean that was her intention after the first change of plans but before what really happened."

"I'm sorry, I don't understand."

"That's all I'm going to say. I've already said too much."

"Your suggestion then is for me to talk to Vidal?"

"There are a lot of people who can tell you part or all of the story. Your problem is to open them up."

That was all I could learn from Amelia's secretary.

"That radio of hers couldn't transmit more than fifty miles, and she did send a message that she only had a half-hour of gas left. I know because I copied the message. She went into the drink close to Howland, and no one will ever convince me otherwise."

Bill Galten of Brisbane, California, who had been listed by the San Francisco *Chronicle* as one of the radio operators aboard *Itasca,* sounded positive when I talked with him by phone. He vehemently denied there had been any discrepancy in the messages supposed to have come from Amelia which were relayed to Coast Guard Headquarters in San Francisco in 1937.

"I was in charge of communications with her plane," Galten continued, "and there was no doubt about what the *Itasca* received or sent. I don't care what the photostats of the log say."

There seemed no sense in seeing Galten, but a letter from Everett, Washington, changed my mind. Leo G. Bellarts, Deputy Director and Radio Officer for Snohomish County, Washington, Civil Defense Office, had been Chief Radioman aboard *Itasca* in 1937. We began a dialogue which clarified Galten's role the morning Amelia and Fred disappeared and explained some of the Coast Guard's confusion.

With his first letter, Bellarts sent a photostat of the organization of the *Itasca's* radio personnel together with the comment that he knew Bill Galten, who was at the time of the Earhart search a radioman third class.

1. This organization will be followed at all times while Amelia Earhart's plane is in the air.

BELLARTS CRM—Handle all plane communications, and log the same. Keep all interested parties informed of the position of the plane and all pertinent data connected with the flight (the Commanding Officer and the Officer of the Deck, the latter will plot the plane positions). In the event of a casualty in either take-off or landing make proper steps to assure the *Itasca* handles all information relative to the casualty and allows no other station to assume responsibilities of communications or dissemination of information. If necessary, use the proper transmitter to block out any superfluous transmission from any unauthorized sources. Prepare a message for action to Headquarters, information to Commander, San Francisco Division and Commander Hawaiian Section giving the extent of the casualty and requesting action to be taken; this message to go in Code A.

CIPRIANTI—Man high frequency direction finder ashore, keeping in direct contact with the ship by means of the portable transmitter as to what time and on what frequency to take bearings. Keep a log as to the time and bearing received from the plane. Familiarize self with operation and calibration of direction finder previous to flight.

O'HARE—Take over watch and handle all incoming and outgoing messages to NPU, NPM and NMC in such a manner as not to interfere with plane traffic. Keep Swan, Ontario, Commander Fourteenth Naval District, Commander San Francisco Division and Commander Hawaiian Section informed.

GALTEN—When plane comes within a thousand miles of Howland Island, man the ship's direction finder and listen in on five hundred kilocycles for the plane and when it is heard, take a bearing, record same with the proper time in a suitable log.

THOMPSON—Relief operator, also send out all homing in signals on the frequency as requested by the plane.

In subsequent letters, Bellarts' comments indicated that with respect to Galten's statements to the press, his memory was at fault. His estimate of the range of Earhart's radio was in error since they heard signals from her plane when she was many hundreds of miles out. Fifty watts of phone on 3105 KCS will carry quite a long way, he pointed out, especially at dawn or early morning hours—a transmitter 1000 feet in the air and airborne will outperform a transmitter on the ground.

Bellarts included his copy of the *Itasca*'s original log of the ten partial or complete messages received from AE. The 0742 Howland Standard Time transmission indicated "gas is running low." The final message, with which I was familiar, had been received at 0843, and read, "We are running North and South on the line 157–337. Will repeat message on 6210 KCS—Wait."

Regarding the final words, Bellarts explained that they took the "157–337" to mean an incomplete sunline position, assuming she was so upset that she failed to send the entire message which would have given the *Itasca* something to go on in the search. They further assumed that she crashed somewhere before arriving at Howland. The "will repeat this on 6210—wait" meant that she was not entirely certain the *Itasca* received her, and she wanted to shift to the 6210, her daytime frequency, and repeat the message. They had receivers on both 6210 and 3105 KCS, but never heard another signal from the plane. It was a possibility that she crashed while she was trying to switch frequency, except that no distress signal was heard or any word of immediate trouble received from her. Also there was no explanation why she would run out of gas at such an early hour. Bellarts accepted the idea that Earhart crashed within two hundred miles of Howland, based on the belief that she ran out of gas right after the last message. If she didn't, he indicated he had no answer as to why they didn't hear something more on 6210 or 3105.

I asked Bellarts about the one position report attributed to Earhart which supposedly had been relayed from Lae, New Guinea, to Hawaiian Section Coast Guard to the *Itasca* at Howland Island, after the disappearance.

8003 Lae New Guinea reports last contact with Earhart plane by Lae radio was at 1720 Friday Gave her position as 433 South 1597 East which is about 785 miles directly on her route to Howland Island 0030

Bellarts replied that the Coast Guard log could not have included that message as the *Itasca* was not aware of it through her own efforts. He was positive that the *Itasca* did not copy that report.

I looked again at the Form 9625 Treasury Department U. S.

Coast Guard Official Dispatch which Eleanor Roosevelt had arranged to be sent to Paul Mantz in 1940. The report Bellarts had denied receiving was dated July 3, 1937, the day after Amelia and Fred disappeared. The routing and text of the message were as above, but several important items were missing. Priority of the transmission was not indicated, and the initials of the operator and duty officer were absent. Apparently no one wanted to accept responsibility for receipt and dissemination of the message's contents. Such reticence is understandable. The message was wrong. It had to be. Averaging less than 115 miles per hour, Amelia certainly would have turned back to Lae and waited for head winds to subside. She would have known that to continue the flight would mean arriving in the vicinity of Howland Island with fuel exhausted. AE and Fred accepted many risks during their years of flying, but nothing as suicidal as proceeding in the face of head winds which could prevent them from achieving their destination. Amelia would have aborted the flight after no more than two hours of such circumstances.

Why then would the position report appear in the official Coast Guard transcript? Bellarts had no idea.

Nor did William Galten. I visited him and his wife at their home in Brisbane, and during the first minutes of conversation, he reiterated his version of Amelia's reports.

"She went down close to Howland," he said, "and that's all there is to it."

"Do you know a man named Bellarts?" I asked.

There was a pause. "Yes . . ." he replied.

The tenor of the conversation changed from then on. Galten did remember Bellarts, as chief radioman aboard the *Itasca*. I told him that Bellarts' account said that there was no message stipulating "one-half-hour of gas." Then I showed him the copy of the *Itasca*'s radio log.

I had brought along a KCBS secretary, Marge Dehrig, to transcribe the conversation, and together we watched in silence as Galten studied the log, concentrating, apparently trying to reconstruct that long-ago day in his mind, against the evidence of the log.

Finally he sighed and said, "I guess I didn't hear what I thought I heard." He went on to say that there was so much confusion in the radio room that morning, it was hard to know what was said.

We discussed the difference between "a half-hour of gas," and "running low on gas." It could have been the difference between the search that was conducted and the one that might have been conducted.

Finally Galten said a surprising thing: "Amelia Earhart never intended to land at Howland Island . . ."

"Why do you say that?" I asked.

"The field wasn't finished the way it should have been, and no one could have landed with all those birds around anyway. There were thousands of them all over that island."

"What did she intend to do?"

"I don't think anyone will ever find out."

"Do you know?"

"No."

"Why do you say it, then?"

"It's just a strong feeling I've had."

"Will you give me the name of anyone I can ask about it?"

"Ask the government. You probably won't get any answers, though."

Galten would say no more. But that was the end of the mystery of the discrepancy in transmissions.

Leo Bellarts later seconded the observation about Howland's nesting birds.

"I remember thinking at the time," he said, "that Earhart could probably land all right, but she would have a hell of a time taking off again. Those birds were all over the place. The bird-watcher societies would have screamed. We killed hundreds of those goonies to try to clear the runways, but it didn't do much good. There were too many of them."

In answer to a request from Commander MacBain in May 1962, I sent a report of the investigation to date to Admiral Smith's office in Washington, D.C. It detailed the apparent lack of cooperation and communication between civilian and military agencies at the time of Amelia's disappearance. Reaction came quickly, but from the Coast Guard, not the Navy. On July 17, 1962, Chief Yeoman Walter Lee of the Coast Guard Marine

Inspection Station in San Francisco called me, and said, "I've been asked to tell you, Mr. Goerner, to obtain a copy of tomorrow's edition of the *Navy Times*. There is some information in it that you should find interesting."

The next day the Coast Guard released the classified report of Commander Warner K. Thompson, who had been the *Itasca's* captain in 1937. Macon Reed, a *Navy Times* staff writer, stated at the beginning of the long article that Thompson's secret file and associated papers had been made available to the newspaper by the Coast Guard in connection with the twenty-fifth anniversary of Amelia's disappearance. If that was the case, the release came sixteen days late. July 2, 1962, was the correct anniversary. I called Reed in Washington, but he gave no additional explanation. The Coast Guard had suddenly presented the *Times* with the information and he had been assigned to write the story.

"I don't get it," he said. "There's evidence that every one of the one hundred and six pages have at some time been photographed with the *CONFIDENTIAL* label covered. Evidently the report has been made available to some people. There are pencil marks in the margins with the word 'include' written several times. At one place, the word 'omit' is penciled, too."

"What does it say?" I asked.

"It reads, 'The Navy emergency direction finder on Howland was powered by *Itasca's* gun batteries, which ran down during the night.'"

"Is the direction finder mentioned anywhere else?"

"Yes," replied Reed. "Thompson noted that a Richard Black of the Interior Department and an Army Air Corps lieutenant brought the gear aboard the *Itasca* at Pearl Harbor. He also wrote that he didn't like the whole business; that he thought the equipment was untried and erratic, and he preferred to depend on the low-frequency direction finder he already had aboard ship."

Thompson's report, together with Coast Guard radio logs, revealed a story of uncertainty and confusion from the moment of Coast Guard involvement to the loss of Amelia and Fred. On June 12, 1937, San Francisco Division sent the following message to CG Headquarters in Washington:

Failure to combine Earhart mission and routine equator island cruise so awkward and embarrassing in variety of aspects it would seem higher authority could compel action on basis of emergency funds. *Taney* will be unavailable law enforcement entire month of July if routine line cruise made by her, and some adverse comment may flow from special detail of *Itasca* to flight cooperation alone.

The U.S.S. *Taney* did not receive the assignment. It was given instead to Commander Warner Keith Thompson and the 250-foot cutter *Itasca* which had already been ordered to depart San Pedro, California, for Pearl Harbor, Hawaii. From Pedro to Pearl, Thompson's log shows he had not been able to learn anything about Amelia's plans. For several days at Pearl, it shows the same thing, but on June 16, the Commandant of the Coast Guard radioed that AE planned to reach Lae, New Guinea, June 23, and would proceed from there to Howland on June 24 or 25.

Richard Black and the lieutenant came aboard with their "borrowed" Navy high-frequency direction finder, and the *Itasca* left Pearl Harbor at flank speed trying to reach Howland ahead of the Electra.

On June 20, Thompson received a message from George Putnam saying that when AE reached Port Darwin, Australia, he (Putnam) would then let the *Itasca* know her radio plans and needs.

On June 21, the same promise of information came from Mrs. Ruth Hampton, Assistant Director of Territories, Interior Department, for Richard Black aboard the *Itasca*. Mrs. Hampton also suggested weather communication with Amelia via American Samoa. Commander Thompson began to complain that four sources, George Putnam, Mrs. Hampton, San Francisco Division Coast Guard, and Richard Black were trying to control the flight communications.

On June 22, *Itasca* radioed San Francisco Division to try to get at least twelve hours notice of AE's take-off. The same day, Black got in touch with a James Kamakaiwi, one of the station force on Howland Island, and urged him to build a large fire to burn all that night. Black was evidently fearful that AE might be flying to Howland the night of June 22.

On June 23, *Itasca* arrived at Howland in the afternoon, and the Navy emergency direction finder was set up on the island while the ship's radio crew manned their stations.

On June 24, *Itasca* learned Amelia and Fred were in Batavia for repairs for at least three days. Everyone relaxed while the ship cruised thirty miles southeast to Baker Island then returned to its anchorage by Howland.

On June 26, San Francisco Division relayed what purportedly was a definitive message from Amelia listing her homing device range as from 200 to 1500 kilocycles and from 2400 to 4800 kilocycles. Division suggested *Itasca* try 333 or 545, and use 3105 for voice. Almost at the same time, a message was received directly from Amelia in which she requested three things: 1. U.S.S. *Ontario* (the Navy weather ship then standing by halfway from Lae to Howland) to broadcast by key the letter N on 400 kilocycles. 2. U.S.S. *Swan* (the Navy plane guard and weather ship standing by halfway from Howland to Honolulu) to transmit by voice on 900 kilocycles. 3. U.S.S. *Itasca* at Howland send letter A on 7.5 megacycles.

Amelia added that she would give a "long call in voice on 3105 kilocycles at a quarter after each hour and possibly at a quarter before each hour."

Commander Thompson was stunned by the two messages. San Francisco Division spoke of low frequencies and quoted Amelia as stipulating her direction finder went no higher than 4800 kilocycles. The second message, directly from AE, instructed him to broadcast a stream of A's as homing signals on 7500—2700 kilocycles higher than Division said her loop would reach. Someone had goofed and badly. Thompson immediately asked San Francisco Division to grant him control of communications and allow him to use Navy relays.

On June 27, copious weather information reached *Itasca*. Included was a copy of an Earhart message which indicated she believed there was a Navy meteorologist aboard *Itasca*. There wasn't. A Lieutenant Love had been left behind, and was doing his forecasting from Pearl Harbor.

On June 28, Thompson tried to solve the communications

riddle with a message to Amelia by way of the Navy. The commander, however, did not refer to the high-frequency Navy emergency direction finder. He simply said, "*Itasca* transmitters calibrated to 7500, 6210, 3105, 500, 425. *Itasca* direction finder range 550 to 270 kilocycles."

On June 29, San Francisco Division reported Amelia en route Darwin, Australia, to Lae, New Guinea, and planning a July 1 take-off for Howland. Also, that day, a message arrived for Black from Amelia. She believed "the *Itasca* will transmit long continuous signal on 3105."

Again there was consternation. AE had previously requested the letter A be broadcast on 7500 kilocycles, and now she apparently intended to home on 3105.

On June 30, Thompson desperately but unsuccessfully tried to learn exactly what Amelia planned.

On July 1, "the entire day," in Thompson's words, "was spent trying to ascertain whether Earhart had hopped."

As darkness fell, first from San Francisco Division, then by press, then by message to Black signed "Vacuum," came word AE and Fred were on their way.

Commander Thompson and his Coast Guard crew braced for a long, difficult night. They figured the plane would arrive sometime after daylight, refuel, and be on its way to Honolulu. Boat parties had been organized in case Amelia overshot the runways and landed in the surf or further offshore. A continual effort was made to clear the birds from the airstrip. *Itasca* radioman Ciprianti was ashore, manning the Navy's new emergency DF. The cutter's searchlights were ready to go on after midnight in case the plane picked up a tail wind and arrived early. The vessel's boilers were scheduled to produce great billows of smoke, beginning at dawn, to guide Amelia to the tiny island from a distance.

By 0600, the tension in the radio room was explosive. Only fragments of messages had been received from the plane, and none contained a position report. At 0615, Amelia broke in clearly, and asked *Itasca* to take a bearing on her on 3105. She whistled briefly to aid the direction finder, and then indicated the plane was approximately 200 miles out. *Itasca* radioed the station on Howland, but AE had not been on the air long enough for the DF to get a minimum. A half hour later at 0645, she again requested a bearing from *Itasca,* and placed the Electra 100 miles from touchdown. The signal strength was good, but the Navy direction finder on Howland still could not get a cut.

At 0718, *Itasca* said by radiophone to Amelia, "Can't take a bearing so good (sic) on 3105. Send on 500."

No reply, as there had been no response to any *Itasca* message during the night; yet AE reported no radio trouble. It seemed she was ignoring *Itasca*'s signals. Those in the radio room pressed closer to the receivers.

Nearly a half hour later, 0742, AE complained she had not been able to reach *Itasca* by radio, but again did not mention any malfunction of her set. She estimated they were over the island, but, at an altitude of 1000 feet, nothing was visible. As if to urge *Itasca* to greater effort, she added, "Gas is running low."

Six minutes later, 0748, in the strongest, clearest reception to that time, Amelia said, "We are circling but cannot hear you. Go ahead on 7500 either now or on the scheduled time on half-hour."

Thompson's agitation increased. Earhart was switching again, attempting to get her own bearing. Why didn't she stay on the air longer on 3105 if she wanted the Navy direction finder on Howland to get a fix? Or why didn't she send on 500 so the *Itasca* could use its gear? What the hell was she doing? He gave the order to resume broadcast on 7500.

Between 0800 and 0803, Amelia acknowledged hearing *Itasca* for the first time.

"We received your signals but unable to get a minimum," she said. "Please take a bearing on us and answer on 3105 with voice."

KHAQQ (the plane's call letters) transmitted long dashes for approximately five seconds on the frequency.

Thompson slammed his fist against the bulkhead. She had done it again. Switched back to 3105 from 7500 as a source for homing signals, and she wanted the *Itasca* to take a bearing on a direction finder frequency the vessel supposedly did not have.

"Call that damned Navy rig on Howland," he ordered, "and see if Ciprianti was able to pick her up."

"Negative," was the answer from the island. AE still had not been on the air long enough for the DF to get a minimum.

Commander Thompson paced the radio shack for a few minutes, but the receivers remained silent. With disgust and despair, he climbed to the *Itasca's* bridge, and scanned the sky above and the distant horizons. In all directions but one, visibility was unlimited. Some forty miles to the northwest, a massive front of storm clouds rose well over ten thousand feet. If Amelia and Fred were anywhere in that area, Thompson reasoned, they could be in trouble. The smoke from *Itasca's* stack would not be visible, much less the island. If a search had to be launched, northwest was the logical direction. For the first time, he felt fear. One of the most famous humans in the world was his responsibility, and in a few minutes, he might be called upon to make a decision which involved her life. Fear turned to frustration. Why had the whole business been so botched up? What was behind the fouled up communications and the secrecy? In his lone communication to her, he had not mentioned 3105 as a homing frequency for the Navy direction finder. In fact, he had not suggested such a DF existed. He had only stipulated 500 and the *Itasca's* gear. Yet Earhart continued to call for a bearing on 3105 and completely ignored 500. She seemed to know of the Navy equipment. If so, why hadn't someone let him in on the plot?

Thompson returned to the charged atmosphere surrounding the ship's radio in time to hear Amelia's final enigmatic utterance.

Sometime between 0844 and 0846, these words burst through the static on 3105: "We are on the line of position 157–337. Will repeat this message. We will repeat this message on 6210 kilocycles. Wait listening on 6210. We are running north and south."

AE was switching to her daytime frequency. There seemed to be a strong note of anxiety in her voice, and all ears strained for her next words. If she was as close to Howland as signal strength indicated, her 6210 signals should be heard clearly.

Instead, there was nothing. The minutes dragged by as Chief

Radioman Bellarts minutely searched the radio band for the sound of the Electra's carrier wave. Still nothing.

At 0900, Thompson knew the decision he feared was imminent. He climbed back to the bridge and leaned against the rail. A seven-knot breeze from the southeast brushed his face, as he stared at the mass of clouds to the northwest.

"That must be where she is," he thought. "South of us she would see Baker Island. Passing overhead, it would be impossible to miss the smoke. '157–337' must be a sunline or a compass heading. If she meant the line to bisect Howland, northwest is the only possibility."

The decision almost made itself. An hour later, at 1000, Commander Thompson ordered the anchor raised, and *Itasca* sped forty miles to the northwest and began to cover a quadrant of ocean. Frustration was only beginning.

For five days, life was chaos for Thompson. Everyone had a different idea of where to search. Putnam and the Coast Guard tried to direct from San Francisco. Admiral Murfin got the Navy into the act from Pearl Harbor, and Richard Black volunteered his thoughts and those of Ernest Gruening and Ruth Hampton in Washington. Even the *Itasca's* crew advanced advice and possible interpretations of Amelia's messages.

Thompson believed the Electra, with buoyancy from its gasoline tanks, could remain afloat indefinitely. Then came word from Lockheed Aircraft that the plane would undoubtedly have broken up and sunk if it landed on water. Messages from Paul Mantz and George Putnam contained the opposite view. The extra fuel tanks had been constructed in such a manner that the aircraft would float.

Ham radio operators began to receive messages attributed to Amelia. Real or bogus, they all found their way to Thompson aboard *Itasca*. Some placed Amelia and Fred in the Phoenix Islands to the southeast. Others had the plane down close to Howland or far to the northeast or northwest. Dozens of U.S. operators claimed to have heard KHAQQ, but there was no official substantiation from any Coast Guard or Navy radio station. Thompson believed most were fabrications, and he classified the others as "products of hysteria."

When another message from Lockheed technicians indicated

the Electra's radio would not work if the plane was in the water, the reports from amateur radiomen were further discounted. Again Mantz and Putnam demurred, saying a special battery had been installed in the cockpit to meet such an emergency, but their comments did not move Thompson. He believed the ham radio operators were trying to confuse him with "criminally false transmissions."

The commander could not make up his mind what to do. Richard Black attempted to piece together the fragmentary information from all the sources, but Thompson would have none of it. He told Black, "The Interior Department has done enough botching."

On July 7, 1937, U.S.S. *Ontario,* the Navy weather ship which had been stationed halfway between Lae and Howland, rendezvoused with *Itasca,* and Commander Warner Thompson was off the hook. *Ontario's* skipper was a senior officer, and he assumed the search responsibility. Nine days later, with fuel down to minimum, *Itasca* ended her service to Amelia Earhart and returned to Pearl Harbor.

During the trip to the States, Thompson wrote his report, sparing almost no one. There was caustic criticism for George Putnam, Richard Black, Ruth Hampton, Ernest Gruening, the Navy Department, the Interior Department, amateur radio operators in general, Amelia and Fred, and even the Coast Guard for permitting itself to be used. Commander Thompson left *Itasca* the end of July 1937 and took command of the cutter *Ingham.* Later he became acting director of the Juneau, Alaska, Division of the Coast Guard. He died there in 1939.

Why was his report classified for twenty-five years?

Thompson's criticism is certainly part of the answer. If it had been released in 1937, reporters would have questioned the involvement of so many departments of government in what had been billed as "a strictly civilian flight." Conjuring answers might have been embarrassing to President Roosevelt. More important, however, were the other enigmas, sufficient to challenge the detective in any newsman's heart. Why was Amelia secretive about her radio plans? Why were her messages to *Itasca* so infrequent and fragmentary? Why did she never send a position report to *Itasca?* Why did she only once acknowledge receiving *Itasca's* signals when the cutter's messages were heard clearly all night by other receivers throughout the Pacific? Why didn't AE broadcast on 500 kilocycles so *Itasca* could use its homing gear? She asked *Itasca* to take a bearing on 3105, but how did she know the Navy emergency DF was available? Thompson had mentioned only the 500 DF in the single message he sent to her before the flight, and yet she avoided the 500 frequency, or suggestion of it, with what amounted to purpose.

In the years since the disappearance, a story has been circulated through the Coast Guard and Navy that Amelia and Fred lost their lives because they jettisoned a low-frequency radio transmitter at Lae, New Guinea, in favor of extra gasoline.

Thompson's report and the San Francisco Coast Guard Division report of 1938 made no such statement, and the rumor was also refuted by Guinea Airways representatives at Lae.

In one of the milder comments of his transcript, Thompson states, "Viewed from the fact that Miss Earhart's flight was largely dependent on radio communications, her attitude toward arrangements was most casual to say the least."

The 1938 Division report, released from secrecy at the same time as Thompson's, maintains AE did *not* know the Navy 3105 DF had been brought to Howland. Written more than six months after the disappearance, the report adds, "To this day, no one in the Coast Guard has been able to find out exactly what radio equipment Miss Earhart did have aboard. Even Mr. Putnam in San Francisco was very badly informed about flight schedules and actual conditions on the plane. Miss Earhart knew the *Itasca* carried a low-frequency direction finder, but she never broadcast on 500 for a bearing and she never chose to explain why not."

Amelia asked that a bearing be taken on 3105, the frequency of the Navy DF, yet Thompson and Coast Guard San Francisco Division officially maintained she did not know such a finder was available.

It would seem obvious she *did* know of its existence, and chose to use the Navy equipment instead of *Itasca*'s low-frequency finder. Why the Coast Guard ignored the apparent might have been explained by Thompson's statement: "The

Navy direction finder on Howland was powered by *Itasca*'s gun batteries, which ran down during the night."

But even that comment was challenged. I called Leo Bellarts for confirmation, and he said, "If Thompson wrote that, he was out of his mind. The gun batteries weren't used. There was nothing wrong with that direction finder. It worked fine the whole night."

The Navy DF seemed to be a key, but two years were to pass before I learned more about it from Richard Black, the man who brought it aboard *Itasca*.

Several months after Thompson's report and the associated Coast Guard documents were released in 1962, a "Letter to the Editor" appeared in *Navy Times*, providing another small link. W. C. Tinus, Vice-President of Bell Telephone Laboratories, was the radio engineer responsible for the design and installation of Amelia's radio communications equipment. In his letter he said he had modified a standard three-channel Western Electric equipment of the type then being used by the airlines to provide one channel at 500 kc and the other two at around 3000 and 6000 kc. A simple modification also enabled transmission to be made on CW or MCW, as well as voice, and a telegraph key was provided which could be plugged in, in addition to a microphone for voice communication.

He said further that several months after her disappearance they received a small package from Pan American Airways at Miami containing her telegraph key, cord, and plug, which she had left in their hangar there. Without these items she could have communicated on 500 kc by voice and could have sent out a suitable signal for direction finding by simply holding the microphone button down for a time. The remainder of her equipment peculiar to the low frequency 500 kc channel probably weighed five or ten pounds, but he did not believe she had left that in Miami or it, too, would have been returned to them. He had no knowledge of whether or not she had left it at some other point.

Tinus' information interested me, but he had nothing to add. Both of us, however, were concerned about what might have happened to the Electra's radio gear during the period between flights and in the time after AE and Fred departed Miami on the second attempt.

About the time I met Richard Black, I also got the answer to the mystery of the missing telegraph key.

In mid-1962, Thomas Devine began to bombard me with letters which propounded one theme: I had excavated outside the wrong end of Liyang cemetery. He was now positive the area shown to him in 1945 was beyond the northern, not the southern perimeter of the graveyard, and if I could arrange clearance with the Navy for him to visit Saipan, he was certain he could lead me to the exact spot. He had tried without success to obtain permission on his own. To the Navy's consternation, he even petitioned the United Nations. The request, however, was quickly referred back to Saipan's "governing authority"; that, of course, being the United States Navy.

I sympathized with Devine, but at that moment, I had no intention of returning to Saipan with or without him.

Ross Game, editor of the Napa (California) *Register* and secretary of the Associated Press, changed my mind.

Ross had invited me to speak before a Napa service organization, and after the presentation, he was on fire.

"That's the wildest story I've ever heard," he effused. "When are you going back to the Pacific?"

"Probably never," I replied.

"Why not? You ought to be out there right now."

"It's too expensive. Besides, I've got my regular program to do."

"Can't CBS spare you for something like this?" he asked. "You've already put a couple of thousand hours into it. That much work shouldn't be wasted."

"If I suggest another trip, they'd spare me all right. Permanently."

"Why? It can't really be a question of money."

"It can and is. KCBS picked up the tab for the two expeditions, and a local station, even though it's CBS-owned, has a budget limiting its activities. If there's no profit at the end of the year, Dundes and a couple of other people may be looking for new jobs."

"But what about CBS News in New York?" Ross continued. "Sending a man to Saipan shouldn't require a second thought."

"That's right, but no one wants the responsibility of giving the go-ahead. We've bombed out twice, and the image has taken a pummeling. I know a lot of the guys are interested, but that's where it ends. There'll be no order to stop, but no one will encourage me, either."

Ross Game is one of the most honest and respected newsmen in northern California, so his next question did not surprise me.

"How much do you believe in what you've found?"

"I can't make up my mind," I replied. "Certainly there's been a lot of dodging by our government. No one had adequately answered any of the major questions."

"Give me an emotional, not a rational, response."

More than two years of frustrations came to the surface with that request. The truth was I had not really analyzed how I felt personally.

"Either I'm completely out of my mind, Ross, or this thing is the damnedest coverup in the history of journalism. A lot of people are running scared for reasons I can only begin to understand. No one laughs at me or puts me down, but every time I begin to follow a lead, those in official places get defensive, doors close and tangibles disappear. From what we've learned, I have to believe Earhart and Noonan were captured by the Japanese and more than a few people in Washington knew about or suspected it long before Pearl Harbor.

"All right. I'll tell you. I'm sore. I don't want to quit. I don't want to give up until there's a final answer. I know it's a hangup, but I feel I owe it to . . . to justice, or something. Doesn't that sound corny? Probably what I really mean is that I want an answer for myself. I've had the tail pinned on me once too often."

Ross smiled. "You don't have to feel embarrassed over an honest reply."

"I know. But I also realize I'm wrong as a journalist to let myself react that way. With that attitude, I can't be objective about anything. Someone else should be making the judgments."

The Game grin widened. "Don't knock your prejudice. If you were the stereotyped cynical newsman, you probably would have quit investigating a long time ago. I suspect some people have depended on that eventual disenchantment. I also have a hunch you're right, and I'm willing to back it. You're returning to Saipan, and to be sure you have a properly cynical approach, I'm going with you."

The next day, Ross and I met with Phil Swift, publisher of the Napa *Register* and twenty-three other Scripps League newspapers in eight western states, and reached agreement: Scripps League would pay for all expenses save my personal transportation. In return, I would write a six-article series for the papers and guarantee an exclusive on any news developed by the expedition, retaining, of course, television and radio rights for CBS.

I was correct regarding KCBS' attitude. Management met Expedition Number Three with studied disinterest. If I wanted to continue, I was welcome to take my vacation, but there would be no official support, financial or otherwise. Jules reminded me, however, that CBS maintained its rights in the investigation because of previous expenditure. The attitude made sense.

I applied to the Office of the Chief of Naval Operations for permission to once more visit Saipan, and expected another battle. Five days later to my surprise the CNO's office responded: "As duly accredited news correspondents to the Department of Defense, you and Mr. Game are authorized to enter and re-enter Guam and the Trust Territory except for certain restricted areas such as Eniwetok and Bikini Atolls, and the Bonin, Volcano and Marcus Islands. Entry into the Trust Territory of the Pacific Islands however requires the approval of the High Commissioner."

Saipan was no longer under Navy control!

A couple of phone calls to Washington, D.C.—to presidential press secretary Pierre Salinger and CBS Correspondent Bob Pierpoint—produced some information.

On January 12, 1962, by order of President Kennedy, Saipan was established as the first provisional capital of the Trust Territory of the Pacific Islands, and transfer of Saipan administration from Secretary of the Navy to Secretary of the Interior was scheduled for July 1, 1962. Trust Territory High Commissioner M. W. Goding and my old friend, Rear Admiral John S. Coye, Jr., Commander Naval Forces Marianas, were effecting the switch, Goding and all personnel of Trust Territory Headquarters were moving to Saipan. There was no mention of NTTU.

Thomas Devine's status remained the same: no permission because he lacked accreditation. We promised him, however, to excavate outside the northern perimeter of the cemetery.

We left San Francisco September 1. The adventure of pursuing Amelia Earhart had only begun.

17

In Honolulu, Ross and I went to see Richard Moritsugu, the interpreter Ralph Kanna believed might have been with him on Saipan in 1944, when the photo of AE was captured, but the Nisei was as obscure as he had been on the telephone. He surrounded himself with wife, children, and the parish Roman Catholic priest, and would not see us alone. Questions regarding his military service were parried by, "That was a long time ago. I don't remember those days."

Finally, he did say, "I remember Mr. Kanna. He was a good sergeant. But I don't remember anything else. We were so busy there wasn't time to think about private matters. You'd better ask Nuno or Higashi. Maybe they can tell you."

The priest let us know the discussion was concluded.

At Guam, we dropped by to see Admiral Coye and were warmly received with conversation and lunch in the quarters which had housed Fleet Admiral Chester W. Nimitz during the last year of World War II.

"I admire your tenacity, gentlemen," Coye began. "There certainly have been enough disappointments."

220

"Did your staff ever locate any more of my film from last year," I began.

"No," Coye answered pleasantly. "As I wrote to you, that which was not returned was improperly exposed."

"Admiral, what's happened to NTTU?" I continued. "I assume you know we've been holding their story."

"Well, the Interior Department has taken over Saipan. Mr. Goding and his staff are occupying the NTTU administration area as headquarters for the entire Trust Territory."

"And NTTU?"

"All personnel have been withdrawn, including the Naval Administration Unit."

"Why?"

"A Washington decision."

"By whom?"

"A number of persons and agencies."

"Is there any possibility NTTU might return?"

"I don't believe so. The change appears permanent."

"Can you give us any help where Amelia Earhart is concerned?" Ross asked.

"Nothing specific," Coye replied.

Ross was determined. "What do you think of the thesis that she went down in the Marshalls and was taken to Saipan?"

Coye smiled. "I say it's an interesting conjecture. If she and her navigator were picked up by the Japanese, Saipan would have been the place for high-level questioning."

"Do you know if that's what happened?"

"No . . . but the Navy does not deprecate your efforts. There is considerable admiration for Mr. Goerner in some quarters."

Coye's remark reminded me of an incident several months before. Admiral Dan Smith, Jr., had finished his tour of duty as Chief of Naval Information in Washington and was assigned to the Pacific Coast to command U. S. Navy Carrier Forces, Western Pacific. Jules Dundes and I received invitations to a reception in the admiral's honor at Treasure Island, and at the party, Smith greeted me warmly, praising my integrity and extolling me to Jules, "Fred is on his way to becoming one of the world's leading experts on the events leading to Pearl Harbor and World War II. He surely has the respect of many people in Washington."

About Amelia, however, Smith had been as cautious as Coye.

"All I can say is you've built a case for a lot more than a crash at sea," he said.

The admiral's compliment had nourished my ego, but it also made me realize that indeed I was being educated in the contemporary history of the Marshalls, Carolines, and Marianas and the islands would make an interesting series of articles or radio and television documentaries. The several million U.S. servicemen who fought for and lived on those bits of earth during World War II might be interested in a pictorial revisit to their battlefields. Ross and I discussed the idea, and decided to include Tinian, Truk, Majuro, and Kwajalein in our itinerary. The Marshalls visit would give us a chance to check some of the information on AE picked up by Eugene Bogan, Charles Toole, and others during the war.

"Except for the Kwajalein area, the Navy is no longer responsible for logistic support and air travel in the Trust Territory," Coye replied to our request for transportation. "The Interior Department has some Pan American Airways pilots on loan to fly a couple of surplus Navy seaplanes on a pretty irregular schedule to Truk and Majuro, but you'll have to take that up with Captain Gordon Findley, Goding's liaison officer. If you can get as far as Majuro, I'll see that a Navy plane flies down from Kwajalein for you."

Findley cooperated, if not enthusiastically. We obviously were compounding his passenger problems. Again a coincidence: the retired Navy captain had served as executive officer for Saipan military government in December 1945 and as officer in charge from January 1946 to April 1947.

"I think you fellows are wasting your time," he said. "How do you expect to find something we were not aware of back in '45 and '46?"

"Did your staff question the Saipanese about Earhart and Noonan at that time?" Ross questioned in return.

"No," answered Findley, "but if such a rumor was floating around, I would have heard it."

"Did you find the natives anxious to discuss Japanese activities?"

"No, you're right there," replied the captain. "They didn't

know Americans the way the Marshallese did. The Boston Missionary Society built schools in the Marshalls long before the war, so the people were glad when we drove the Japanese out. The Saipanese, however, had no contact with Americans, and they resented and were afraid of us."

"Is it possible then," asked Ross, "that they kept some things to themselves?"

"Yes, I guess it is," said Findley. "And as you said, we never asked them about it. If you want to be sure of your testimony, why don't you take a Chamorran from Guam with you? Someone like José Quintanilla. Big Joe commands respect and is used to questioning people and sifting fact from fiction."

Quintanilla is Guam's police chief, a position not as modest as it might sound. With a mixed civilian-military population of more than 70,000, the island has the problems of any fair-sized American city which is part military reservation. The difference is that Guam is larger than the average city, giving Quintanilla more land to police. He has an advantage in that Guam is difficult to escape from, but the island also has some of the world's thickest jungles which, as I mentioned in an earlier chapter, probably still hide Japanese from World War II.

I had met Joe the year before through the press secretary to the then Governor Bill Daniel of Guam, and found him articulate and thoughtful. He knew of the investigation, having assisted the two Air Force officers, Gervais and Dinger, as they questioned Saipanese living on Guam in 1960, and he had said, "I felt the people we talked to were telling the truth. There was no reason for them not to." Ross and I decided he would be valuable.

The big, barrel-chested Chamorran wanted to accompany us, and took his two-week vacation to do it. He even included his assistant, Detective Lieutenant Eddie Camacho, who had relatives on Saipan and knew the history of most of the families. The next morning, we boarded one of the Trust Territory's ancient SA-16 Albatross seaplanes and quivered the 115 miles north to Saipan.

Fathers Sylvan and Arnold met the plane at Koebler Field, and on the way to what had been Naval Administration Headquarters, apprised us of changes. The shift of control had altered the island's atmosphere. The natives now traveled in relative freedom and seemed gayer and more communicative. Johnson and all of NTTU had departed along with Bridwell, Hippe, and their crew. The eleven spy-training complexes in the jungle were being dismantled, but as Coye had indicated, the spy-school town was now occupied by Department of Interior personnel. Bridwell's quonset village, which had fronted for the CIA, currently housed visitors to the new "Capital of Micronesia," and the Officers' and Enlisted Men's Clubs were open to the natives. The NTTU night club, at which I had spoken the year before, also catered to anyone who had the price. The three spas did not please the Fathers. Some Saipanese were spending their meager earnings on liquor; collections at church, therefore, had suffered.

Joe, Eddie, Ross and I were assigned the two-bedroom quonset which Commander Hippe and his family had occupied. From the porch, I could see Bridwell's old quarters and beyond, the "Presidential Suite" and memories of my nocturnal visitor.

"What's with our old friend, Francisco Galvan?" I asked Father Sylvan.

"He's got plenty of money, but where it comes from is a mystery. That pile of scrap is twice as big, but he still hasn't been able to arrange for a ship to pick it up."

Joe and Eddie reacted visibly to Galvan's name.

"Is Galvan's family name 'Kobei'?" asked Joe.

"That's right," said Father Arnold.

Joe nodded. "I know him."

"I do, too," said Eddie with a bitter note in his voice. "He collaborated with the Japanese when they invaded Guam in '41. He came with them as an interpreter."

Father Sylvan explained our several encounters with Galvan, and I related the rainy night sequence when Francisco had faced me with a machete.

"Everyone on the island says he knows about 'the two white fliers,'" added Father Arnold.

"That figures," said Eddie. "'Kobei' was a honcho with the Jap military police."

(I should state here that "Kobei" is not the real family nickname. I have changed it, like "Galvan," to protect not Francisco, who merits no such consideration, but his family, who are decent and upstanding people.)

Ross was confused. "I understand about Francisco Galvan," he said, "but what's 'Kobei' got to do with him?"

Joe and Eddie laughed.

"Chamorran families get a little mixed up sometimes," said Joe. "When there are several children who have the same first and last names, a family name is also given to help with identification. Within our society, the family name is used more than the regular name, so when we say 'Kobei' we know which Francisco Galvan we're talking about."

"You leave Mr. 'Kobei' to me," said Eddie.

"You sound as if you have something against him," Ross said.

"Eddie does," said Joe. "It goes back to the war."

The captain stared at his detective lieutenant for a moment, then added, "And Mr. Camacho will keep his hands off Mr. 'Kobei.' The Guam Police Department is not a revenge bureau."

Eddie stared back and then broke into a grin. "Okay, Joe. Relax. I just get a little hot when I hear his name."

I looked at the two Guamanians. Quintanilla had a kind manner, but his questions and commands were incisive. When he moved, his thick body projected a strength that would tolerate no argument. Eddie was younger and Joe's physical opposite; yet he matched the strength with quickness and agility. They would be formidable opponents for anyone, and having them on our side gave me a secure feeling.

The next morning Father Arnold took Ross, Eddie, and Joe to visit some of the witnesses we had found in 1960 and 1961. Father Sylvan and I waited at the mission house while Mariano, the cook, rounded up the native "diggers" so excavation could begin according to Devine's new instructions. As we sat at the dining table renewing our friendship, there was a soft, rapid tapping on the screened door leading to the porch. Through the mesh I recognized a twisted face; it belonged to Francisco "Kobei" Galvan. Father Sylvan let him in, and Francisco's eyes never left mine as he crossed to the table. He stood for a moment, then pulled the old Seabee cap from his head and began to speak to Father Sylvan in Chamorran.

"He wants to ask a favor of you," Father Sylvan translated, "and he says he's willing to do one for you in return."

Galvan continued to stare at me intently.

"Ask him what he was doing in my quonset last year," I replied.

The question had no apparent effect. Francisco merely shook his head and growled a brief answer.

"He says he has never meant any harm to you."

"What's the favor?"

Again there was a quick exchange in the Spanish-sounding language, then Father Sylvan said in a sober tone, "He wants you to get permission from the Navy or the Interior Department for a Japanese ship to come in here and pick up that pile of scrap he's got down at the harbor."

"Ask him why he doesn't discuss that with Goding or Coye."

Anxiety and tension began to cloud the Chamorran's face. His words broke through the façade of bravado and became a stammer of pleading sounds. The accompanying gesticulations were almost uncontrolled. Father Sylvan fastened his huge hands on Francisco's shoulders to still him. Slowly composure returned to the dark face, and with it, the realization his explosion had betrayed him. His eyes darted furtively at me as he struggled to measure his speech and regain position.

Father Sylvan turned to me with an odd expression.

"It appears," he began, "that 'Kobei' has received several large amounts of money from a Japanese company for his scrap with the understanding that only a Japanese ship can pick it up. Our government will not permit Japanese vessels to visit any of the islands, and this has our friend in a real bind. He has to give back the money, a good portion of which he has already spent, or get this wedge for the Japanese. He's afraid of what will happen to him if he can't do either."

"What's he bargaining with?" I asked.

Father Sylvan managed a wry smile. "That's the kicker," he said. "'Kobei' says he'll tell you where the woman flier is and what happened to her."

I tried not to show any particular reaction. Should I play along and try to bluff him, or simply reject any deal? I could not change State Department policy even if I wanted to. It was a strange game. Japan, wanting a foothold again in the Pacific Islands, was using a man whose chief power for negotiation resided in information detrimental to the country he sought to benefit. Obviously Japan did not know Galvan was willing to divulge secrets about Amelia Earhart to accomplish his purpose.

"Ask him what he knows about the woman flier," I said.

Francisco looked sharply at me, and muttered only a few words in reply.

"He says he'll talk about it only after the arrangements for the ship have been made," said Father Sylvan.

"Tell him that's impossible. I won't make any effort in his behalf until I know the extent of his information."

To that sally, Francisco merely shook his head.

"Tell him then," I said, "it will be much better if he gives the facts without attempting to profit by them. The American government will have a more kindly attitude toward him if he cooperates."

That approach received the same response.

Father Sylvan then suggested that withholding information about the death of an American citizen before World War II could result in great trouble for him should the truth be learned from other sources. It was the same technique we had used with Francisco in 1961, and it achieved no more success. "Kobei" slapped the old cap back on his head and strode from the room, slamming the door behind him. He shouted some words through the screen before disappearing around the building.

"Pardon me, Frederick," said Father Sylvan, "but he says you are an unprintable word, and if you have anything else to say to him he'll be at the Saipan Style Center this afternoon."

Ross, Joe and Eddie were excited when they returned to the mission at noon. They had talked with a half-dozen witnesses and were convinced they told the truth.

"None has a single reason to lie," said Joe. "Even allowing for exaggeration, the pieces fit."

"There's no doubt in my mind," agreed Ross. "It's beyond belief they could invent that story."

I disclosed Galvan's visit, and excitement increased.

"Why don't you let me handle 'Kobei'," pleaded Eddie. "I'll get what you want."

"Roughing him up won't work," said Joe. "Besides, if I let you work him over, there won't be enough left to talk."

Eddie grinned. "I'll do my best."

"Keep your hands to yourself," warned Joe. "The decision is Fred's."

What to do with or how to further approach Francisco were difficult questions. I couldn't make a deal with him, nor could I miss the chance of getting the information we needed. If we sufficiently angered him, however, he might destroy whatever evidence existed. But did he know where AE and Fred were buried? If he knew we had recovered the wrong remains in 1961, why had he searched my quonset armed with a machete? Was his information in the form of testimony, or did he have tangible proof?

"Let's talk to him again this afternoon," I said. "He said we could reach him at the Saipan Style Center."

"If you don't mind," said Father Arnold, "Father Sylvan and I will not accompany you. If there's possibility of conflict in a public situation, we shouldn't be involved. You and Ross will be safe with Joe and Eddie."

The Saipan Style Center is a ramshackle four-room combination restaurant-bar-dancehall-trinket-shop on the road leading north from Chalan Kanoa. It attracts coastguardsmen from the Loran station and a few Department of Interior employees, but native Chamorrans comprise the bulk of its trade. Two Saipanese girls, chosen for their voluptuousness, serve come-ons with the drinks. (Hard liquor was permitted on the island when the Navy and CIA departed.) The place takes its name from two oddly clothed manikins which dominate a dirty, insect-specked window fronting the trinket shop, a not-too-large room filled with tables loaded with cheap Japanese-produced items ranging from paper fans to mechanical toys. The rest of the building is cooled by a huge air-conditioning unit which forces an icy flow through rooms separated from each other by long strands of beads at the doorways. The temperature is always twenty degrees below the island reading, and the shock of entering the chilly gloom stuns the senses. Windows are heavily curtained or boarded, and the only light comes from colored bulbs irregularly spaced along the walls. A garish jukebox, stocked with rock-and-roll and rhythm-and-blues records, is the feature of the bar. Its kaleido-scopically changing hues and sounds completes an atmosphere of furtiveness and unreality.

As Joe, Eddie, Ross, and I walked through the room; a half-dozen apathetic drinkers glanced at us as we entered the bar. The barmaids brightened.

"Where's 'Kobei'?" Joe asked one of the girls.

She made a distasteful face. "He's back in the restaurant. You friends of his?"

"Yes," said Eddie. "We've known him a long time."

"Do you want me to tell him you're here?" she asked.

"No," said Joe. "We'll just surprise him."

Galvan was sitting alone at a table toward the rear of the low-ceilinged room, sucking up large forkfuls of a stringy, glutinous seaweedy substance. After each inhalation, he washed his throat with deep swallows of beer. Two men were drinking and talking at a table near the entrance; otherwise, the room was empty. As we approached, Francisco saw me first and there was a flash of cunning, but when he recognized Joe and Eddie, hostility reclaimed the face and his eyes projected fear.

Eddie translated for Ross and me.

"Hello, 'Kobei'," said Joe. "Things seem fine with you."

A grunt was Galvan's only reply.

"You remember me, don't you?" said Joe. "Captain Quintanilla from Guam?"

Again a grunt.

"You're being talked to, you snake," snarled Eddie.

The words came with such force Galvan choked on a mouth-ful of food and the explosion sprayed half-masticated particles over the table and on the sleeve of Eddie's shirt. With revulsion, Eddie brushed the mess from his arm and prepared to resume attack, but Joe pushed him into a chair.

Meanwhile, Francisco struggled back to a degree of composure.

"Understand you had a talk with Mr. Goerner this morning," said Joe.

This time Francisco nodded but made no sound.

"What do you know about the man and woman, the fliers the Japanese captured before the war?" Joe continued.

"I know of them," Francisco muttered.

"Do you know what happened to them?"

Again a nod.

"Where did the Japanese capture them?"

"I know," said Francisco.

"Well, where?" Joe prodded.

"I not ready to say."

"Did the Japs kill them?"

Francisco shrugged his shoulders.

"You were an important man with the Kempeitai, weren't you?" said Joe.

At that question, Francisco squirmed in his chair and averted his eyes.

"I was small man," he replied. "They not tell me if they kill spies."

"You're lying," said Eddie. "You were honcho with your Jap friends. You forget I was on Guam in '41 when you did their work."

"I had to help them," said Francisco. "They made me."

"You didn't have to beat and torture your own people," Eddie shouted.

Francisco started to stand, but Joe's stare halted him.

"Sit down, 'Kobei'," he said. "Mr. Goerner says you want to make a trade. What is it?"

Words began to tumble from Francisco as they had at the mission with Father Sylvan.

"I will tell only if Japan ship come for scrap. I have contract, but Americans will not let ship come. They say Trust Territory ship later, but I need Japan ship. It cost much money if I don't get."

"What will you trade?" asked Joe.

"What he wants," said Francisco, pointing to me. "I will tell of man and woman and plane. Not here. Far away. Japanese catch and bring them to Saipan. I know more than anybody."

"Do you know where they are buried?"

"No," Francisco hastily answered. "I know almost, but not perfect. I did not have to do with death."

"Could you show us general place they are buried?"

"Yes . . . but not until ship come."

"Forget about the ship for a minute," said Joe. "I seem to

remember that you told Tony Palamo on Guam last year that a Japanese-American from Los Angeles, a woman who appeared to be white, was the one executed before the war, and that the story about 'the American woman flier' was untrue."

Francisco began to look frantic.

"Tony lies," he said.

"Do you want me to bring Tony over here?" said Joe. "Will you call him a liar to his face?"

Francisco thought for a moment, then said, "Tony not understand right. Woman hanged as spy was different. She come from Japan, but we learn she really American. The other one, pilot, was with man. Japanese Navy took them."

"What was the name of the woman who was hanged?"

"Too long ago to remember."

"Were you there when she died?"

"No," Francisco again answered quickly. "I only hear from Japanese."

"How did the woman pilot die?"

"I say no more until ship comes."

Joe asked more questions, but Galvan returned to his nauseating blue-plate special and focused attention on the opposite wall.

"I think that's all you're going to con out of him," said Eddie. "You want to try it my way now?"

"What's your way?" I asked.

"'Kobei' may run into some trouble tonight, that's all. Missing a few teeth and with a couple of bent ribs he might be ready to tell us the truth."

"It sounds appealing," I said, "but I don't think so."

"I vote against it, too," said Ross. "Giving this guy a few lumps he deserves is a temptation, but there are too many negatives. Any evidence we got that way would be open to criticism, and beside that, I don't want to think a story is worth violence. If he's responsible for the deaths of Earhart and Noonan, leave it for a judge and jury."

"I'm glad you feel that way," said Joe, "because I couldn't let it happen. Eddie blames 'Kobei' for things the Japanese did during the war, but if we use the same tactics, we're no better than they were."

During the exchange, Francisco apparently ignored us, but

19   Radio direction finder recovered in September 1961 from Tanapag Harbor, Saipan. An identification plate proved it was of Japanese manufacture, ending speculation that Amelia Earhart had crash landed in the harbor. *Author's Photo*

20   Liyang ("The Cave") cemetery, Saipan, 1961. Photos taken here in 1945 by Thomas E. Devine of West Haven, Connecticut, showed the same cross. *Author's Photo*

21 This angel in Liyang cemetery served as a reference point in instructions supplied by Thomas Devine which led the author to an unmarked grave site outside the cemetery. *Author's Photo*

22 Father Sylvan Conover at grave site outside Liyang cemetery where remains were found in September 1961. The cross and stones were placed here by natives after the site had been excavated. *Author's Photo*

23 Father Conover with Pedro Sakisag who, from photographs, identified as Amelia Earhart a woman he had seen at Tanapag Harbor in 1937. *Author's Photo*

24 Father Conover with Jesús Bacha Salas who occupied a cell next to that of an "American woman flier." *Author's Photo*

25 Navy Commander Paul W. Bridwell with José Pangelinan who was the first witness to testify that Amelia Earhart had died of dysentery and Fred Noonan had been beheaded. *Author's Photo*

26 View from Mount Tapotchau of northern end of Saipan Island in 1961. The jungle hides eleven installations of Naval Technical Training Units, where agents were trained. *Author's Photo*

27 View of eastern side of Saipan, 1961, showing Kagman Airfield which was used by the CIA in bringing agents to the island for training. *Author's Photo*

28   Interior of NTTU Club where author addressed CIA training staff in Saipan, 1962. *Author's Photo*

29   At nationally broadcast KCBS news conference in San Francisco, November 1961, the author (at table, right) is questioned by newsmen about package of remains being flown in from Saipan. Don Mozley, KCBS Director of News, sits at table with Goerner. *Author's Photo*

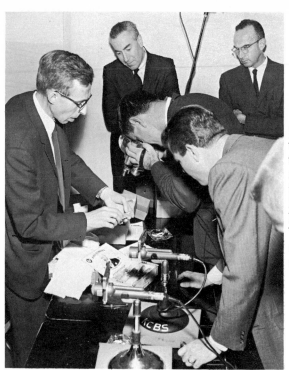

30 Dr. Theodore McCown, University of California (Berkeley) anthropologist, announces at December 1961 news conference his finding that the remains were not those of Amelia Earhart and Fred Noonan. Center background is Jules Dundes, CBS Vice-President and General Manager of KCBS Radio, San Francisco. *Author's Photo*

31 Guam police chief, José Quintanilla, back to camera, and author questioning native Saipanese in September, 1962. Napa, California, Register *Photo*

32 Thomas E. Devine who claims that he was shown the Earhart-Noonan grave site on Saipan in 1945. *Napa, California, Register Photo*

33 Attempting to pinpoint grave site during 1963 expedition are, left to right: Father Conover, Matthew Katz, and Thomas Devine. *Author's Photo*

34   Pre-war Japanese photo of Garapan City, Saipan, captured during 1944 invasion. *Napa, California, Register Photo*

35   Pre-war Japanese photo of Garapan cemetery. The large gravestone to the right of center was unearthed during 1963 excavations. *Napa, California, Register Photo*

36   Matthew Katz removing a bit of a skull from one of the eight unmarked graves excavated near old Garapan cemetery, Saipan, on the 1963 expedition. *Napa, California, Register Photo*

a slight shock had gone through him each time his name was mentioned and there was no mistaking the tone of Eddie's remarks. The lull in conversation made him more nervous. I decided on a gambit which, if he was sufficiently frightened, might collapse him.

"Tell him," I said to Joe, "this is his last chance. If he tells the truth now, I'll forget the stunts he's pulled, but if he continues to withhold information, I'll inform the American authorities of his attitude and try to make certain that no Japanese ship is given permission to transport his scrap."

Joe relayed the threat, and Galvan erupted. With a violent push, he thrust the table against us, spilling beer, food, and utensils on the floor.

"You not stop 'Kobei'," he screamed. "I fix you good."

His eyes were maniacal; his face contorted to hatred. Almost without looking, he grabbed an empty beer bottle from the next table, but at the same moment, Eddie scooped a knife from the floor and jumped in front of us. He feinted his shoulders left, then right, and Francisco began to back toward the door.

"Go ahead, 'Kobei'," said Eddie. "Use that bottle, and I'll cut your throat out."

The battle was over. Francisco Galvan fled the Saipan Style Center, and disappeared down the road at a speed uncommon to a man his age. The incident extinguished any hope 'Kobei' would provide answers. The next day he left for Guam and did not return until we departed.

During the next week, we worked the northern perimeter of Liyang cemetery. First Joe and Eddie followed Devine's instructions; then Ross and Father Arnold; finally Father Sylvan and I. The conclusion was the same: The southern end, where we had excavated the year before, more closely fit the maps and photographs. Devine's orientation seemed exactly reversed, but Ross and I decided to go ahead as Devine wished. The natives chopped the jungle to clear ten yards from the northern boundary, and seven holes were dug across the area. We all took turns monitoring each excavation, and plenty of items, including 50-caliber machine-gun ammunition, clips of Japanese rifle cartridges, rotted fabric, shirt buttons, combat goggles, and broken sake cups were found, but no human remains. Some of the things were three to four feet beneath the surface, a fact indicating that a bulldozer had probably turned them under.

In heavy jungle on a small hill immediately east of the cemetery, I located the demolished houses referred to by Robert Kinley, the Marine who had found a snapshot of Amelia. Little more than foundations remained. The natives had stripped them of metal and every usable piece of wood. One of the houses had a cellar, as Kinley indicated, and near the building was the small shrine or temple consisting of four stone columns, two of which were marked with characters later identified as Chinese writing; the translation is still incomplete. Experts can only speculate that the area represented something like a convent operated by a man and woman named Young. Either one or both of them held religious titles and academic degrees, including M.D., Ph.D., and LL.D. There are no records of the Youngs on Saipan, and the Saipanese do not know or care to tell who the couple was, when they lived, or how they died.

A few yards east of the house is another small hill which could have held the Japanese command post Kinley and his squad blasted in 1944. A large mound of rocks and coral covers the western slope. If the tunnel's entrance lies beneath the debris, it would take earth-moving equipment a week or a month to open it.

The evening we abandoned the Devine excavation, I walked about a mile south to the area which had been the temporary cemetery for the dead of the 2nd Marine Division. There I fulfilled Robert Kinley's wish. With a bottle of Jim Beam whiskey brought from San Francisco, I saluted each direction, and repeated his toast.

Further search for the grave seemed useless, but we did make progress with testimony. Departure of NTTU and the Navy had loosened tongues, and the combined persuasion of the Fathers, Joe and Eddie gave additional confidence to the natives. The story of "Kobei" running from the Style Center had quickly circulated, depreciating Galvan's fearsome image established under the Japanese. Even Francisco's brother was disenchanted.

Bridwell had taken me to see Vicente "Galvan" in 1960 as one of the men "who should know if Amelia Earhart was ever on Saipan," but Vicente, along with the other Bridwell "leads," had seemed nervous as he denied knowledge.

He was a changed man in 1962.

I was walking along the main Chalan Kanoa road toward the Mission House when Vicente pulled up in his jeep, and with English miraculously improved in two years, politely offered a ride.

My reticence showed.

"You do not have to be afraid," he said through a broken-toothed smile. "I do not fight for 'Kobei.' What he has done is wrong. What I answered to you when you were with the commander was wrong, too."

I climbed in beside him, and the jeep leaped forward in traditional bone-pounding flight.

"In your search for information about the woman flier," Vicente yelled above the roar of the engine, "many who know of her have not helped you."

"Why not?" I hollered back.

"For some, it was to protect their jobs. The Navy and NTTU wished you to be discouraged. For others, it was being afraid to speak. The Japanese were very hard with people who talked, and there still are Japanese sympathizers here."

"Well, will you talk now?"

Vicente grinned at me as the jeep bounded over a king-size rut, jabbing a comb through my back pocket where it hurt.

"I do not blame your impatience," he said. "You have worked hard."

The vehicle's brakes locked, and it literally slid to a stop before the mission. Father Sylvan helped extricate me, while the blobby, 250-pound Vicente jumped lightly to the ground.

"I think the Father would like to hear this," I said.

"I am glad to tell him," said Vicente. "The woman you look for, along with a man, were picked up by the Japanese in the Marshall Islands. I heard this from Japanese officers. Many of us knew this. You should ask José Villa-Gomez, Manuel 'Deda' Sablan or Ben Salas. They also heard it."

"I talked to Sablan and Villa-Gomez in 1960," I said. "Did someone get to them, too?"

"They knew it was not wise to give information. I am not sure they will talk to you now, but you should try."

"What else do you know?" I asked.

"It is possible the woman and perhaps the man were brought to Saipan from the Marshalls, but they did not fly their plane here."

"What happened to it?"

"You should talk to Antonio Díaz about that. He was a driver for Japanese Commanding Officer at Tanapagchico Base. Tony knows much."

"Well, what happened to the man and woman after they got here?"

"It is possible they did not leave island."

"You keep saying 'possible.' Do you know these things for sure or what?"

"I only try to help now," Vicente said quietly. "I did not participate in the events, so I must say it is possible they have happened."

"Have we been looking in the right place for their remains?" asked Father Sylvan.

"I do not think so. There may be confusion about the area and the woman."

"I've felt we're in the wrong area," said Father Sylvan, "but what do you mean about the 'woman'?"

"The Japanese had many political prisoners, including several women. It is possible this fact has deceived some of the witnesses you have spoken to."

Captain Quintanilla had come out of the Mission House and joined us, and Vicente's last statement brought Joe into the conversation with information I didn't know he had.

"The woman we're concerned about," he said to Vicente, "was held by the Kempeitai at Kobayashi Royokan in Garapan. That was a sort of hotel the Japs took over in 1936 to house important prisoners."

"Where did you get that tidbit?" I asked, amazed.

"The Chamorran woman who owned the property lives on Guam now. Vince knows her: Concepcion 'Chande' Díaz. I questioned her a couple of years ago when those two Air Force officers were nosing around. She said the Japs held a woman as a spy sometime around '37 and '38 and the description she gave matched Amelia Earhart."

"It is possible," added Vicente.

"According to this Concepcion, what happened to the woman?" I asked.

"As I recall, she simply said the woman died," said Joe.

"Does 'Kobei' know a lot about this?" said Father Sylvan.

"Yes. But not as much as he claims," said Vicente. "He worked with the Japanese, but he did not know all their secrets. They looked down on natives. The Japanese feel superior to Chamorrans."

"What did you mean when you said we weren't digging in the right place?" I asked.

"Liyang cemetery," said Vicente, "was not dedicated until 1940. The old cemetery was located in Garapan City, but the Japanese wanted that property and ordered the Chamorran people to dig up the graves and move the caskets and bones to Liyang. This was started sometime during 1938 or '39. If the woman died before then, she would have been buried outside Garapan cemetery; after 1940, outside Liyang."

"Do you know which?" said Joe.

"Either place is possible."

"Does anyone know for sure?" said Father Sylvan.

"It is possible," said Vicente. "Along with Tony Díaz, you might talk to Vicente Sablan, José Attao, Gregorio Arriola, Felipe Seman, Juan Pangelinan, or Francisco Pangelinan. All were drivers for the Japanese high brass. 'Deda' Sablan was with the police and Kempeitai. Ben Salas and Joaquin Seman are on Guam now, but they know some things."

"Eddie and I reached them two years ago," said Joe. "Joaquin started to talk and then said he was afraid of 'Kobei.' Ben Salas said the man and woman the Japs called 'fliers' were buried in unconsecrated ground outside of Liyang. 'Kobei' tried to threaten him, too, but Ben is a strong man. He told 'Kobei' to swim back to Saipan."

Joe's revelations continued to amaze me.

"I would have told you and Ross before," he explained, "but I felt I should remain silent about information I learned while working with Captain Gervais and Captain Dinger."

I had to smile. That kind of integrity was typical of Joe.

"Be careful about which cemetery," said Vicente. "The people believe there are several unmarked graves outside Liyang, but there were some outside Garapan, too. Also, there are seven unknown graves marked only with crosses inside Liyang. The Japanese had many secrets."

"There must be three dozen graves with plain crosses inside Liyang," said Father Sylvan. "Which are the unknowns?"

"I do not know," said Vicente, "but I'm sure someone does. You should talk with many more people. Juan Ada was a civilian judge under Japanese. Saipan's Mayor Ignacio Benavente may know something. Joaquina Cabrera did laundry work at Kobayashi Royokan where, as Captain Quintanilla said, many prisoners were kept."

Vicente gave another ten names, and then, a happy man with a clear conscience, he swung his big body into the jeep, and wheeled down the road in a cloud of coral dust. Father Sylvan, with some pride, explained Vicente's sudden cooperation. The Pope had given Vicente a decoration because two of the Chamorran's daughters were nuns and one of his sons had recently been ordained a priest. Vicente was now bent on living up to his children.

The leads were productive.

Villa-Gomez said, "Japanese officers spoke to me of one American woman flier and one man captured near Marshall Islands before the war. They were found somewhere near Jaluit Atoll, but I do not know what was done with them. It is possible they were brought to Saipan. I told this two years ago to Mr. Patton, the secret policeman for United States government."

I later learned that Joseph M. Patton had been a special agent for H. G. Hirshfield, Intelligence Officer for the then Commandant of the Marianas Sea Frontier, Admiral Wendt. Patton had conducted his investigation in December 1960. It was to be April 1963 before the U. S. Navy grudgingly showed us a part of Patton's report.

Manuel "Deda" Sablan also had heard the Japanese brag of capturing "the woman flier who spies." Sablan claimed to have seen the woman, and his description fitted Amelia. He was, however, evasive as to where and in what circumstances he had seen her on Saipan.

Antonio Díaz offered more.

"The woman flier," he said, "was brought to Saipan. It is also possible her plane was brought here. Do not believe anyone who tells you she flew the plane to Saipan. The Japanese one day unload it from ship at Tanapag, and they take it on big truck to Aslito Field. The officers talked about it as her plane."

"What condition was the plane in?" I asked.

"I do not know," said Díaz. "It was not wrecked or I would remember."

"Did you notice the color or the identification numbers?" said Joe.

"It was silver and some other color," replied Díaz. "There were numbers I suppose, but I do not recall them."

"Was it a warplane?" asked Father Sylvan.

"No," said Díaz. "It was a two-motor kind I had never seen before."

"Was there a man with the woman?" asked Joe.

"I heard it said there was, but I did not see him," said Díaz. "They say he injured his head."

"What happened to the man and woman?" asked Eddie.

"I do not know for sure, but I think they did not leave the island."

"You mean they died here?" said Father Sylvan.

"It is possible," replied Díaz.

"What happened to the plane?" I asked.

"I did not see it again," said Díaz.

Juan Ada remained mute about his years as a judge while Japan used Saipan. Benavente, the mayor, pleaded ignorance on the grounds he and several other Chamorrans had been sent to Yap Island to work by the Japanese in 1937. William Reyes was obsequious in his protestations of cooperation and unable to verify any misdeeds by the Japanese. In 1960, Maximo Akiyama had believed Reyes would provide corroboration for Josephine's story. His disappointment had been apparent when Reyes defended the Japanese and said no women had ever been held by them.

Ross probed Reyes' chauvinism by asking, "Aren't things better for you now than they were under the Japanese?"

"You Americans always think that," fumed Reyes, "and you're always wrong. The Japanese were strict, but they did something with the people and the island. There was plenty of work, and the Saipanese had money to spend. We didn't want to be 'liberated.' You have brought us nothing but poverty. You use Saipan for any purpose you like and expect us to accept your handouts with gratitude. The Japanese felt superior to most Chamorrans because they were, but they did not act superior to me because I am a teacher. Americans act superior to all islanders."

"Would you want the Japanese to return," asked Ross, somewhat startled.

"Yes, I would welcome it," said Reyes, "and they will come back. You beat the Japanese with guns and planes, but you cannot beat them economically. Saipan is near Japan and very far from America. There is no way you can compete. One day the United Nations will make you open the islands to Japanese trade, and then we loyal Saipanese will have the place we deserve."

Akiyama's brother-in-law, José Matsumoto, was not enthusiastic about being questioned again, particularly by Joe and Eddie, but he did reiterate his support of Josephine's story. He had heard from the Japanese about two American fliers, a man and woman, who supposedly had flown to Saipan to spy. He continued to maintain he had not seen them or their plane.

Albert Kamiyama was similarly inscrutable. Joe and Father Sylvan tackled him first, then Ross, Eddie, and I. A few grunts mixed with smiles and shakes of his head were our answers. Kamiyama's neighbors were more communicative. They said he had worked as a photographer during the Japanese occupation, and because he had married a Chamorran woman, as with Matsumoto, he was permitted to remain on Saipan when all other Japanese, Koreans, and Okinawans were repatriated. In 1962, he operated a photographic service together with a small restaurant and bar, and appeared to be nearly as affluent as Matsumoto. They felt he had considerable knowledge of Japanese activities on Saipan, but there was no apparent way to get him to talk.

Mrs. Joaquina M. Cabrera brought us closer to the woman held at Kobayashi Royokan than any other witness. Father Arnold, Father Sylvan, Ross, Eddie, Joe, and I crowded into the front room of her tiny house in Chalan Kanoa, and listened to her halting recital.

"I did laundry for the Japanese and the prisoners who stayed there."

"How old were you then?" asked Father Sylvan.

"I was twenty-five or twenty-six," said Mrs. Cabrera. "It was 1937 or 1938."

"Just take your time and tell us what you know about the woman," said Father Sylvan, as the six of us leaned forward to catch her words.

"One day when I came to work," she began, "they were there . . . a white lady and man. The police never left them. The lady wore a man's clothes when she first came. I was given her clothes to clean. I remember pants and a jacket. It was leather or heavy cloth, so I did not wash it. I rubbed it clean. The man I saw only once. I did not wash his clothes. His head was hurt and covered with a bandage, and he sometimes needed help to move. The police took him to another place, and he did not come back. The lady was thin and very tired. Every day more Japanese came to talk with her. She never smiled to them but did to me. She did not speak our language, but I know she thanked me. She was a sweet, gentle lady. I think the police sometimes hurt her. She had bruises and one time her arm was hurt. She held it close to her side. Then, one day . . . police said she was dead of disease."

There was a long pause while the Fathers and Joe and Eddie absorbed what they had heard, then Father Sylvan translated for Ross and me.

"Are you sure she died of disease?" asked Joe.

"That is what police said," answered Mrs. Cabrera.

"What did the woman look like?" said Father Arnold.

Mrs. Cabrera closed her eyes for a moment as if visualizing the scene of twenty-five years before, then said, "She was tall for a woman, and her hair was short like a man's. But she had a thin, pretty face. It had look of kindness and suffering."

"What about the man?" said Eddie.

"I did not see him well because of the bandage," replied Mrs. Cabrera, again closing her eyes. "He was thin and tall is all I can remember."

"How long was the woman here before she died?" asked Joe.

"It was many months. Perhaps a year. I am not sure."

"What happened to the man?" I asked.

"I heard he died, too," she said.

"Died? Or was killed?"

"Just dead."

"Where was the woman buried?" said Ross.

"It is possible near Garapan," Mrs. Cabrera said carefully. "I am not sure."

"Do you mean Garapan or Liyang cemetery?" said Father Arnold.

"Garapan."

"Does any part of Garapan cemetery still exist?" I asked Father Arnold.

"No," he answered. "There's nothing but jungle there now. I don't think anyone is even sure of the location."

It was obvious in the first minutes of conversation that M. W. Goding, High Commissioner for the Trust Territory, had too many problems to permit him real interest in Amelia Earhart. Ross and I had dinner with the Commissioner and his wife in their spacious home which had been occupied until July by Mr. Johnson, Commandant of NTTU, and we traded questions and answers most of the evening. I told him of the entire investigation with particular emphasis on the Francisco Galvan incidents.

"Don't worry," he replied. "Galvan won't get his Japanese ship. U.S. policy won't permit the Japanese to set foot in the Trust Territory, much less establish a trade relationship. Aside from that, though, I can't help you very much. We just moved in here, and there's a lot of getting acquainted to be done."

"Do you want to discuss the propriety of the Central Intelligence Agency using Saipan for ten years?" I asked. "The Department of Interior must have some thoughts."

"No, thanks," laughed Goding. "I don't want to be quoted on that one. Just say I'm pleased that Headquarters is inside the Trust Territory for the first time, and I'm not complaining about the quarters we inherited from our departed friends."

"Some of the people don't like American Administration," said Ross. "They'd like the Japanese to come back."

"A few feel they could hold better positions under the Japanese, or profit more, but the bulk of the people don't support that philosophy," answered Goding. "I hope I can make you understand the problem. The Trust Territory covers an ocean area of more than three million square miles, larger than the United States. In that area is 687 square miles of land comprising two thousand one hundred and forty-one islands of which ninety-six atolls and separate islands are inhabited with a population of close to eighty thousand. For over ten years, the funds available for administration of the whole territory averaged less than six million dollars a year, appropriated under a statutory ceiling of seven million five hundred thousand. I don't mean that a lack of appropriations was entirely responsible for the inadequacies of the past, but it was a mighty important part of it. The first thing I faced when I took this job in the summer of 1961 was to secure legislation setting a new ceiling and to initiate a greatly increased budget program. A new authorization of seventeen and one half million dollars was fixed by Congress this year, and under this ceiling the appropriations for 1963 and 1964 fiscal years have been more than doubled."

I liked Goding. A heavy-set man in his early fifties, he gave the impression of dedication not only to his job, but to the product of his efforts: the welfare of the Micronesian people. By nature a calm man, he projected thoughtfulness and capability. His reply to Ross' question was strong.

"Anyone who intimated that is irresponsible," he said. "The UN Trusteeship Council meticulously monitors our administration by sending visiting missions to the area every two to three years and by requiring our government to submit a detailed annual report that usually runs more than three hundred printed pages. Additionally, we are questioned extensively in open annual sessions of the Council at the United Nations Headquarters in New York. I've served as Special Representative of the United States at the UN, and despite thorough examination, no representative on the Council, except that of the Soviet Union, has seriously suggested we have failed to meet our obligations."

"How did your administration make out in last year's report?" asked Ross.

"The 1961 UN inspection team was critical in a number of important areas, but it was also quite laudatory in others. There was no great embarrassment to the Department of Interior or the United States."

"Isn't it true that the same team visited Saipan last year and gave the Navy extremely high marks for its administration?"

"Yes," said Goding.

"Isn't it also true the Navy had done too much for the Saipanese compared to what the Interior Department was capable of doing for the natives of the rest of the Trust Territory, and the discrepancy was hard to explain?"

"You'll have to talk to the Navy about that."

"We understand your position where Saipan's past is concerned," I said, "but now that you have control, why is almost all the northern end of the island still off-limits to natives and visitors?"

"Because the property belongs to the government," said Goding, "and because between five hundred and a thousand acres of it are strewn with hand grenades, a small caliber ammunition dump which was ineffectively decontaminated after the war. We've closed the area to protect the natives and our own personnel. Three military explosives specialists have been detonating the stuff for nearly a year, and they have a long way to go."

"Why is the property considered as belonging to the United States?" asked Ross. "I'd think the natives would be the rightful owners."

"Provisions for custody of property on Saipan were set by Admiral Nimitz's Military Government Proclamation Number Eight in 1944, which stated in Article Two that all abandoned, all state and all private property was subject to seizure under international law. Land claims were collateral duty for the military government officer, but the problems of land ownership were insolvable. Land records were scattered or destroyed by the invasion, and the few recovered were insufficient to determine ownership. Originally, most of the land did belong to the Chamorros, but over a period of years it had been leased to the Japanese development companies serving as a front for the Japanese Navy and Army, so when we invaded about seventy-five-percent was government held. It was impossible for our military government to do more than locate available records and interrogate the people concerning ownership. As you know, we still have a Land Claims Office; solution to this problem is going to be long range."

"That sounds like a long answer meaning we are free to use the Trust Territory of the Pacific for almost anything we please," said Ross.

"The interpretation is yours," said Goding.

"The interpretation," replied Ross, "belongs to anyone willing to invest modest study. The Nike-Zeus military facilities at Kwajalein, the atomic tests at Bikini Atoll, the CIA spy-school on Saipan—none of them would on the surface appear to be in the best interests of the Micronesian natives."

"I again refer you to the Pentagon in Washington," said Goding, "but take this thought with you. President Kennedy, many members of Congress, and I, are determined to give the people of these islands a fair shake. We have built and are building hospitals, elementary and junior high schools, airfields and new harbor facilities, and we're trying to develop the economy of each area. With more hard work, a little luck and some cooperation from you newsmen, we may be able to bring Micronesia into the twentieth century."

Goding waved at us from the porch, and called, "I hope you find Amelia Earhart."

"I refer *you* to the Pentagon in Washington," I shouted back, not realizing the aptness of the statement.

We had planned to visit Tinian anyway, but the Reverend Father Roy Richter, O.F.M. Cap., gave us special reason. Fathers Sylvan and Arnold said he had taken part in the invasion of Saipan and Tinian in 1944 as a Navy enlisted man, and after seeing the devastation, decided to spend the rest of his life helping the people of the two islands. He was one of the oldest men ever ordained a Catholic priest, and in 1962, his parish consisted of 420 Chamorro and Carolinian natives, the total population of Tinian. He was the only American on an island nearly forgotten by the world, and he might know something about Amelia Earhart.

Tinian, ten and a half miles long with a maximum width of five miles, is smaller than Saipan and topographically its opposite. Tinian is fairly flat with a slight elevation at both ends. In 1944, the island was intensely cultivated with sugar cane; ninety percent of the arable land, 39 square miles, or approximately 25,000 acres, had been planted in cane in square and rectangular fields, separated by irrigation ditches or clumps of trees for windbreaks. The U. S. Marines who invaded Tinian said it reminded them of the slopes of Aiea above Pearl Harbor. It was open and nearly park-like in appearance, a huge checkerboard except for a few hills and a tableland at the southern end. The civilian population of about 19,000 was centered at Tinian Town, on the southwest coast where Sunharon Harbor offered the only break of any size in the rocky shoreline, and at the three airstrips at Ushi Point on the northern end of the island.

The tough question facing American planners in 1944 was where to land? The coastline was as ugly as the rest of Tinian was attractive. The land breaks off into the water in a series of jagged water-carved coral cliffs, rising in some places to 150 feet. The natural barriers would tear the flesh and clothing of anyone who tried to negotiate them. Beaches suitable for landing craft, with exits through which tanks and other vehicles could move quickly, were rare. The best lay in front of Tinian Town, but they were defended by the largest concentration of Japanese guns and troops. The few beaches on the eastern coast were exposed to winds and had been heavily trapped and mined. That left two beaches on the northwest coast opposite the airfield. They were only 60 by 160 yards in length, separated from each other by approximately a thousand yards. Because of their small size, the Japanese believed they were inadequate for a major invasion, and therefore did little to fortify them. Through those tiny funnels on July 24, 1944, poured more than 15,000 U. S. Marines, soldiers, and Seabees, in one of the most perfectly executed invasions of World War II. The cost of the initial landing to American forces was only fifteen killed and two hundred wounded. Marine Corps Major General Harry Schmidt, who had commanded the 4th Marine Division at Kwajalein and Saipan, was designated as Commander of all ground troops at Tinian. General Schmidt later plays an important role in our investigation of the mystery of Amelia Earhart and Frederick Noonan.

The official fight for Tinian lasted nine days with the U.S. finally committing more than 40,000 men to oppose the 9000 fanatical Japanese defenders. On the evening of August 1, 1944, General Schmidt declared the island "secure," although three months of mopping-up operations were necessary to burn and blast the last Japanese from their caves. One cannot say the cost of capturing Tinian was cheap; not when 389 of your men are killed and 1816 wounded. But compared to Saipan and other invasions and the eventual uses to which the island was put, there can be a consideration of value received. The Japanese lost 5000 killed; only 252 surrendered and became prisoners. More than 3000 of the enemy military personnel were officially unaccounted for due to cave warfare and suicides.

The strategic use of Tinian in World War II can only be estimated. It was developed into the greatest B-29 base in the Pacific, and was, by August 1945, the world's largest airdrome. The Seabees built airfields for two Army Air Corps B-29 wings (the 313th and the 58th) as well as for large numbers of Navy and Marine Corps aircraft. North Field had four parallel strips, each 8500 feet by 500 feet. The first B-29 landed there, December 22, 1944. West Field had a 6000 foot runway for naval planes and two 8500 foot strips for B-29s, and received its first plane, April 2, 1945.

The changes since the war were astonishing. Though Tinian lies only three nautical miles south of Saipan, it took more than three hours for our M-boat to make its way across the channel, move down the western shore, and circle into the harbor where Tinian Town once stood. Not a sign of life was visible. The jagged cliffs are the same, but the island's surface has been swallowed by heavy jungle. There is no resemblance to the agrarian scene that greeted American forces in 1944, or the asphalt vista left by the fliers and maintenance specialists who abandoned the "world's largest airdrome" at war's end. The Seabee breakwater endures after two decades of typhoons, a great tribute to the men who built it.

There was small welcome at the dock. Two natives wandered over and secured the lines thrown ashore, then, without a word of greeting, walked down the pier and disappeared into the jungle. A few minutes later, a jeep driven by Father Roy Richter hurried down the pier to break the spell. A gentle-mannered man in his late fifties, the Father was hungry to see and talk to us.

"All the natives moved down here to the south end of the island a couple of years ago," he said, "and built a village they call San José. They had to because it was impossible to keep up the roads any more."

"Don't planes land here any more?" Ross asked.

"There haven't been any regularly scheduled planes for years," said the Father. "The admiral used to fly over from Guam occasionally when the Navy controlled Tinian, but since the Department of Interior took responsibility we haven't had even a Piper Cub. The jungle consumes more of the airstrips each year. Pretty soon it'll be hard to tell a plane ever landed here."

"What do you know about Amelia Earhart?" I asked, in due course. "Father Sylvan and Father Arnold thought you might have some information."

"Not very much," replied Father Richter. "I am of course aware of your efforts to find an answer to the mystery, but I have never heard anything but vague rumors from the natives. A few of them have said that the Japanese captured an American woman flier, but I've never met an eyewitness."

"There is a man on the island," he continued, "who might be able to help you. He runs a little quonset-hut hotel for the few visitors we get from Guam or Saipan. Albert Hoffschneider knew a lot about Japanese activities. You may enjoy meeting his daughter, too. It is bad for her living on Tinian. She is unmarried, and there are no boys here of whom her father approves. Most of the young men have gone to seek employment on other islands."

Ross and I were not prepared for Daisy Hoffschneider. A smiling, dark-haired, twenty-three-year-old girl, with beauty-contest figure clad in blue jeans, opened the door, and we stared. Albert, born of a German father and Marshallese mother, had married a Carolinian girl, and daughter Daisy inherited the best characteristics of each strain. She possessed a sweetness and attractiveness that is difficult to describe. With perfect English, she invited us to follow her onto a wide, cool, screened porch where her father was playing chess with a friend.

Albert Hoffschneider knew little about Amelia and Fred, and what he knew was traceable to my endeavors in the islands. Born in the Marshalls, he had spent the greater part of his life at Koror in the Western Carolines, and had come to Tinian after World War II, hoping to better the economic condition of his family.

"I only met one American before the war," said Hoffschneider. "He came to Koror when I was still a young man."

"Do you remember his name?" I asked.

"Yes. It was Ellis. Mr. Ellis was a trader, or so he said."

"What year?"

Hoffschneider paused for a moment as if counting to himself, then replied, "I believe it was 1922 or '23."

I remembered the story of United States Marine Corps Lieutenant Colonel Earl Hancock Ellis, who smuggled himself into Japan's Mandated Islands at that time and filed a controversial War Department report regarding future events between America and Japan. Ellis had returned to the Pacific, and met a mysterious death at Koror.

"What happened to Ellis?" I asked.

"He died," said Hoffschneider.

"How?"

"Poison."

"Suicide?"

"No, the Japanese killed him."

"How do you know that?"

"Two friends told me," said Hoffschneider. "William Gibbon was English, and he talked many times with Mr. Ellis. Gibbon knew the Japanese Police Commissioner ordered Ellis killed for spying. José Telei told me, too. He was chief of native police under Japanese."

"People who knew Ellis say he used to get drunk a lot," I said. "Was he drinking much when you saw him?"

"Yes," answered Hoffschneider, "but that did not kill him."

"A Navy man was sent by the United States from Japan to bring back Ellis' body," I said. "Did you see that man?"

"I saw another American but did not meet him," said Hoffschneider. "Telei said he was poisoned, too, but I do not know if he died."

"What happened to Ellis' body?" I asked.

"The Japanese cremated it," said Hoffschneider, "so no one can tell he was poisoned."

"What happened to his belongings?"

"The Japanese took them and searched everything."

"Has anyone ever told you that Mr. Ellis was really a colonel in the American Marine Corps?"

"I knew he was not a trader," answered Hoffschneider. "He looked everywhere around Koror, and told William Gibbon that there was going to be a war between Japan and the United States."

We had sought help with a young mystery and had gotten the answer to an older one. The mysterious death of Colonel "Pete" Ellis—who penned a 30,000 word document entitled *Advanced Base Operations in Micronesis,* predicting war between Japan and the United States, a report classified Top Secret in Washington in 1921, twenty years before Pearl Harbor—was murder. Young U. S. Marines who attend classes in Ellis Hall at the Marine Corps Station, Quantico, Virginia, may find special meaning in the last line of the inscription on a memorial plaque honoring the colonel who tried to protect his country from a threat few could recognize: HIS HEART WAS DAUNTLESS AND FULL OF COURAGE.

Ross and I prevailed upon Father Richter to drive us to the area on Tinian where the atomic bombs were assembled and loaded in 1945. It's a trip of only a few miles, but it took more than three hours. The four-lane roads that once accommodated hundreds of vehicles carrying tens of thousands of men plunge into jungle darkness and serve as avenues for the snail and the vine. Only one road to the north remained passable, and even on it we were forced to stop the jeep a dozen times to cut away voracious vegetation. It seemed as if we were moving through a long tunnel pierced by occasional shafts of light which splashed the surface with a flickering chiaroscuro. Bright sunlight at the end of the tube appeared a mirage. As we approached, it seemed to grow more distant.

Finally, we reached the aperture, and Father Richter swung

the jeep onto one of the huge B-29 runways. The effect was overwhelming. A sheet of asphalt more than a mile and a half long by four hundred feet wide stretched before us. The jungle had consumed fifty or so feet on both sides and was beginning to erupt through the surface at various points, but nonetheless it appeared ready to launch or receive an aircraft at any moment. Heat from the afternoon sun reflected in waves, and the mass pulsed as with energy.

"During the war," said Father Richter, "there wasn't a bit of jungle on this end of the island. The runways and hundreds of planes were visible for miles. Now nothing can be seen from offshore, and one has to fly directly over the island to glimpse the airstrips."

He steered the jeep into a taxiway leading from the main strip, and stopped beside what had once been a bomb-loading pit. The area was covered with vines and thick growth, but one could trace the outlines of a revetment large enough to accommodate a B-29. A narrow, four foot white stone column topped with a weather-stained bronze plaque stood at the front of the pit. I leaned over and read:

> From this loading pit the 1st atomic bomb ever to be used in combat was loaded aboard a B-29 aircraft named "Enola Gay" and dropped on Hiroshima, Japan August 6, '45. The Bomber was piloted by Colonel Paul W. Tibbets, Jr. USAAF of the 509th composite group 20th Air Force USAA Forces.

Seventy-five-yards down the taxiway, there was an identical setting; this plaque read:

> From this loading pit the 2nd atomic bomb ever to be used in combat was loaded aboard a B-29 aircraft named "Bock's Car" and dropped on Nagasaki, Japan August 9, '45. The bomber was piloted by Major Charles Sweeney USAAF of the 509th composite group 20th Air Force USAAF Forces. On August 10, '45 at 0300, the Japanese emperor, without his cabinet's consent, decided to end the Pacific war.

I walked down the main runway about a quarter of a mile, lost in my own reactions, absorbing the impact of those two statements of history. The entire future of mankind was shaped, perhaps irrevocably distorted, because of two ten-thousand-pound burdens borne by birds of battle from the field on which we stood. The birds were now extinct, but the effect of their cargoes still made man tremble, and would continue to do so for the rest of time.

Father Roy Richter drove us back to the dock and a surprise. Daisy Hoffschneider, traveling bag in hand, was already aboard the M-boat. She had decided to visit a cousin on Saipan for a few days.

Before we left Saipan in September 1962, Joe, Eddie, Ross, and I sat down with Fathers Arnold and Sylvan at the mission house and thoroughly discussed the investigation.

Our conclusions were that Amelia and Fred were captured in the Marshalls and brought to Saipan, possibly by the Japanese seaplane tender *Kamoi*, which may also have brought their plane. Probably there was more than one woman among the prisoners on Saipan, but description of the white woman held at Kobayashi Royokan almost perfectly fitted Earhart. There might be some exaggeration in the testimony, but the bulk of it had to be accepted. The general area of burial, however, remained obscure. It could be either Liyang cemetery or the old Garapan graveyard site. There was speculation as to whether a positive answer could even be found on Saipan. We all felt U. S. Navy or Marine Corps Intelligence must have information which had not been released, and the investigation should continue.

Again it was difficult to thank and say goodbye to Fathers Arnold and Sylvan. Their friendship had become an important addition to my life, beyond the fact the search would have been impossible without them. That they had similar feelings was evidenced by Father Sylvan the morning we departed.

"I won't come to the airfield, Frederick," he said. "It made me too sad to see you leave last time. I think you know I want you to get the answer, but it would also make us happy if you return again next year."

At Guam, we learned from Tony Palamo (the Associated Press stringer who filed the first Francisco Galvan story in 1960 and broke the 1961 story of the remains) that "Kobei" had been busy trying to keep his word about "fixing" us.

"He didn't mention he'd had a run in with you," said Palamo. "He simply came into the office and started spilling his guts. He said the Japanese did capture Earhart and her navigator, but they were never brought to Saipan. A Japanese captain told him they were picked up near Satawan Atoll and taken to Japan."

"What did you do with that garbage?" I asked.

"I sent it to AP in San Francisco."

"You sent that story out without checking it any further?" said Ross.

"Sure," returned Palamo. "Galvan was real big with the Japs during the war. With all the copy about Earhart, I figured it was a story that would get some space."

"You knew I was on Saipan," said Joe. "Why didn't you wait and find out what I thought about it?"

Palamo had no adequate answer to that and most of the other questions, but there was no sense in additional criticism. The damage was done. Palamo's report of Galvan's story had found its way into many American newspapers, to confuse further an already perplexed public.

Truk! The rock-like, forbidding sound carried great impact to American military forces in the Pacific during World War II. The true strength of Japan's "Pearl Harbor" was not known to U. S. Intelligence, but rumors called it "immense."

Japan came to Micronesia in 1914 with plans. Civilian headquarters for the South Seas expansion remained at Truk only until 1922; then it was shifted to Koror, and Japanese military moved into the Marshalls and central Carolines. By the middle 1930s, Japan's propaganda mill was grinding out the phrases: "Truk—Gibraltar of the Pacific"; "Truk—Japan's impregnable fortress"; "Truk—the unsinkable aircraft carrier." Truk was top-secret, and Japan intended it to stay that way. U. S. Naval, Marine Corps, and Army Air Corps Intelligence desperately wanted the truth, but there was no method of obtaining it without risking an international incident and possibly war. In 1935, the U. S. Marine Corps Schools, Quantico, Virginia, forged detailed plans for the capture of Truk. The basis was "Operation Plan 712-H" which had been prepared for the Marines in 1921 by Colonel Ellis.

How strong was Truk?

What would an invasion cost in men and material?

Those questions plagued American leaders during 1942 and '43. Admiral Chester Nimitz felt that Japanese strength should be tested before amphibious assault was undertaken. In December 1943 he received a preliminary draft of GRANITE (code name for the Central Pacific Operations plan) which called for air attack on Truk, March 20, 1944, with landings in the atoll complex beginning August 15, 1944. Quick successes in the Marshalls, however, caused Nimitz to move the air strike ahead. Admiral Marc A. Mitscher's Fast Carrier Task Force 58 did the job well, giving Truk the first trim of what was to become the famous "Mitscher Haircut." The fliers would have had greater success but for enemy detection of a U.S. scout plane over Truk on February 4, 1944. The Japanese high command was alerted, and the Combined and Second Japanese fleets quickly departed for the Palaus. When American torpedo and dive bombers struck February 17 and 18, 1944, most of the big game had fled. There were, however, plenty of targets of opportunity. Over two-thirds of the 365 Japanese land-based planes were destroyed, and approximately 140,000 tons of shipping were beached or sunk. U.S. losses were considerable, but the carrier pilots brought welcome news to Nimitz: Truk could be bypassed. For the remainder of the war, Liberator and Mitchell bombers flying from bases in the Marshalls and Gilberts, and American submarines always on station, neutralized Japan's "Pearl Harbor."

On August 28, 1945, a message was dropped on Dublon Island, Truk Atoll, from a U.S. plane, directing the Japanese to surrender. Two days later the U.S.S. *Stack* (DD406) moved into Truk lagoon, and Brigadier General L. D. Hermle, USMC, accepted the largest-scale enemy surrender in the Pacific Ocean Areas from Admiral Michi Sumikawa and General Shunzaburo Magikura. Propaganda had placed the Japanese forces at 130,000. The actual count was a little more than 38,000.

Captain Gordon Findley did his best to discourage Ross and me from making the flight on his Trust Territory Airline.

"Several months ago," he said, "one of the seaplanes had a

bit of a problem landing at Koror. It struck a submerged object which ripped the whole bottom out."

"When does the next flight for Truk leave?" asked Ross.

"The flight to Truk two weeks ago was a lulu," continued Findley. "They lost one engine just past the point of no return."

"Captain," said Ross, "the news fails to disquiet us. When do we leave?"

"I can't guarantee what you'll be getting into," returned Findley. "If you have any mechanical trouble out there, it could be quite a time before spare parts could be flown to you."

"Captain . . ."

Our old Albatross groaned and droned for hours at five thousand feet, dodging massive white cloud layers over the vast expanse called Pacific. About the time we began to believe the earth's land had vanished everywhere, mountaintops of Truk's eleven islands emerged on the horizon. Colors changed with each minute of approach, shading from palest turquoise to deepest forest green. Surrounded by an enormous coral ring, more than forty miles across at widest point, the lagoon is one of the most beautiful areas in the world, yet, strangely, the aura of mystery instilled by Japan's propaganda remains.

A still usable Japanese-constructed airstrip on Moen saved us the apprehension of a water landing. The mountainous island is home and headquarters for Interior officials who administer to the 22,000 natives of the 180,000-square-mile district. Distad (district administrator) Robert Halverson met the plane, and immediately put us aboard a World War II LCM for a tour of the harbor. Ship wreckage is piled on beaches and reefs, but little of it represents Mitscher's carrier strike: the present hulks were victims of post-war typhoons. There are, however, many still visible indications of Japan's central Pacific search for aggrandizement—called "South Seas Development." Along the shore of Dublon Island, one can see the carefully constructed permanent concrete docks from which Japan's great fleets were serviced and repaired. Rusted machine guns protrude from slits in pillboxes built into the docks, and bits of shattered equipment litter the surfaces. Offshore rides the huge buoy where the *Yamato*, Japan's largest, most powerful, "unsinkable" battleship regularly moored. *Yamato*, never able to use her eighteen-inch batteries, was finally sunk near the Philippines by more than a dozen U.S. bomb and torpedo hits.

I liked the Trukese people. Taller and leaner with a more sharply pronounced facial structure than the Polynesian or Chamorro people, they are sensitive to the attitudes of others and extremely friendly and courteous to strangers. The smallest demonstration of good will wins their confidence and cooperation. Most are quiet, with nonassertive behavior during any formal occasion. They seem to consider it impolite to contradict directly a statement or refuse another's request, and there is great enjoyment of protocol and social custom.

The people we questioned apparently knew nothing of Amelia and Fred, but they were not reticent to voice dissatisfaction with American administration policies and indicate their desire for a return to Japanese rule. I asked Halverson about the situation.

"It's true," he replied. "Some say they want the Japanese, but what they really want is more money to spend. They had more goods and services with the Japanese, but they've forgotten the exploitation. You were asking what preparations the Japanese made before they attacked Pearl Harbor. The first airfield was constructed on Eten Island in 1931 by conscripted native labor. The Trukese don't want any more of that. With the new Trust Territory budget, we should be able to jack the economy up to a level where we don't have any more complaints."

Early the next morning we flew east to Ponape, another of the islands Nimitz decided to bypass. The Albatross thrust its way through a heavy rainstorm until a little before noon when Ponape's two-thousand-foot peaks burst from the ocean as they must have for American bomber crews who flew the first attack strikes in April 1944. The Japanese landing field had long since disappeared, so our pilot, Captain Robert Graham of Bend, Oregon, set the ship down within the reef and taxied more than a mile to what had been the main ramp for an enemy seaplane base constructed on a small island rising from the center of Ponape Harbor. Graham lowered the wheels into the water, then gunned the plane onto an ascending concrete ramp, pockmarked with bomb craters. The structural steel struts of an immense hangar remain at the end of the ramp, and a volcanic hill behind is honeycombed with tunnels, machine shops and gun positions.

The jungle grows in, around, and over the grotesque skeleton which once housed the best aircraft of the Japanese Imperial Navy.

Ponape never has a water shortage, with its average yearly rainfall of more than 200 inches. Rain-laden clouds find the island as filings seek a magnet, obliterating the lagoon with downpour, giving way only to a fresh cascade. Maynard Neace, Department of Interior Distad, took us ashore while the plane was being refueled, but the natives politely shook their heads when asked about white people captured by the Japanese before the war. They had not seen Americans until September 17, 1945, when the first U.S. service personnel came ashore from the U.S.S. *Hyman* where General Masao Watanobe and Captain Sunao Naito had surrendered a Japanese garrison of nearly 14,000 men to Commodore B. H. Wyatt.

Ponape's gasoline truck forced us into an overnight stay. Originally an Air Force castoff to the Navy which in turn discarded it to the Interior Department, the vehicle was so rusted the gas had to be strained by hand through a chamois cloth. By the time our Albatross got full tanks, it was too late to make Majuro in the Marshalls. We stayed the night at the new Department of Interior hotel, a collection of cubicles by one of the vilest-smelling coral roads in the South Pacific.

During the night, a radio message from Kusaie Island, 350 miles southeast of Ponape, called for an emergency airdrop of serum and medicine to stem an epidemic which had advanced beyond the abilities and supplies of Kusaie's practitioner, a native who had studied with a doctor for less than a year. Old Albatross drew the mission. As there is no field on Kusaie or even a reef-protected stretch of water for a seaplane, it was decided we would drop succor by parachute.

I had flown a lot of air miles in rough weather, but none compared to our mercy detour. We hit Kusaie shortly before noon in close to typhoon weather. Driving rain beat against the cabin ports making it impossible to see, and Captain Graham estimated gusting cross winds at fifty miles per hour. I expected Graham to abort; instead he bored in to five hundred feet, then leveled off along the shore. The rain subsided for a moment, and

Ross pointed to mountain peaks as formidable as those on Ponape.

Because the vials of medicine might shatter should they strike the ground, it had been arranged by radio to parachute the package into the lagoon. The target was to be a bright red outrigger boat manned by natives. Co-pilots Paul Oakes of Fort Wayne, Indiana, and John Copeland of St. Louis, Missouri, opened the top half of the main hatch, then each wrapped a leg around cabin seats and gripped the belt of Flight Engineer Max Gorrell of San Francisco, California, as he leaned out of the hatch, package and parachute in hand. Graham made two passes over the lagoon, but rain obscured the boat. On the third run the air cleared and Gorrell dropped the cargo. We could see a red boat churning through the water as Graham banked the Albatross to the left tumbling his co-pilots and daredevil engineer into a heap, preventing the possibility of anyone going through the hatch. Gradually, as we pulled away from Kusaie en route to Majuro, the weather eased and the roller-coaster effect lessened. It was not a routine experience but neither was it extraordinary for Graham and his crew. I began to understand and appreciate the uncertain scheduling of Captain Findley and his Trust Territory Airline.

Majuro was as I had imagined, a long, narrow, palm-tree-studded coral atoll, at its highest point only a few feet above sea level. Captain Graham set the Albatross down on the same airstrip that accommodated U.S. fighters and light bombers during World War II. The Marshalls had come first in the steppingstone operation, and with special historical significance, for they were the first pre-war Japanese-held islands to be wrested from the enemy. Kwajalein, the world's largest atoll in the central Marshalls, was prime target. By fall, 1943, it had become headquarters for the Japanese fourth fleet and boasted considerable airpower. Majuro, to the south, was second in importance because of its excellent lagoon suitable for fleet anchorage. On January 29, 1944, U.S. carrier-based planes began pre-invasion air assaults. Fifteen thousand tons of bombs were dropped on Kwajalein with optimum effect; not a single enemy plane remained operational. Then, in a comic opera landing on January 30, the Majuro attack force composed of Marine scouting parties and elements of the 106th Infantry Regiment of the 27th Division moved in on that island with great caution, discovering, with pleasure, that the Japanese had fled. Rear Admiral H. W. Hill, under the command of Admiral Raymond Spruance, quickly moved his ships into Majuro's spacious lagoon which was to serve nearly every U.S. naval vessel before the end of the war.

Majuro is little changed since the war. When the Navy and Marine Corps left for home, the usual mementoes remained. Piles of abandoned metal that once served some purpose disintegrate along the main road which traverses the causeway linking the islands. The Department of Interior has constructed a few new buildings, but many of the old quonsets remain, and the wooden frame of a Japanese weather station still dominates the main village. The vast lagoon, that once received the greatest fleets the world had even seen, is beautiful as ever, but only one small sailing schooner rode at anchor the late afternoon we arrived.

Peter Coleman, Marshall Distad, met us at the plane with unhappy news.

"The captain in charge at Kwajalein," he began, "radioed this afternoon that you would not be permitted to enter their area. They won't send a plane for you, and the Navy forbids us to bring you there."

"Why not?" said Ross, startled. "We have clearance and we're both accredited by the Defense Department."

"I don't know," said Coleman. "They've a lot of top-secret testing on the Nike-Zeus antimissile missile system. Maybe that's the reason."

"What kind of testing?" I asked.

"It's an Army project," replied Coleman, "but the Navy still controls the atoll. They call it the Pacific Missile Range Facility. One of those Atlas intercontinental ballistic missiles is fired down range from Vandenberg Air Force Base in California and then Kwajalein tries to intercept it. It's quite a deal."

Ross and I exchanged glances that absolved Coleman of blame for the restriction.

"Have you ever heard of a native named Elieu?" I asked. "He's supposed to have been on Majuro sometime during 1944."

Coleman's countenance brightened.

"You bet there's an Elieu," he said. "In fact I can take you over to headquarters to meet him if you like. He teaches at the Trust Territory school and is one of our best and most loyal employees."

Elieu's brown, open, sincere face was the same as the one in Eugene Bogan's photographs, though eighteen years had added forty pounds to his frame, giving him a stocky appearance. Unlike most of the Micronesians with whom we had talked, Elieu showed no discomfort in our presence. He entered Coleman's office with confidence, exchanged greetings in a relaxed manner, and waited with interest for our questions.

"Do you remember a man named Eugene Bogan?" I began.

Elieu smiled as he said, "I remember Mr. Bogan very well. He was the first military government officer here at Majuro. I was fortunate to work with him for many months. How is he? Do you bring a message from him?"

"Mr. Bogan is fine," I said, "and he sends you best regards. He's a successful lawyer now in Washington, D.C."

"That is good," said Elieu. "He was a smart man, and I am not surprised that he has done well."

"Mr. Bogan said you might be able to help us find two American fliers who disappeared in this area before World War II."

Elieu thought for a moment, then said, "I only know of one flier, a woman."

"Is this the woman you spoke to Mr. Bogan about?" I asked.

"Yes. I remember he seemed very interested when I told him."

"Do you recall the year?"

"It was 1937. I did not see the woman. I only heard about her from a Japanese friend named Ajima. He worked for the trading company and used to travel to all the islands. He said one American woman came down in a plane near Jaluit and that she was picked up by a Japanese ship."

"Is it possible there could have been a man in the plane?"

"Yes, but Ajima only spoke of the woman. It was very unusual that a woman would be doing such things."

"What did he say about the woman?"

"He said she was a spy and that she was taken away by the military."

"Where was she taken?"

"I assumed to Jaluit, but she could have been taken to Kwajalein or someplace else."

"Ajima did not say what happened to her?"

"That's right."

"What happened to Ajima?"

"I don't know. He disappeared at the time the United States began to occupy our islands, and I never heard from him again. He is probably dead."

"Did he describe the woman?"

"Not that I remember. He just said it was an American woman."

"Did Ajima describe the plane?"

"No."

"Where did you learn to speak English so well?" I asked.

"From Miss Hoppin at the mission at Jaluit," said Elieu.

"Would that be Miss Jessie R. Hoppin of the Boston Missionary Society?"

"That is right," said Elieu with amazement in his eyes. "Did you know Miss Hoppin?"

"No, but I have heard much about her," I said. After I related the tale of Colonel "Pete" Ellis, Elieu nodded his head.

"Miss Hoppin spoke of the man Ellis. She nursed him while he was at Jaluit. The Japanese did not like him. He was always trying to enter forbidden areas."

"Elieu, do you know any other Marshallese who may have information about the American woman flier?" I asked.

"No one around Majuro any more," he said. "It may be that some people at Kwajalein could help you."

"The Navy won't let us go there," I said. "What about Jaluit, or Ailinglapalap, or Mili?"

"It is possible someone would know," Elieu said, "but it is difficult to reach those atolls now. Jaluit had a big typhoon two years ago which blew away many people and almost all vegetation. Many people have moved to better islands. It might be a month before you could get a boat to those places unless Mr. Coleman can arrange transportation."

Coleman was not encouraging.

"The field trip ship is not due in here for two weeks," he said, "and the next voyage down to Jaluit isn't for more than a month."

We took some pictures of Elieu and tape-recorded his statement along with a special greeting for Eugene Bogan.

"Mr. Bogan," said Elieu during the recording, "I will never forget the time we inoculated all the children at Majuro for yaws disease. Your faith in me gave me much pride."

We had dinner that evening at Coleman's home, and met Dwight Heine, District Administrator of Education for the Marshalls and president of the Marshallese Congress, the outspoken yet powerless elected representatives of the Marshallese people. Heine, a native in his mid-thirties educated at Honolulu, was critical of American policy even though his salary was paid by the Department of Interior.

"It is the responsibility of the United States," he said, "to bring the people of the Marshalls into the twentieth century. You can't continue with your double standards. You use some of the atolls for your own purposes without regard to the wishes of the inhabitants, and then when you deign to hire a Marshallese, you pay him only a fraction of what you pay the employees from stateside."

"What's happened at Kwajalein?" I asked.

"There are over three thousand Americans living there now," answered Heine. "Most of them are civilians with some kind of specialist ratings, and they live in air-conditioned homes and work in air-conditioned offices. They have bowling alleys, libraries, five theaters and four night clubs to enjoy in the evening, and during the day, they can swim in their swimming pools or go marlin fishing, boating, diving, shelling or use the nine-hole golf course. Also available to your people are tennis and basketball courts and the softball and football fields. You use our islands and work the people, but what do you give us in return? Do you see anything around Majuro that looks like what I've described at Kwajalein? You've built some schools and medical facilities, but where are the houses, the pleasures that your people enjoy? What has been done to help the economy of these islands? We're still trying to make a living out of copra products. It simply can't be done. The United States has to develop some industry here and support it for a long time to come. You can't give people a taste of what life can be like and then not give them the means to attain it."

"Do the Marshallese people really want that kind of life?" asked Ross.

"The older people don't care much," said Heine, "but the young ones do. A lot of them go away for educations, and they never come back because there is no way for them to earn a living and there are none of the conveniences that they've gotten used to. Your leaders are always talking about our learning the ways of democracy. You had us elect leaders and establish a Congress, then denied us the power to implement the legislation of that body. It's the most ridiculous rhetoric in the world, and you could only guess at the frustration it produces."

"If your Congress did have power, would you throw the United States out of the Marshalls?" I asked.

"Of course not," replied Heine. "We need help, and we believe in the ultimate good intentions of the United States."

"What would you do about the nuclear testing that's gone on at Bikini and other places?" I asked.

"We would end it forever," said Heine. "The Marshallese people do not like that at all. It has injured us."

"In what way 'injured'?" said Ross.

"The people of Rongelap were caught in fall-out which blew the wrong way from one explosion. No one knows yet how seriously injured they are. The Atomic Energy Commission sends doctors down here every year to check for physiological changes. You got more than one hundred human guinea pigs out of that experiment."

"The United States has tried to make amends," protested Coleman. "The people were moved to a new island and given better facilities than they had before, and the U. S. Congress is considering a bill right now to pay reparations to the Rongelapese."

"We appreciate that," said Heine, "but the fact is it shouldn't be necessary."

"What about the Nike-Zeus business at Kwajalein?" asked Ross. "Would you eliminate that?"

"We need the employment, so we accept it," said Heine. "But

don't get the idea we are pleased with the situation. Kwajalein is the largest atoll in the world and one of the most important to us. We would certainly use it for other purposes if we had the chance."

"What about the Japanese?" I said. "Were things any better when they controlled the Marshalls?"

"No!" said Heine in what approximated an explosion. "The Japanese were bad. They closed the islands from the rest of the world, and forced the Marshallese to work. When the war came, they took all of the food and let our people starve. Then they killed many Marshallese because they thought we would cooperate with the Americans."

He told us of many cases of oppression, torture and murder, all documented in Washington.

Finally I changed the subject. "We have a project that deeply concerns us. In your opinion, is it possible Amelia Earhart and Fred Noonan were picked up in this area by the Japanese?"

"Of course it's possible," said Heine, "and the Japanese would have been outraged in 1937 to have their secrecy violated. I do not personally know of this incident, but I would believe anything Elieu said. He is an honest man."

"Where could we get the information we need?" asked Ross.

"I would suggest you ask the people around Kwajalein," said Heine.

With frustration and disgust, Ross and I boarded the Albatross the next morning to begin the long flight back across the Pacific to Guam where we could get a Pan American Airways flight to San Francisco. It was ridiculous. Kwajalein was closed to us in 1962 for no apparent or announced reason. It was the kind of obstacle that made us even more determined to get some answers.

Those answers would come too late, though, for Amelia's mother. Mrs. Edwin Earhart died at the age of ninety-five in Medford, Massachusetts, October 29, 1962.

18

The tape recordings made during the 1962 trip were used by KCBS for an hour-long documentary titled *The Silent Thunder*. The show sketched the U.S. 1944 Pacific invasions and recounted the look of the island battlefields seventeen years after the war. As I prepared for the broadcast, Commander John Pillsbury, Public Information Officer for the 12th Naval District, arranged a meeting for me with one of the people to whom this book is respectfully dedicated—Fleet Admiral Chester W. Nimitz. It was the first of many meetings and the beginning of a friendship I shall treasure all my life.

The mind which guided the destiny of the Pacific war and commanded nearly three million men had not weakened. He spoke of Pearl Harbor, the Battle of Midway, the invasion of the Marshalls and the bypassing of Truk, the Marianas campaign, Iwo Jima, Okinawa, the decision to drop atomic bombs on Japan and the day of the Japanese surrender aboard the U.S.S. *Missouri* in Tokyo Bay. His recall of detail was almost complete. It was difficult, however, to reconcile the warm, gentle-man-

nered, gray-haired man before me with the legendary admiral
who affected the course of history.

"*The Silent Thunder*," he said. "That's a good title. Let's hope,
with the help of the good Lord, the thunder stays silent."

As the interview concluded, Commander Pillsbury mentioned
Amelia Earhart, and the admiral looked at me with new interest.

"So you're the man who refuses to give up," he said. "I
thought your name was familiar. Several people from Washington have mentioned you, and I remember hearing you speak of
the investigation on the radio."

There was only respect in his voice, so I chanced the big
question.

"Is there anything you can tell me, sir, about Amelia Earhart?"

Admiral Nimitz looked straight into my eyes for a moment,
then he carefully answered. "Not a great deal. I remember hearing during the war that some things that belonged to her had
been found on one of the islands. I don't remember which one,
and I didn't actually see the material. Most likely it was
channeled through Joint Intelligence at Pearl Harbor."

"Some people think I'm crazy for pursuing this thing so long,"
I said. "Do you feel I'm wasting my time?"

"You seem quite rational to me," smiled the admiral.

There was an awkward pause until I became aware that he
did not intend to say any more on the subject. On the way back
to San Francisco from the admiral's house in the Berkeley hills,
I weighed his remarks. He had seemed to be encouraging me,
but he also had been cautious and obscure. Commander Pillsbury supplied part of the answer.

"Don't forget," he said, "that the admiral, even though he's
seventy-seven, is still on active duty. There's a limit to what he
can tell you, particularly if the matter concerns classified information. I'd take what he said as definite encouragement."

The documentary was more of a success than I could have
hoped. CBS scheduled it three times because of letters from the
public and reactions of critics, but the greatest satisfaction came
from Nimitz. Immediately after the initial broadcast, he telephoned congratulations, and the next day sent his Marine orderly
to the station with a hand-written letter commending my report-

ing of our interview and the narration of the principal events of the Pacific war.

During the next few months, I had cocktails and dinner with Admiral and Mrs. Nimitz several times, but he said no more about Amelia and I did not press the issue. It was not until the night Commander John Pillsbury retired from the Navy that the admiral reached me indirectly with more encouragement.

Members of press, radio, and television in San Francisco who have occasion to cover military affairs gave a dinner party honoring Pillsbury at the Fort Mason Officers' Club, and toward the end of the evening, John took me aside for a private conversation.

"I'm officially retired now," he said, "so I'm going to tell you a couple of things. You're on the right track with your Amelia Earhart investigation. Admiral Nimitz wants you to continue, and he says you're onto something that will stagger your imagination. I'll tell you this, too. You have the respect of a lot of people for the way you've stuck at this thing. Keep plugging. You'll get the answers."

His words were welcome, but the question was where to plug. After three years of investigation and three trips to the Pacific, the avenues to final answers seemed as blocked as ever. There was the possibility of locating the other two Nisei interpreters whom Ralph Kanna believed might have been with him the day the photo of Amelia was taken from the Japanese soldier during the invasion of Saipan. I worked on William Nuno first, and after checking dozens of telephone directories for California cities, found his name listed in the Pasadena book.

In 1963, he was working for the U. S. Post Office in Pasadena, and he recalled Kanna, Dick Moritsugu, and Roy Higashi without hesitation. He had no recollection, however, of having seen a photo of AE, or of interrogating any captured Japanese soldiers in regard to her.

"Dick Moritsugu spent a lot more time with Kanna's outfit than I did," he said.

I explained that we had already talked with Moritsugu.

"Well, I can only say this to you," continued Nuno. "Amelia Earhart's flight could have been considered an early-day U-2 mission. If the Russians had not wanted to reveal for political purposes that they had captured Francis Gary Powers, he would have been 'lost at sea,' too, and no one would have heard anything more about him."

William Nuno apparently had nothing to back his interesting analogy. He said his opinion had developed from what he had heard and read.

In closing, he said, "You might want to talk to Roy Higashi. He lives in Seattle, Washington, now."

When I reached Mr. Higashi, he simply said Ralph Kanna was but a dim memory, and he had never had anything to do with Amelia Earhart.

Mr. E. H. Dimity of Oakland, California, had a positive contribution. He identified himself as President of International Weather Control, Inc., and a member of the board of directors of the Amelia Earhart Foundation, a non-profit corporation formed in 1937 after Amelia's disappearance "to conduct an expedition to clear up the mystery" and "to inspire the study of aeronautical navigation and the sciences akin thereto." World War II, according to Mr. Dimity, had interfered with the foundation's plans for a Pacific search expedition. He believed "there was a great deal more involved in Amelia's flight than most people suspected," and he invited me to look at some of the material which had reached the foundation over the years.

Among the mass of letters and photo-copies of logs, I found two documents which seemed of great importance. They were duplicates of messages copied by three operators at the Navy radio station at Diamond Head, Oahu, Hawaii, in the first days after the disappearance. On the Fourth of July, 1937, the station had received carrier waves on 3105 kilocycles at approximately 15 to 20 minutes past the hour during the night. At one point a man's voice had been heard, but it was undistinguishable. On the night of July 7, 1937, a woman's voice had been heard saying, "Earhart calling. NRU1—NRU1—calling from KHAQQ [Amelia's call letters]. On coral southwest of unknown island. Do not know how long we will . . ."

At that point the carrier wave had faded, but a few seconds later the woman's voice broke in and said, KHAQQ calling. KHAQQ. We are cut a little . . ." The wave faded a second time, and the voice was not heard again.

"How did you get these?" I asked Dimity.

"One of the operators gave them to me," he replied. "He felt somebody should know about them."

The CIA was not able to keep its promise about giving us an exclusive on the Saipan spy-school story. The aerospace editor of a Honolulu newspaper had visited Saipan after our 1962 expedition, and put enough pieces together for an expose. The paper printed his story, telling something of NTTU's mission and the involvement of CIA. I immediately checked with Mr. Winter in San Francisco, who in turn reached John McCone, head of the CIA in Washington. There were apologies. No clearance had been given for the Honolulu publication. The CIA position was that we were free to go ahead with our story, but the request was made that it be treated gently. That evening I did a two-minute report for the CBS *World Tonight* program with only a few more details than the Honolulu newsman had disclosed.

With Saipan's security structure somewhat relaxed, we went to work on the possibility of a trip to the island for Thomas Devine. He still believed we had not found the correct area for excavation, and was convinced he could lead us to the exact spot. A letter to M. W. Goding, High Commissioner of the Trust Territory whom we had met the year before, produced the needed permission. Ross Game and my other friends at the Scripps League of Newspapers and Associated Press were still deeply interested and an agreement was reached whereby Ross' people would pay all of Devine's transportation and personal expenses. I dug deep for my own travel costs, and Matthew Katz, my business manager, had become so embroiled in the project that he decided to make the trip, too.

On December 1, 1963, Thomas Devine, a pleasant-faced, Irish-appearing man in his mid-forties, arrived in San Francisco armed with maps, photos and absolute confidence, and the next day, he, Matt, and I departed for Guam and the fourth expedition to Saipan.

Fathers Sylvan and Arnold met the plane at Koebler Field, and I had the definite feeling of a homecoming. Arrangements were quickly made to rent a car and a small house near Chalan Kanoa, and that afternoon we took Devine to Liyang cemetery.

Already his consternation was evident. The growth of the jungle since the years he had served on Saipan was something he could not have imagined from our reports. I showed him how several of his photos matched some of the markers in the graveyard, and how we had come to the conclusion that his directions to us had been reversed.

For several hours he clawed his way through the jungle outside the northern perimeter of the cemetery, then walked a quarter of a mile or so up the beach trying to orient his eighteen-year-old memories.

"It's so changed," he said, shaking his head. "I have the feeling we're too far south. Some of the pictures match all right, but it's possible they were taken by one of my buddies. The graveyard I remember was a temporary one, and it was much closer to Garapan City and the Japanese jail."

We counseled that night with the Fathers, and decided to eliminate Liyang cemetery as a possibility before attempting to locate the graveyard that had once existed near Garapan. With a crew of ten natives equipped with machetes, we spent the next four days clearing an area fifty yards wide and deep north of Liyang, and Devine plotted the distances he remembered. A half-dozen holes were then dug with completely negative results. By the end of the week, we all agreed that Tom's initial reactions had been correct. The area he had been shown by the Okinawan woman in 1945 was at least a half mile to the north.

Johnny Pangelinan, a young Chamorran who worked at the Land Claims Office, made a find in the archives which considerably narrowed the search. It was a Japanese map with a scale layout of the plots and streets in what had been Garapan City. The old graveyard was clearly marked, and a Department of Interior surveyor spent a day roughly marking what had been the boundaries. Devine's enthusiasm immediately returned. The area was much more familiar to him, and when we hacked our way into the crumbling Japanese prison, the distances he recalled seemed identical.

"I'm sure we're near it now," he said. "I remember walking past the jail many times, and the graveyard was right where the surveyor has placed it."

While this had been going on, Fathers Sylvan and Arnold,

together with Matt, had been visiting all the villages on the island, asking for the help of anyone who knew of the old cemetery and its connection with the two American fliers. Remedios Jons, a small, shy Chamorran woman in her mid-fifties who lives in a tiny house near San Roque Village, responded to the plea. Before the war, she and her sister had been shown the unmarked grave of an American man and woman outside the cemetery by a Japanese soldier. The soldier had mentioned that the man and woman had been fliers and were killed as spies. She believed the area she had been shown was outside the southeast corner of Garapan cemetery, but which would have been north of a temporary graveyard that had been used for a few months after the 1944 invasion.

Excavation by hand would have required months, but Commissioner M. W. Goding supplied a bulldozer together with operator, and we had the area cleared in a few days. Then, slowly and carefully, we began to scrape away the surface coral and dirt. Matt and I rode the blade of the 'dozer as it removed a cautious six inches of ground with each cut. About three feet down, the first shattered gravestone appeared. The name *Pangelinan* became discernible as it was pieced together. Obviously we were inside the boundaries of the cemetery. Gradually the bulldozer turned up the earth to the south, but when no graves were found at a five to six foot depth, we moved the giant machine beyond what appeared to be the north end of the graveyard. On December 22 and 23, 1963, we found the remains of eight people, all in separate graves. None had been buried in caskets and none was identifiable. (Dr. Phillips had not been able to locate the impressions he had made of Fred Noonan's teeth, but enough other dental information on Amelia and Fred existed to make it clear the recovered skulls did not qualify for further study.)

I wanted to continue excavation, but on the evening of the twenty-third a report was received by radio at the mission that a typhoon with winds in excess of one hundred miles per hour had taken a course directly toward Saipan. The Fathers advised that we take the morning plane to Guam as the expected blow might interrupt transportation for several weeks. Reluctantly I directed the 'dozer operator to fill in the deep cuts we had made.

Before leaving Saipan, Tom Devine revealed additional information. Not only had he been shown a gravesite in 1945, he had been an ear and eyewitness to two strange scenes at the captured Japanese air base, Aslito Field, at the south end of the island. One day he had overheard a conversation among several high-ranking officers outside a closely guarded hangar to the effect that the plane inside had been identified as Amelia Earhart's. The conversation had turned into a squabble over what unit was going to receive credit for finding the plane. According to Devine, one of the officers then said, "This is top-secret. No one is going to get any credit. Wally Greene has identified the plane, and that's an end to it."

The next night Devine had gone back to the field to see if he could get a look at the plane, and had witnessed its destruction. As he watched, a civilian two-motored transport was rolled out of the hangar, drenched with gasoline, and burned into rubble. Devine believed the "Wally Greene" who had been mentioned was Wallace M. Greene, Jr., G-3 staff officer for the 2nd Marine Division on Saipan in 1944–45, the same Wallace M. Greene, Jr., who became Commandant of the U. S. Marine Corps in 1963.

Tom Devine said he was revealing the information for the first time because he had been unsuccessful in pinpointing the gravesite as he had promised he could do.

The morning of December 24 we said goodbye to the Fathers and boarded the Trust Territory plane for Guam. Matt decided to go to Japan for a vacation-business trip, but I headed back for San Francisco. It was a dismal Christmas Eve. The end of the fourth twelve thousand mile trek to the Pacific, and still no final answer for Amelia and Fred was in sight.

19

On Thursday, January 2, 1964, Ross Game called from Napa.

"Something strange has happened," he began. "I know how many times your hopes have been up and I'm a little reticent to start building them again—but I just received a call from a man in Sacramento; his name is Henson. He read a couple of the stories you wrote for us and Associated Press while you were on Saipan last month, and . . ."

". . . And he was shown a gravesite, too, in 1944 or '45, and he's sure he can take us right to the spot . . . ?"

There was no jocular response from Ross. He just drew a deep breath.

"Not exactly, Fred. Mr. Henson says he *recovered* the remains of Earhart and Noonan from an unmarked grave outside a native cemetery on Saipan the latter part of July 1944!"

Now it was my turn to be silent.

"I'm going to drive up to Sacramento and see him tomorrow morning," Ross continued. "He says he's got something in his garage that may help us."

I was cautious—too often burned. "Are you sure this guy is for real?" I asked.

"Well, he sounds fine on the phone. He has a government job in Sacramento, and he certainly would be jeopardizing that job if what he told me is phony. I'll call you tomorrow when I know more about it."

The following evening Ross gave me the information: Everett Henson, Jr., worked for the Federal Housing Administration as an appraiser. He was an intelligent, reserved man in his mid-forties, who had served with the 2nd Marine Division during World War II and fought through the battle of Saipan in 1944. Sometime in late July or early August 1944, his company had been bivouacked just south of what was left of Garapan City. One evening a Marine captain had asked for volunteers from Henson's platoon for a patrol the next morning. The captain mentioned there was some digging connected with the detail and it would probably take most of the day. Henson and a friend, Private First Class Billy Burks, had volunteered. The captain, whose name was Griswold, had first taken them to a partially demolished house on a hill some distance away. The house had been occupied by a Japanese admiral, and Griswold directed Henson and Burks to look for anything of American origin. In what appeared to be a carriage house just below the main house, Henson had found attached to a wall a large aircraft propeller of U.S. manufacture, although some Japanese characters had been marked or painted on it. The captain ordered the prop removed from the wall.

Griswold had then taken the two privates to a small native cemetery south of Garapan near the Japanese hospital and fairly close to the western shoreline. He told Henson to walk around the graveyard in one direction and the captain and Burks would circle it the other way; they were to look for graves outside the boundary of the cemetery. Henson found a small area marked by coral or rocks which had been painted white. He called Griswold and Burks, and the captain had carefully coordinated the area against some notes or a map he had, then ordered them to dig. About three to four feet down, two skeletons had been found and the remains were placed in containers the captain had brought with him.

While they were excavating, Henson had asked the captain what was behind the whole thing. Griswold replied, "Have you ever heard of Amelia Earhart?"

When Henson answered he had heard of her, the captain added, "I think, then, that's enough said."

On the way back to the encampment that evening, Captain Griswold had admonished both Henson and Burks to say nothing of the afternoon's activities.

I spent a good part of the night thinking through Henson's story. If he was telling the truth, and Ross seemed to think he was, then I'd been blind. The Marines were the first ashore in most of the invasions of the Pacific islands and it made sense they would have found the bulk of intelligence information. If this Captain Griswold's mention of the name Amelia Earhart was a joke, it was a macabre one, and certainly Earhart wasn't a name someone would have picked at random.

If the remains recovered in 1944 were those of Earhart and Noonan, why hadn't it been announced at the time? Such a revelation not only would have solved the mystery, it would have produced strong propaganda to be used against Japan during the remainder of the war. And where were the remains today?

Locating Billy Burks seemed to be the best course. Henson had provided Ross with Burks' Marine Corps serial number from records he had stored in his garage, but tracing Burks after twenty years could take the rest of a lifetime. Even if we did find him, would he remember the incident?

I recalled then the letters from Robert Kinley of Norfolk, Virginia, who had found the photograph of Amelia together with the Japanese officer; Kinley had been a Marine. There was Devine's information about a "Wally Greene" having identified AE's plane at Aslito Field in 1944. If "Wally" really was General Wallace M. Greene, Jr., another Marine was closely connected to the story.

I drove to Sacramento to see for myself.

Everett Henson, Jr., lived up to Ross' billing. He was quiet, introspective but pleasant, and spoke with a soft midwestern accent. He'd been with the FHA for a number of years and liked his job as appraiser. I tried to ask him every pertinent, and by now almost standard, question.

"Mr. Henson, did you ever tell this story to anyone else?"

"Yes, I did," he replied. "I told my family about it and a couple of close friends, too."

"Why did you wait until now to contact Ross Game or me? This investigation has been going on for nearly four years."

Henson gave a way-of-the-world smile and then replied, "I did try to contact you, Mr. Goerner. I guess it was three years ago, 1961, when there was all that publicity about sending bodies that were supposed to be Earhart and Noonan to the States. I tried to call your office at CBS in San Francisco, but your operator gave me a real fast shuffle and said you couldn't be reached, so I figured the hell with it."

"Then why are you coming forward now?"

"I saw by the paper that you were out on Saipan again, still looking for what we dug up in 1944, so I decided it was time to save you some sweat."

"Ross said the captain who was with you cautioned you not to say anything about the incident. Does that bother you?"

"No. Why should it? That was twenty years ago. I can't figure out what difference it makes now. Beside that, I wasn't part of Intelligence so I wouldn't have to keep quiet. I was a PFC, and a lot of guys have told me what happened to them during the war."

"Can you give me any more details about the cemetery?"

"Well, it was a small graveyard. You could walk around it in three to four minutes, maybe less. There were stone markers and crosses in it and some kind of a statue, an angel or the Blessed Virgin or something. There was also some sort of a wrought-iron fence around the whole thing."

"Where was the cemetery located, Mr. Henson?"

"As I told Mr. Game, it was somewhere near the Jap hospital, fairly close to the ocean and it was south of Garapan. Our encampment was in that area."

"How deep, again, was the grave?"

"It must have been three or four feet. We were down to our waists or a little more when we found them. In other words, we could still see out of the grave and kind of jump up rather than climb out."

"Are you sure the remains of two people were in the grave?"

"Yes, sir, I am. We came across some shin bones and leg bones first, and then the rest of them; there were two skulls. That's all of that kind of digging I ever care to do."

"What did Captain Griswold do with the remains?"

"He stored them in some kind of containers. I can't remember whether they were packs or metal containers or what. Anyway, he was real careful with them."

"This grave was definitely outside the cemetery?"

"It was. Definitely. Maybe ten yards more or less. There weren't any markings, just some white-looking rocks, coral probably."

Nothing Henson had said matched the cemetery area we had worked in 1961 and 1962, the one Tom Devine had finally rejected on the last trip, but it did fit descriptions of the graveyard closer to Garapan which had been bulldozed at the end of the war.

It was near the latter that we had found the eight unmarked graves in December '63. I began to understand what might have happened to Devine. He had pictures of "Cave" cemetery, but actually he had been shown Garapan cemetery in 1945. Tom had arrived, in the last days we were on the island, at the right site, but according to Everett Henson, twenty years too late.

But why would the Okinawan woman have shown Devine the gravesite of "two American fliers, man and woman" if Henson, Burks, and Griswold had already recovered the remains?

There was a possible answer: after the invasion, most of the natives had been held many months in an internment camp near Susupe in the southern part of the island. The Okinawan woman had probably been a part of that group. It was during that period that Griswold and company could have completed their job. When the woman returned to her shack, she did not know the grave had been disturbed.

Devine happened by some months later, but by then the grave area was covered with grass, and the vignette was enacted which plagued the ex-soldier from Connecticut for two decades.

"What about Captain Griswold?" I continued the questioning. "What do you know about him?"

"Not too much," Henson replied. "He wasn't a part of our outfit; I know that for a fact. I have the complete battalion roster in my old seabag out in the garage, and his name isn't listed."

"Well, where did he come from?"

"I don't know that either. I do remember seeing him several times before Burks and I were asked to volunteer for the digging. He was interrogating captured Japs, and I saw him talking to a lot of the natives down at Susupe. He was also going through the companies picking up souvenirs the guys had collected. We were allowed to keep a lot of stuff, but it had to be passed by Field Intelligence first. They had a stamp they'd put on things if it had been checked and found okay."

"Do you know if Griswold was looking for something special?"

"He was the day we went with him, but I don't know if Earhart was his only job."

"Do you have any idea of his first name?"

"No, I've thought and thought, but I guess I never heard it. I do remember he said the Griswold Stove Manufacturing Company was in his family. It was in the East somewhere. At least that's what I think he said. I've a pretty good memory, but it gets tough after twenty years."

"Are you sure about the Amelia Earhart statement?"

"Yes, I'm positive. Something like that is impossible to forget. If it had been some unknown person, I might have forgotten the name, but she was as famous as anyone can be."

"Again, about Griswold. Did you see him after that day, or have you seen him since the war?"

"I'm not sure whether we saw him in the next couple of days after the digging, but I don't think so. The truth is that he seemed to disappear. I sure haven't seen him since the war, but I'm pretty certain I could pick him out of a group of men."

"What about Burks?"

"I haven't seen Billy since the war, either. In fact, I haven't seen him since Saipan. Our outfit was broken up after the Tinian invasion and I don't know exactly when he got back to the States."

"What do you know about Burks? How old was he? What kind of a person was he? Where did he come from?"

"Oh, Billy was a nice guy. He was a little younger than I, about twenty-three or -four I guess. As I recall, he came from

Texas originally, but he used to talk a lot about California. I think he was living out here when he enlisted in the Marines."

"What part of California?"

"I can't be sure . . . but I have a hunch it was Southern California somewhere."

"Mr. Henson," I concluded, "I don't want to be rude or ungrateful, but I think I have to ask this question. Do you hope to make some money or gain some fame by telling this story?"

Henson stared at me for a few seconds and then said, "I suppose you did have to ask that question, so I'm not offended. No, I'm not looking for anything. I just decided this thing has gone far enough. There's something wrong with this whole business about Earhart and Noonan. I think we dug up their bodies in 1944, but twenty years later it's still claimed nobody knows what happened to them. That grave was there when the Japs controlled the island, so they must have killed them; or Earhart died of dysentery as you think. Anyway the Japs had them. They died on Saipan at least a couple of years before a lot of Marines did. I guess you might say they knew what was going to happen to the United States a long time before most of us, and they paid more of a price for that island than a lot of us, too."

As I drove back to San Francisco that evening, I tried to put some of the pieces together. Henson apparently was telling the truth, but his word would never stand alone. We would have to find Burks. Griswold would be too tough. We only knew his rank and that he had been with Intelligence or possibly OSS, and even if we could locate him, that fact he was with Intelligence might preclude his disclosing anything about the incident.

A thought occurred: if Henson's story was corroborated by other testimony, it would mean the U.S. government had held the remains of Earhart and Noonan for twenty years without notifying the next of kin. It would also mean that three of my four trips to Saipan had been a total waste.

The following week the U. S. Marines were again brought to the center of the investigation by a letter from Warren Hasse, general manager of KPDN Radio in Pampa, Texas. Hasse, who had been following our efforts for some time, wrote about a friend of his, a W. B. Jackson. Hasse had known Jackson for more than twenty years, and he believed his friend had some information which might be vital in settling the Earhart-Noonan question. Jackson, according to Hasse, had been with the Marines during the invasion of the Marshall Islands in 1944, and had found some of Earhart's personal effects. Enclosed with the letter were Jackson's home address and telephone number in Pampa. Hasse closed by saying Jackson was one of the most honest men he had ever known, and we could completely depend on what he said. I immediately called Jackson, and what he related was important. I asked him to send me a letter containing the information; this is the gist of what he wrote:

In February 1944, on the Island of Namur, Kwajalein Atoll, Marshall Islands, three Marines brought a suitcase from a barracks. They disclosed that the room they found it in was fitted up for a woman, with a dresser in it. In the suitcase they found a woman's clothing, a number of clippings of articles on Amelia Earhart, and a leather-backed, locked diary engraved *10-Year Diary of Amelia Earhart*. They wanted to pry open the diary but when Jackson explained who Amelia was, how the government had searched for a trace of her, and that this should be taken to Intelligence, they closed the suitcase and started toward the Regimental Command Post with it. That is the last Jackson saw or heard of it.

Again, why hadn't Jackson made his information known before 1964? His answer was about the same as all of them. He hadn't thought his knowledge of sufficient importance. He didn't want publicity, and in any case, the federal government must have all the facts because the diary and personal effects had been turned over to Intelligence.

Less than a week later I received a telephone call from a former Marine captain, Victor Maghokian, living in Las Vegas. He, too, had seen several of the stories I had written on Saipan, and he believed he had information which would contribute to the effort. His story closely paralleled Jackson's. He said that about February 18 or 19, 1944, he was ordered to check out a story that a Makin Island native, Rudolph Miller, was around the Kwajalein Atoll. He was found about a day later and brought aboard their ship, the *Kane*. Miller said that he had been rescued by the Marines on Tarawa and now was a native interpreter for the U. S. Navy. Subsequently, on an island close by, Maghokian talked to some of the natives through the interpreter. They told him that sometime in the year 1937 a white woman and a white man were in the Kwajalein Atoll area for a short time and then were taken away by the Japs to another island.

He added that "one of their men" found a diary and some personal belongings that were supposed to belong to Amelia Earhart.

I checked both ways: Maghokian had never heard of Jackson, and Jackson only vaguely remembered a captain named Maghokian. Yet twenty years after an event, they had both come up with the same story. There was just too much testimony from too many reputable people to draw any but one conclusion: Earhart and Noonan had gone down in the Marshalls and were captured by the Japanese. There was Eugene Bogan, the Washington, D.C., tax attorney, who had been the senior military government officer at Majuro. Charles James Toole in the office of the Under Secretary of the Navy, who had gathered similar information in the Marshalls. Elieu, the most trusted and respected native in the Marshalls, had told the same story he told in 1944. Now Maghokian and Jackson with much more to add. There had been another half-dozen letters from former military personnel indicating they had heard from natives or comrades that "two American fliers, a man and woman" had crash-landed in the Marshall Islands before the war and had been held prisoner by the Japanese. Even Commander Bridwell had volunteered his belief that Earhart and Noonan had not flown their plane to Saipan, but had gone down in the Marshalls.

But where in the Marshalls? Was it Ailinglapalap as Bridwell believed, or between Mili and Jaluit as the Japanese trader Ajima had reported to Elieu? If Tom Devine was right, and General Greene, the Commandant of the Marine Corps in Washington, D.C., had been involved in the mystery to the point of identifying AE's plane on Saipan in 1944, then a Japanese ship, perhaps the carrier Kamoi, had plucked the Electra from the water or the shore and transported it to Saipan. The Japanese had been great record-keepers; there must be records extant which would detail the entire sequence of events. But where were those records? We had tried everything to locate them. Where were the pictures found at Saipan? The diary and personal effects located at Kwajalein? We already knew beyond doubt that the State Department and Navy Department had classified files which had never been made available. Serious discrepancies in letters to me from both departments clearly indicated the existence of the files. The State Department even had gone so far as to name the date in 1960 when the Navy had communicated to State that such files were on hand. Tom Devine had been shown part of a classified Navy file on January 7, 1963, in an effort to persuade him to drop his interest in the case.

There was something tremendous behind the disappearance of Amelia Earhart and Frederick Noonan in 1937. I thought back to the words of Commander Pillsbury the night he had retired: "The admiral wanted me to say to you that he thinks you should continue the investigation, and I want to add to that, don't you ever give up. You're on to something that will stagger your imagination!"

Now was the time to place the evidence in the hands of someone who had real power within the government and someone who might be able to convince the Department of Defense that justice should be done. We chose U. S. Senator Thomas H. Kuchel of California. In April 1964, Ross Game, Matt Katz, and I went to Washington, D.C., for two weeks with three purposes: (A) Get the classified report from the State Department. (B) Get the classified report from the Navy Department. (C) Get a statement from General Greene and determine how deeply the Marine Corps had been involved.

A and B were difficult. C was impossible.

20

Several efforts had already been made to get a statement from General Greene before the April 1964, Washington, D.C., trip. Robert Pierpoint, CBS Washington correspondent, had made inquiries, as had Norman Hatch, press officer for the Pentagon. The general initially replied, "I would like more information to refresh my memory."

A complete statement containing Devine's allegations was sent to General Greene through Norman Hatch, and again the general had been asked to comment. The statement also included testimony and eyewitness accounts concerning other areas of the investigation which had been volunteered by the former Marines. The names of the individuals were excluded. Ross and I had become apprehensive that if the names were given the investigation could be stalled indefinitely while each person was interviewed and his information "evaluated" by the Pentagon. By the time we reached Washington, there still had been no comment from General Greene.

Our first attempt to see the general was made through Norman Hatch at the Pentagon. Hatch got in touch with a Colonel Adams,

Greene's aide, and hours later Adams replied, "The general's terribly busy this week and says he can't see Mr. Game and Mr. Goerner. Besides the general says he doesn't know what all this Earhart business is about."

We asked Adams to remind the general of our letter to him in response to his request for more information. Again several hours later Adams telephoned to say General Greene not only didn't recall the letter, he couldn't remember having asked to have his memory refreshed. Fortunately Ross had brought along a copy of the letter Norman Hatch had sent requesting the information and a copy of the letter containing our statement and questions which had been returned. More time passed before Colonel Adams responded that General Greene now recalled the situation, but felt he had nothing to contribute on the question of Amelia Earhart. We protested that we had come to Washington with the primary intention of seeing the general and getting an official statement from him. The next day Colonel Adams replied that General Greene was preparing the budget and couldn't possibly see us that week. We inquired about an appointment for the following week. Several hours later Colonel Adams allowed that the general was going to be tied up all of the next week, too.

Ross and I then appealed to Senator Kuchel, and Ewing Hass, the Senator's Chief Administrative Assistant, began conversations with General Greene through Colonel Adams. It was finally decided that we should see Colonel Randolph Berkeley, G-2 Intelligence Officer for the Marine Corps, as preface to an audience with the general. The Berkeley appointment was set for the end of the week.

In the days before that meeting, we made some progress. At the Pentagon, we sat down with Captain James Dowdell, the Public Information Officer I had met at Pearl Harbor in 1962 who was now Deputy Chief of Naval Information.

"We'd like very much to have access to the Navy's classified file or files regarding Amelia Earhart," I began.

"I understand, Mr. Goerner," Dowdell answered, "that you have been informed on several occasions that the Navy has no classified information on the matter."

"Yes, Captain, that's true," I returned. "The Navy has indicated the Earhart affair is strictly of civilian concern, that the Navy has conducted no investigation into her disappearance and the Navy had no connection with Amelia in 1937 other than to send the *Lexington* and other vessels on a search mission. I have five or six letters stating that attitude. I also have a letter from the State Department dated Sepember 12, 1963, which reads, 'The Department of State was informed on December 24, 1960, by the Navy, the administering authority for Saipan, that a full investigation by the Commander Naval Forces Marianas had been made into the allegations that Amelia Earhart had been imprisoned or executed on Saipan.' I also have a letter, dated April 1, 1963, from one Thomas E. Devine of West Haven, Connecticut, in which he states that on January 7, 1963, at Hartford, Connecticut, a conference was sought with him by an agent of Naval Intelligence, and that the agent allowed him to see the classified photos and reports of the investigation of Earhart and Noonan conducted on Saipan by the Office of Naval Intelligence. Devine says he was told that "something must have come up" because ordinarily no non-government person is allowed to see classified matter.

Captain Dowdell took the photostats of the letters. He looked them over for a moment, then telephoned Naval Intelligence.

"Do you or do you not have a classified file down there regarding Amelia Earhart?"

The answer was affirmative and Dowdell made arrangements for us to peruse the material as soon as permission could be gained from the Chief of Naval Intelligence. The captain's attitude toward me in particular had been cool since I entered the office. Questioning him, I discovered that he had heard a broadcast I had done in which the CIA Saipan spy-school was mentioned and he felt that I had broken faith with the military and jeopardized national security. When he learned the truth, that I hadn't violated secrecy and had been cleared by the CIA to do the broadcast, our relations improved immediately.

"You'd better get the CIA to send a letter to everyone concerned here in Washington," Dowdell suggested. "A lot of people here think you blew the whistle on the Saipan operation. It'll make things a lot easier if you do."

I made a mental note to contact Mr. Winter when I returned to San Francisco.

The classified file Naval Intelligence finally showed us wasn't much, but it did contain a few things that made sense to me. Some of the natives Bridwell had first taken me to in 1960 had been questioned again and the testimony was different. José Villa-Gomez, for instance, told the Navy there was nothing to the story that the Americans had flown their plane to Saipan but the Japanese had talked of taking an American woman flier prisoner in the Marshall Islands. Jesús Salas had told the Navy the same thing. The Japanese had bragged about capturing American fliers, a man and woman, near Jaluit in the Marshalls. The Navy investigator had also interviewed Mrs. Antonio Blanco, Josephine Akiyama's mother, on Guam, and Mrs. Blanco had stated that her daughter did tell her of the two Americans, the fliers, before the war and that she had warned her daughter not to discuss what she had seen with anyone for fear of Japanese reprisal. Two items in the file were of particular interest. There was a letter from Commander Bridwell to the Commandant of the Marianas deprecating my investigation, and a report from a naval intelligence officer on Bridwell's information. There was no explanation why Bridwell had tried to steer me and the Navy away from the trail. The answer could have been in a section of the file we were not permitted to see. Dowdell explained that that portion did not concern itself directly with Amelia Earhart but rather was a report on Commander Bridwell and the operation of the Naval Administration Unit on Saipan and as such could not be made available to the press at least for the present. Captain Dowdell also seemed quite anxious to convince us that we had seen everything the Navy had to offer where Amelia and Fred were concerned.

"That's all there is," he said. "I've checked with ONI. You do believe that's all there is?"

"I can't say I do, Captain Dowdell," I replied. "There was such a long time when the Navy denied it had anything at all that it's a little hard to accept protestations of faith and innocence now."

"Are you satisfied that Amelia Earhart was not on a secret mission for the Navy when she disappeared?"

"I don't know that either, Captain. It seems that everything we have come up with points to a possible mission. Whether it was for the Navy, the Army Air Corps, the Marines or whomever, there was more to that flight than a couple of civilians seeking publicity. The harder the Navy tries to disclaim any interest in them, the more I suspect the Navy was deeply involved."

Captain Dowdell was pleasant when we left, but I'm sure he was glad to see us depart. The Public Information Office is a Navy department most officers are happy to leave themselves.

The next day we checked through the available Amelia Earhart record file at the National Archives. This one had been thoroughly perused by literally hundreds of people. Everything in it pointed only to the possibility that AE and Fred had gone down at sea and were forever lost; everything, that is, but a lot of items that apparently had no reason for being included in the file at all. There were copies of dozens of requests, dating back ten years or more, from the U. S. State Department to numerous foreign countries, asking for permission for U. S. Navy planes to fly over their territory. Almost without exception, the countries, including many allied to the U.S., had replied negatively. In the Earhart file, there was a whole history of the Navy's frustration with the State Department regarding foreign over-flights, and not one of the incidents was connected to AE. Why were they in this particular file?

There were also copies of many requests from private individuals to the U. S. Navy asking for assistance for long-distance flights in many parts of the world. Here is an example of one of the letters. It was dated June 4, 1934, and addressed to Chief of Naval Operations, Washington, D.C. It was a request that the Navy supply a special kind of hub shank and propeller blade for an aircraft that was to make the first Recognition Trade Flight from New York City to Moscow, Russia. Only the Navy had those particular items, and it was guaranteed they would be returned after the flight.

J. K. Faussig, Rear Admiral United States Navy and Acting Chief U. S. Navy, answered the letter and a copy was attached to the original request. The United States Navy would not and could not cooperate on a private flying venture.

Again, here was material seemingly unconnected to Amelia Earhart but included in her "official" government file. The casual researcher would simply have pushed it aside. The documents really didn't mean a lot to me until a few months later. Now I believe that someone at some time included them in that file knowing that eventually a person with sufficient background would recognize the implications.

The State Department came next, and they too disclaimed the existence of a classified file until I called to their attention the closing line of a letter written to me September 12, 1963, by Richardson Dougall, Acting Director, Historical Office, Bureau of Public Affairs, Department of State, in which he said that the Department's records relating to Amelia Earhart contained little classified information, and none of relevance to my questions.

However "little" the information might be, I wanted to see it and judge for myself its relevancy to Amelia. The file was made available and Mr. Dougall could not have been more wrong. It was a strange collection of material, but not strange that it was classified, from the standpoint of what we already knew.

There was a letter to the State Department from Amelia Earhart's mother written in 1949. It pleaded with State to find out from the Japanese what had happened to her daughter.

"There were things Amelia could not tell me," Mrs. Earhart wrote. "I know she was under verbal orders from the Military."

Also in the file was a notation that AE's plane had been "delayed at Port Darwin, Australia, due to an irregularity in health certificates." Another notation indicated that a Sergeant Stan Rose had carefully repaired and tested the Electra's radio equipment at Port Darwin. Two other letters concerned equipment aboard the plane. The engines carried by the Lockheed were not those listed in publicity releases to the public. Two new Pratt & Whitney Senior Wasp military-version engines had been installed instead of the 550 h.p. Wasp Juniors. The new engines gave the plane half again as much power and a cruising speed of 200 or more miles per hour. An extra telegraph system had also been installed to be used in the event of emergency.

There was a letter, dated March 1944, indicating a U. S. Navy lieutenant commander had reported learning that an American woman with a male companion had come down near Jaluit Atoll in the Marshall Islands several years before the war. The name of the lieutenant commander was not included in the communication.

The diplomatic exchanges between Japan and the United States at the time of AE's disappearance were also included in the file. One reply from Japan was a clear and definite refusal for U.S. planes to fly over the Marshall Islands to search for Amelia and Fred. The Japanese had been unusually blunt.

One strange item in the classified file bordered on the bizarre. France's state department had sent a communication dated October 30, 1938, to the U. S. Department of State which said that a French housewife, a Genevieve Barrat of Soulac-sur-Mar, France, had been walking down a beach and picked up a bottle which had floated ashore. In the bottle was a note which read, *Amelia Earhart and Fred Noonan are prisoners Jaluit Atoll, Marshall Islands.*

There was plenty of reading between the lines to be done where the State Department file was concerned. Mrs. Earhart's letter spoke of a possible "mission" and significantly the State Department's answer to Amelia's mother was missing. The delay of the plane at Australia because of "health certificates" had added meaning. The mysterious William Miller had met the plane there. Was the "mission" just starting or ending?

The radio gear had been completely repaired and checked at Port Darwin. Where did that leave all the people who had said AE's radio was not functioning properly? And the emergency "telegraph system," how and under what circumstances could it operate? Nothing about such a system had been made public at the time of the flight. Most significant was the proof that the engines had been changed. The added power altered every computation that had publicly been made for the flight. With those engines, the Electra was faster and had a higher ceiling. With better than a 200-mile-per-hour cruising speed, Amelia could have flown in a number of directions and still kept her estimated time of arrival at Howland Island which had been based on the speed produced by the lesser-powered engines. The report that she checked in with Lae, New Guinea, about 800 miles en route to Howland averaging 111 miles per hour had to be phony; either that or the plane was encountering nearly one-hundred-mile-per-hour head winds, and if that had been the case AE certainly would have turned back to Lae rather than chance a continuation of those winds throughout the rest of the flight. What I had noticed about the 0615 and 0645 messages received by the *Itasca* had been correct; the Electra was averaging two hundred miles an hour!

The inclusion of the Marshall Islands information had meaning, too. The State Department must have suspected that Amelia and Fred had ended their flight there. Why else would such information be classified, especially something as seemingly ridiculous as a French woman finding a note in a bottle?

One small mystery within the mystery was solved before we got to the meeting with Colonel Berkeley. I located Richard Black who had been aboard the *Itasca* the morning of the disappearance and who had later become a Rear Admiral, USN. He is now working on special projects for the Navy's History Office in downtown Washington. Admiral Black had quite a career even before his Navy days, a career which included one of the famous South Pole expeditions with Admiral Byrd. In 1937, Black was working for the Interior Department and colonization of Howland Island was one of his responsibilities. He had populated the island with Hawaiians and had helped with construction of Howland's airfield.

It became obvious as our conversation progressed that Admiral Black did not look with disfavor on the theory that Earhart and Noonan had gone down in the vicinity of the Marshalls and had been taken to Saipan by the Japanese. He also had some comments about the mysterious Navy radio direction finder which had been set up on Howland Island as Amelia began her flight from Lae, New Guinea.

"I brought that DF aboard the *Itasca*," said Black. "It was given to me by a Navy man at Pearl Harbor and it was a very hush-hush deal. Actually it was an experimental model of some of the direction finders we used during the war.

"I've thought for many years," he continued, "that there was a great deal more to Amelia's disappearance than simply missing Howland and going into the drink."

U. S. Marine Corps Headquarters is located in the Naval Annex building alongside Arlington National Cemetery; not as posh as the Pentagon but a lot more accessible. It was there we kept our appointment with Colonel Randolph Berkeley, G-2 for the Corps. Considering the running battle we were having trying to get an appointment with General Greene, I expected open hostility from Berkeley, but he was warm and friendly and listened patiently to the whole story.

"Can you reveal the names of the men who have given you this information?" was the colonel's first question.

I explained why we did not wish to go through that process and Berkeley nodded, whether in agreement or disbelief I could not tell.

"We'd just like simple answers to these questions, Colonel," I said. "Does the Marine Corps have a classified file on Earhart, or did the Corps collect information on Earhart and Noonan during the war and turn it over to another Service? Did General Greene identify Earhart's plane at Aslito Field on Saipan in 1944? Did the Marine Corps recover the remains of Earhart and Noonan?"

"I frankly don't know the answers to those questions," Berkeley replied. "We have a lot of our classified files right here in this building, but it'll take a couple of days to check these things out. Why don't you come back, say next Tuesday morning at ten. We should have an answer by then, and perhaps we can arrange a chat with the general."

As we were leaving Berkeley added, "If those remains were recovered, I wonder where they would be now."

"Perhaps across the road in Arlington Cemetery," I offered. "I hope they still aren't in the containers Captain Griswold was carrying."

"Well, we should have some idea next Tuesday," said Berkeley. "I'll see you then."

We didn't see Colonel Berkeley the following Tuesday. When we showed up for the appointment, we were told that the colonel had left Washington on leave and no one had any idea where he had gone. We didn't see General Greene, either. He had also left Washington for destinations unknown. Alas, even Colonel Adams could not be located. Presumably he was with General Greene, wherever *he* had gone.

We reported the situation to Senator Kuchel's office, and it was decided that we should work up all the information available on the investigation so the Senator could approach the Defense Department fully armed. Before we left Washington, we had several lengthy discussions about what might lie behind the enigma of Earhart and Noonan, trying to answer the one big question: Why had the information about them been suppressed for so many years? This is the conclusion we reached.

Amelia and Fred were captured and held by the Japanese in 1937 and the U.S. military either knew it or strongly suspected it. President Roosevelt was also aware of the situation. But what could be done about it? The United States was in a mood of isolationism and our military forces were anything but prepared for conflict. To have ordered the carrier *Lexington* and its accompanying forces to search the Marshall Islands in the face of Japan's refusal to permit such a search could well have precipitated World War II, at least in the Pacific area, in 1937. Roosevelt certainly would have been committing political suicide by issuing the order.

The U.S. military had been suspicious of Japanese use of the Mandated Islands for many years, and Japan was preparing itself for war. When would Japan strike against the United States? How advanced were her bases in the Mandates? Were the airfields active? How was the Japanese Navy using the harbors? Those questions had to be answered to provide security for America.

Earhart and Noonan were serving their country. They were on a reconnaissance mission, almost parallel to the U-2 flights of the 1960s, but with that mission went the hazard that always must be faced by spies. If you're caught, your country can do nothing to help you. Perhaps the plan had been for Amelia and Fred to fly first over Truk, then down over the Marshalls to Howland Island, or perhaps the plan had called for them to pretend to be lost and actually to land in the Marshalls; the supposition being that the Japanese would never dare to hold anyone as famous as Amelia.

The first tangible evidence that AE and Fred had been held by the Japanese came with the February 1944 invasion of the Marshalls. The information could have been held in the hope that they might later be found alive; the information was probably only fragmentary. Then, Saipan, and the full knowledge of what had happened to them. The timing could not have been worse for AE and Noonan. It was just four months before the national election, and President Roosevelt, seeking his fourth term, was having a tough duel with Thomas E. Dewey. The opposition was making political capital out of any and all military reverses of the war and the general state of unpreparedness before Pearl Harbor. If the Republican forces had found anything as volatile as the abandonment of Earhart and Noonan in 1937, Dewey could well have become President. The American public would have forgotten its pre-war isolationist attitude; Japan was now the hated enemy. Every newsman in the country would have questioned why Earhart and Noonan had been held by the Japanese and why we had done nothing about it. The fate of AE and Fred therefore remained classified. As it developed, the issue could have swung the election. The polling was close, Dewey losing thirteen states by less than three percent of the popular vote; those thirteen states alone would have given Thomas Dewey the electoral count he needed for victory.

Unfortunately, President Roosevelt died in 1945 before the end of the war, and doubtless President Truman had no wish to qualify FDR's memory in any way by releasing the Earhart information, nor was he going to jeopardize his own chances for the presidency in the 1948 election. Truman was victorious in 1948, but the matter of Amelia and Fred had slipped deeper into the classified files and there seemed little sense in releasing it.

Then, in the early 1950s, the whole future of Saipan changed when President Truman switched control of the island from the Department of Interior to the Navy and the Central Intelligence Agency went to work building its super spy-school. Even if someone had thought of giving the vindication of truth to Amelia and Fred during the years that followed, it would have been impossible. Photographers and newsmen, the government reasoned, would have clamored to go to the spot where the world's most famous aviatrix had died, and the thirty-million-dollar Saipan secret would have been out in the open and probably on the floor of the United Nations. In 1960, when we had begun our investigation, Saipan's CIA operation was in full swing. The timing again could not have been worse for Earhart and Noonan.

By 1964, though, the threat of disclosure of the CIA on Saipan had been removed. The question now was, after all the years and all the delays, how would the information be released? Someone was going to have to take responsibility and there appeared to be no volunteers.

What about Japan? Why had she not admitted culpability long before? The answer was that there was nothing to be gained and a lot to be lost. Japan had never admitted the illegal use of the Mandated Islands prior to World War II. In the War Crimes Trials in Tokyo in 1946 and 1947, Japan had stated that the airfields and bases in the Mandates before the war had been used for "cultural purposes and for aiding fishermen to locate schools of fish," and the United States had accepted that answer. If Japan was forced to admit Earhart and Noonan, she would also be forced to admit the reason for holding them, the fear that they would tell what they had seen. The revelation would document charges of Japan's misuse of the League of Nations Mandate, a violation of international law, and could cause serious loss of face for Japan. Then, too, Japan still had interest in the islands of the Pacific and hope that Okinawa and perhaps some other territory could be returned to her through the United Nations. An uproar about Amelia Earhart might endanger those chances.

U.S. relations with Japan were touchy in 1964, too. There were the American bases in the Japanese home islands, and the possibility of the establishment of a Polaris Submarine-tender base in Japan. Japan was also contemplating the possibility of trade with Red China which might not be in the best interests of the United States. These and other considerations could militate against the release of a final answer to an old mystery.

That was how we saw it when we returned to San Francisco at the end of April 1964 and faced the task of finding Billy Burks.

21

Everett Henson had supplied Burks' Marine Corps' service number from which Norman Hatch at the Pentagon traced the enlistment address. Henson was right about Southern California. Burks had lived in East Los Angeles. Ross Game arranged with Associated Press in Los Angeles to check the residence.

"No Billy Burks there," came the reply, "and no one in the neighborhood ever heard of him." The landlord did not have records dating back to the 1940s.

How would you begin to trace a man after twenty years?

I started with the telephone directories for major California cities, but there was no listing. A friend of Ross' at the FBI suggested gas and electric company records.

Score! A Billy Burks had lived in Huntington Park near Los Angeles in 1953. There was, however, no record of a forwarding address. Ross stopped in Huntington Park during a business trip and found another dead end. The house had been rented a dozen times since 1953, and no one recalled an ex-Marine named Billy Burks. It was many months before we came across another lead.

Meanwhile, Matt Katz pursued some answers in Tokyo. He

managed a conference with two directors of Nanyo Boeki Kaisha, the post-war export company which had been associated with Nanyo Kohatsu Kaisha, Japan's pre-war South Seas Development front in the Mandated Islands. Both men had been on Saipan during the 1937–41 period, and before they learned the real purpose of Matt's visit, several pictures of pre-war Garapan were produced, including one of Garapan cemetery which matched Henson's description of the graveyard around which he, Burks and Griswold supposedly excavated. A large tombstone engraved with the name PANGELINAN appeared in the foreground of the photo. It was the same marker we had recovered in December 1963. When Matt asked about Amelia and Fred, the tenor of conversation changed completely. Tension filled the room, and the meeting abruptly ended. In the confusion, Matt came away with the photo.

Matt then talked with a member of the Foreign Affairs Section of the House of Representatives of the Japanese Diet, and they became quite friendly. At one point, the official admitted that Japan had violated the League of Nations Mandate prior to World War II.

"Everyone knows Japan did this thing," he said, "and I think it is senseless for us to deny it now."

"Would you be willing to tell the press what you've just told me?" asked Matt.

"Yes, certainly I would," the Japanese replied.

With the help of Ken Yamaguchi, Chief of Foreign Relations for the newspaper combine Yomiuri Shimbum, Matt called a press conference for the next morning, but forty-five minutes before the conference was scheduled to begin, the Representative telephoned that he could not keep the appointment, and his statement of the previous afternoon should not be released. Someone had alerted the Diet member to the explosiveness and possible repercussions his comments might produce.

The night before Matt returned to San Francisco, he appeared on a Japanese national television program similar to America's *I've Got a Secret*, and asked viewers with knowledge of two American fliers, a man and woman, on Saipan before the war, to address him in care of the Japanese network. An acquaintance of Matt's at the television station had consented to forward to San Francisco any correspondence received.

It was July 1964 before six letters finally arrived. Each had already been opened and studied. The number of extraneous marks on each letter left no doubt of that. Five of the six letters were from individuals who suggested other persons who might be able to contribute information. The sixth was from a woman whose husband had served with the Japanese Navy on Saipan.

"My husband is now dead," wrote the woman, "but I remember his speaking of an American woman flier. He had his picture taken with her. I enclose the picture."

There was no photo in the letter when it arrived in San Francisco. Matt later learned that the letters had never reached his friend. They had been forwarded from an unknown source. Obviously there was going to be no cooperation from Japan where Amelia Earhart and Frederick Noonan were concerned.

Help came from Washington, D.C., however, from an unexpected source. One of the highest ranking and most respected members of the U. S. Department of Commerce wrote to me July 31, 1964, and offered to assist on a quasi-governmental basis. He had been following the investigation and felt he might be able to reach people in Washington on terms a newsman could not achieve. (I omit his name by request. He fears criticism from some quarters because of his cooperation; however, should the Senate or House of Representatives launch an investigation into the Earhart matter, he has indicated I may reveal his name, and he will testify.)

I accepted his offer, and by October 1964 he uncovered the information I have recounted in an earlier chapter about William Miller. Then he began to bombard nearly everyone in government and the military for information.

On October 27, 1964, Elizabeth B. Drewry, director of the Franklin D. Roosevelt Library, Hyde Park, New York, wrote of discovering correspondence in the archives which gave some indication of the depth of presidential involvement in the final flight. Roosevelt had first arranged for the Navy to refuel the Electra in flight over Midway Island. Then he had arranged for allocation of funds to the Bureau of Air Commerce for construction of a landing field at Howland Island for Amelia's use. Miss Drewry ended her letter with the note that while there was evidence of President Roosevelt's interest in the search for Amelia Earhart, there was no record of any action taken by him.

A letter to former President Dwight Eisenhower was answered by Colonel Raymond C. Ball, Chief, Historical Services Division, Headquarters Department of the Army, Office of the Chief of Military History, in Washington, D.C.

> This office holds a memorandum dated 5 June 1961 from Dr. Arthur M. Schlesinger, Jr., then Special Assistant to President Kennedy, asking that "all the War Department and Navy documents on Amelia Earhart be made available." Research conducted in this office, the Office of the Assistant Chief of Staff for Intelligence, and the World War II Records Division, National Archives and Records Service failed to locate any pertinent information. A file titled "Earhart, Amelia, Information Regarding Location Of Grave Of" is held by the Office of Naval Intelligence and contains information on the Earhart case. Should you wish to explore this source it is suggested that you contact that office."

The file referred to by Colonel Ball had not been shown to us by the Navy when we visited Washington.

Our Department of Commerce contact nosed about the Pentagon and received comments ranging from interesting to very doubtful.

From General Lucius D. Clay: "There's more to the Earhart business than anyone suspected. I'm not a part of it myself, but I would like to see it told."

From a staff assistant in the Secretary of Defense office who refused to be named: "There is a complete file on what happened to Earhart right here in the Defense Department."

From another source who would not let his name be used: "President Roosevelt knew all about Earhart's mission. Amelia was commissioned a Major, and Noonan a Lieutenant Commander."

The only fact for basis of the statement appears to be that Amelia was given the wings of an "Honorary Major," 381st Army Air Corps Reserve, in San Francisco in 1929.

A letter was also sent to former President Harry S. Truman by our helpful friend in Washington. His was not, however, the first letter sent to Mr. Truman asking about Amelia and Fred. CBS Vice-President Maurie Webster wrote in 1960 as did I in 1961 and 1962. None, to this writing, have been answered. Truman is known as a good correspondent, but it is conceivable that his integrity will not permit him to answer in the negative if he does know something. He may feel that any information concerning President Roosevelt's years as chief executive should not be revealed by his successor; therefore, the only answer is not to answer. Admiral Nimitz concurred in the logic of this analysis.

The Department of Commerce sleuth also had some constructive suggestions regarding the possible recovery of Amelia and Fred's remains by Henson, Burks and Griswold. He felt the officer in charge of an exhumation party might have been an M.D., and if the remains were taken to Washington, possibly they could have been stored in the classified vaults and files of the Armed Forces Institute of Pathology. Following this theory, we located a Dr. Griswold in Louisville, Kentucky, who had served on Saipan in 1944, but he denied any knowledge of Earhart and Noonan. At the Institute the initial reaction was that the subject did not "ring a bell" with the people presently there, but the possibility should not be eliminated.

In his eagerness to contact everyone who might help, our Mr. X tried a number of people I had already reached. One letter went to Admiral Nimitz, who relayed it to me for answer.

"I feel you're the best qualified to comment on this subject," said Nimitz, giving me another jot of encouragement.

Several evenings later I had dinner with Admiral and Mrs. Nimitz, and out of context of the conversation, he turned to me and said, "You do feel Miss Earhart and her navigator went down in the Marshalls, don't you, Fred?"

"Yes, sir, I do," I replied.

The admiral nodded his head and smiled. By then I knew him well enough not to press the subject. It was simply his way of telling me to go on.

During those 1964 months, the search for Billy Burks continued, but it was not until September that we got a real break. Matt Katz managed through a friend to obtain a photostat of

Burks' last California driver's license which had been issued August 21, 1961, by the San Pedro office of the California Motor Vehicles Department. The address listed was in Wilmington, California. Burks' previous license had been issued in Texas. The California license had expired on the birthdate, 1963. Matt immediately visited the address, but it was another dead end. Billy had moved, and no one knew of him or when or where he had gone.

In October I decided to take the last two weeks of my vacation and pound Los Angeles pavements. I started first with the Wilmington address, but Matt had been thorough. No one in the neighborhood could help. Next I tried the post offices and the possibility of a forwarding address; nothing there. The American Red Cross in Long Beach had no listing for a Burks, but the woman in charge suggested I try local credit bureaus. The San Pedro office came through.

A 1962 address in Long Beach, California, was a court of apartments, and again I was too late. The manager had been hired only a few weeks before and knew of no Burks. The former manager still lived in the court, but was not home.

"Perhaps," suggested the new manager, "you could get some information at the bar up the street. A lot of people from the court go there."

I showed Burks' driver's license picture to the bartender at the place.

"What do you want with him?"

"I'm with CBS. This fellow was a Marine in 1944 and we're looking for him in connection with a story," I answered.

I showed him my CBS identification, credit cards, and driver's license.

"Okay. That's enough," he said smiling. "Sure, I remember Billy. Hell of a nice guy. Quiet. Never caused any trouble. Just used to sit here occasionally and have a drink. I don't know what happened to him. He stopped coming in here a year or so ago."

"Do you have any idea where he might have gone?"

"Nope. But you might try a place over on Anaheim Boulevard. I think he used to stop in there occasionally."

He gave me the address; it was a smaller edition of the first bar.

"What's it to you?" was the reply when I showed Burks' photo there.

The same dialogue ensued, with the bartender finally admitting he had worked at the place only a month and didn't recognize the picture.

"There's a fellow who comes in here at night, though, who might know him," he said. "He's an old-timer and knows most of the neighborhood people."

That night the old-timer consumed a couple of beverages paid for by me, then volunteered that he had seen Billy Burks the week before at the California Unemployment Office in Long Beach.

It took two days for the manager of the office to get permission from his superiors to tell me that Mr. McGillicutty had been wrong; no one by the name of Burks was registered.

Somewhat despondent I went back to the apartment courts, and this time the former manager was home.

"Yes . . . yes, I do remember the name," she said. "It was a man and his wife. She was a nurse I think. Yes . . . they moved away a little more than a year ago."

"Did they leave a forwarding address, or do you know where they went?"

"No . . . I don't seem to recall."

I was walking out of the court when she reopened the door and called to me.

"Wait a minute. I do have an address . . . at least for his wife. I remember now. They went back to Texas."

The ex-landlady had what I can only describe as an amazing book in which she had kept the names and addresses of everyone who had ever corresponded with her. Mrs. Billy Burks had written her a letter; the address was in Dallas, Texas.

When Information revealed no phone listing, I turned the job over to the director of news at KRLD-TV, the CBS affiliated station in Dallas. In one day, he had good news. Billy Grant Burks and his wife were still living in Dallas. The happy report included Burks' address and telephone number.

During the ten months since Ross had called me with Henson's information, I had pondered the right way to approach Burks if he were found. I had decided the best way to avoid leading him was not to mention Amelia Earhart before he did.

I enjoyed a small ripple of satisfaction that evening when Billy acknowledged his name to the long-distance operator. Through a series of questions it developed he had been with the 2nd Marine Division on Saipan and after the war had lived in the Los Angeles area, then Texas, Los Angeles again, and finally he had moved back to Dallas in 1963. He was now planning to open a television repair shop and had great hopes for it.

"Mr. Burks, do you remember the names of any of the men you served with during the war?" I asked.

"God—let me see," he said. "It's been so long. Well, sure . . . there was Kinsell . . . and Yonke . . . and Ev Henson . . . and 'Candy' Bob Kirkpatrick—those names really take me back."

"Have you seen any of them since the war?"

"No . . . no, Mr. Goerner, I haven't. Why?"

"Do you recall having been asked to excavate for human remains while you were on Saipan?"

"Yes . . . how the hell do you know that? I'll never forget it. It was sometime just before or just after we finished fighting on Saipan?"

"Do you remember who was with you at the time?"

"Yeah . . . I guess I do. It was Ev Henson, I think, and some officer. Some guy in Intelligence."

"Can you remember the officer's name?"

"Not right off, I can't. He was a captain or a major or something."

"Could you describe for me exactly what happened?"

"Not exactly, I couldn't, Mr. Goerner, that was twenty years ago."

"Please try."

"Well . . . seems to me we went out near some old graveyard there on Saipan and this officer had Ev and me dig up some bodies. That's about all there was to it, except it was a lousy job. I don't remember if I volunteered or if I was picked to do it. If I volunteered, I was out of my mind."

"How deep did you dig?"

"Oh . . . it couldn't have been very deep. Three or four feet maybe. If it'd been any deeper than that, Ev and I would have given up. We were never known to impress people with our work."

"What did you find?"

"Oh . . . it was a couple of people. There was nothing but bones. You know that was the funny thing about it. They were just buried as they were; no box, no clothes like, nothing. It was real funny."

"What did the officer do with them?"

He put them in something, a box or a can or something like that."

"Then what?"

"He took 'em away. I don't know what he did with 'em. That was the last I saw of him. He just took them away."

"I'm going to speak three names, Mr. Burks, and I want you to tell me which one sounds the most like the officer's name. Carlson . . . Griswold . . . Butler."

"Griswold! That's it. Griswold. That was the guy's name. I'm sure of it. Captain Griswold or Major Griswold. He was always around the area buggin' the troops about their souvenirs, and he was questionin' the Japs and the gooks down at the compound."

"Did Griswold tell you anything about the remains you recovered?"

"Yeah . . . he said not to say anything about what we'd done."

"Did you?"

"Yeah . . . we told a few guys around. I haven't thought about it though since the war."

"Mr. Burks, this is important. Did Griswold say who the people were?"

"Yes, sir, he did. I know what you're trying to get me to say. Griswold said we dug up that flier, Amelia Earhart."

"Why do you think I was trying to get you to say that?"

"What the hell else would you be askin' me so many questions for? You wanted to know who it was we dug up."

"Did you believe what Griswold said?"

"Sure. Why not? He wasn't laughin' when he said it. Beside, come to think of it, he didn't say it to me."

"What do you mean?"

"He said it to Ev. Ev was always asking questions. It used to make some of the officers mad."

"Do you know that an investigation into Amelia Earhart's disappearance has been going on for a long time?"

"So what? As I said, I haven't thought about it. It wasn't my business anyway. When you're a PFC, you keep your mouth shut."

I arranged a conference call the following evening to get Henson and Burks together, and their entire ebullient conversation was recorded at KCBS. A lot of it, however, will never be aired. Their vocabulary was much too pungent.

Not too strangely, my "ripple of satisfaction" was gone. I realized deeply, perhaps for the first time, that AE and Fred had become a part of me. I never met them; yet they changed my life.

In a way, I did not want to know any more, but it was too late to stop. There were too many people committed.

22

In January 1965, Ross Game and I prepared a proposed release for Associated Press, detailing the major points of the investigation. The report, more than twelve feet in length in wire service form, was sent to Senator Kuchel in Washington, together with a request for a conference among ranking members of the Defense and State Departments and representatives of CBS, Scripps League Newspapers, and Associated Press. We also suggested that President Johnson be asked to attend. No one in Washington had seemed willing to accept responsibility for release of information about Earhart and Noonan, and we anticipated the possibility that it might require direct permission from the President. There was more than enough evidence to produce a national news story without the conference, but all concerned had long ago agreed every attempt should be made to cooperate with the government and no story should break until we had taken every possible step to determine how much of what we knew or suspected was correct.

A number of major questions remained. Did General Greene identify Amelia's plane on Saipan in 1944? His only statement to us throughout 1964 had been made by way of a Defense Department Public Information Officer, indicating that there was nothing he could tell us which would help. And what of the remains Henson and Burks had recovered? Where was Captain Griswold?

Ewing Hass, Senator Kuchel's Administrative Assistant, took the report to Secretary of Defense McNamara's office for appraisal and decision.

Several days later, a McNamara aide returned the material to Ewing, advising, "There is a great deal more to this Earhart matter than anyone suspected. There are some possible international repercussions and even some political overtones for this country. The Defense Department will have to have clearance from Department of State before any classified information can be released or we can officially comment."

Ewing immediately took the summary to the State Department where it was agreed the Public Affairs and Far Eastern Affairs Sections would study it and reply within a few days. The days stretched to weeks, then a month. Early in February 1965, I telephoned Jonathan Moore, Special Assistant to the Assistant Secretary for Far Eastern Affairs, and asked about the delay.

"Your report is requiring a lot of study," said Moore, "but I think you're going to get the clearance you need. I don't think Japan's reaction will really affect anything. That's just my opinion, though, there are still two or three people looking at your findings. I'm sorry I can't give you a definite time when you'll get your answer, but it shouldn't be too long."

February 19, 1965, Senator Kuchel received a five-page letter from James L. Greenfield, Public Affairs, U. S. State Department.

With disappointment we read, "The Department of State is in no position to give official verification. It was the Navy Department which conducted the search for Miss Earhart, and any detailed account of that search and subsequent investigations would have to come from the Navy."

Of the several hundred points made in our presentation, Greenfield took exception to five, and each rebuttal was made to absolve the State Department from any responsibility where Amelia and Fred were concerned. No explanation was given of the long-classified State Department file, and there was no comment on any of the other evidence presented. Greenfield's only references to what we had found in the file were, "The alleged 1949 letter from Miss Earhart's mother to the Department, expressing the view her daughter had been on a government mission in 1937, has not been located, and there is no trace in the finding aids for our files that such a letter ever was received."— and—"There is no evidence of a Japanese refusal for American ships to search the Marshall Islands."

Strange indeed that two statements copied from State Department classified files a year before had disappeared.

"What do you make of it?" I asked Ewing Hass by phone.

"As far as I can see the State Department is getting out from under," he replied. "I think we're free now to push as hard as we want at the Defense Department. I'll see that Tom [Kuchel] gets the picture on this thing, and then we'll insist on the conference you want."

Even with the Senator's help, it was not easy. The stalling continued until March 29 when Ewing notified us that General Greene had finally consented to a meeting on April 6.

"If you can come back here for a couple of weeks," he said, "I'm fairly sure we can get you in to talk with some other important people, too."

The following day I received a call from Admiral Nimitz.

"Now that you're going to Washington, Fred," he said, "I want to tell you Earhart and her navigator did go down in the Marshalls and were picked up by the Japanese."

It was a rewarding moment. After five years of effort, the former commander of U. S. Naval Forces in the Pacific was telling me it had not been wasted.

"Admiral, how did you know I was going to Washington?"

"You forget," he chuckled, "I'm still on active duty as an adviser to the Secretary of Defense."

"Where can I get the evidence we need to sew this thing up?" I said.

"Well, there is one person in particular I want you to call. That's General Harry Schmidt who lives now in San Diego. He commanded a part of the Marine Forces during the invasion of Kwajalein in 1944. I think he can tell you what you want to know."

Admiral Nimitz even supplied Schmidt's home address and telephone number.

"And do something else for me," he continued. "When you get to Washington, drop in to see Admiral Eller, Chief of the Department of Naval History, and Admiral Bernard Austin of the Interamerican Defense Board. I'll write them letters that you're coming. Tell them everything you know. I want them to be aware of what's going on."

"Can I quote you on this, Admiral Nimitz?"

"When the time comes for you to do your story, I'll be happy to have you quote me. Good luck."

Immediately I called General Schmidt in San Diego, and after a two-minute introduction, said, "Admiral Nimitz told me to call you. He said you might be able to clear up the Earhart mystery for us."

There was a long pause, then Schmidt replied, "I have the highest regard for Admiral Nimitz, but I thought by now just about everybody knew what happened to Amelia Earhart."

"No, sir, we don't have all the facts. Won't you tell me what you know?"

"Well, if Admiral Nimitz thinks you ought to know, maybe I should," said Schmidt. "Did you say you have an appointment with General Greene on April 6?"

"Yes, sir, that's right."

"Well, let's leave our talk until then. I'm not a well man, but I'll go back to Washington for this. I don't want to miss that discussion."

At last it seemed to be breaking. I headed for Washington the last week of March, with Ross Game and Matt Katz scheduled to join me the following week for the meeting with Greene. Senator Kuchel and Ewing Hass greeted me warmly and appeared optimistic, even excited.

"I think you've got it, my boy," said Ewing. "You have too much now for anyone to dispute it."

Admiral Nimitz had written the letters as promised, and Admirals Eller and Austin rolled out the blue and gold carpet.

Eller listened with deep interest as I outlined the investigation, then said, "That's an incredible story, and a lot of it figures. I'll tell you frankly, though, the Office of Naval History doesn't have a thing to my knowledge that would help you. Contrary to the ideas of some people, we do not have access to classified information. We deal only in what has been cleared. Go ahead, though. Swing as hard as you can. You have Chester Nimitz on your side; you couldn't have a finer, more respected, and for my money, more influential man."

Admiral Austin, who had been Nimitz's Chief Aide during the late stages of World War II, was as interested as Eller, but no more helpful.

"I heard some scuttlebutt about some things of Earhart's being found during the war," he said, "but I never saw tangible evidence. Most of the Japanese intelligence material picked up on the Pacific islands was sent to Joint Intelligence at Pearl Harbor for evaluation. What would have happened to the things you're seeking, I don't know. They could have been siphoned off by high-level order, but I couldn't even begin to guess where they would be today."

Back I went to the Office of Naval Information in the Pentagon and our old friend, Captain James Dowdell.

"I'd like another look at the Navy's classified Earhart file," I said.

"I've got to hand it to you, Goerner," he said, "you never give up. All right, you can see it this afternoon."

At first, the report appeared the same. There was the Navy's 1960 investigation with the transcripts of native testimony and the conclusion, "The questioning indicated that subject may have been brought to Saipan by Japanese military." The same signatures of H. G. Hirshfield, Intelligence Officer, and Joseph M. Patton, Special Agent, were affixed. Further down in the file, however, some interesting bits of information had been added since our first perusal the year before. One notation was, "Alvan Fitak, former Marine Lieutenant, gathered information about Amelia Earhart in the Marshall Islands." Another read, "6 October, 1949, (A) OP-323M5 File, #P-7229, Lt. Colonel William C. Humbred, USMC, OP-331, has information about Earhart in Marshall Islands." Nothing more about the two Marines or their testimony appeared in the file.

Near the bottom of the thick folder another piece of evidence had been added. A terse, U. S. Navy message with no heading stated, "At 1030, the morning of the disappearance, Nauru Island radio station picked up Earhart on 6210 kcs saying, 'Land in sight ahead.'"

I blinked my eyes. Nearly two hours after Amelia had supposedly run out of gas, a radio station in the British-controlled Gilbert Islands had received her voice. Why was that message not included as part of the 1937 search? What had she sighted? Was that the extent of the message?

At 10:00 A.M., April 6, Ross, Matt, and I along with Ewing Hass shook hands with the Commandant of the Marine Corps, Wallace M. Greene, Jr. Two brigadier generals and a colonel stayed to listen to our discussion. Neither general was named Schmidt.

Greene, a slim, dapper man of medium height, was perfunctory in his greeting. He seated us on a couch, and arranged himself in a chair with a note pad and pencil in his hands.

"You're here about Amelia Earhart," he opened, leaving the next line to me.

"Yes, sir," I replied. "What do you know about her?"

"Nothing very much," he said quickly. "I want to make it quite clear at the beginning of this meeting that I had nothing to do with identifying either her or her plane on Saipan as has been alleged. I have nothing to offer that could help you."

"Why, sir," I asked, "was it so difficult then for us to get you to state that last year when we were in Washington?"

"I passed that information along in an official memo to the Defense Department," he said.

Ross and I glanced at each other.

"We never received any word of that memo," I said.

"A copy of it can be made available, I'm sure," said Greene. "You men don't seem to believe me. I didn't have a thing to do with Amelia Earhart. I'm not used to protesting my innocence."

The level of the general's voice rose considerably during his last two sentences. It was evident he did not intend to be pushed further.

"We of course accept your word, General," I said. "You can understand, I think, why we wanted to hear from you personally."

Greene nodded and tension decreased.

"I have a portable tape recorder with me," I continued, "and with your permission, I'd like to play portions of a conversation between two former Marines who have stated they recovered the remains of Earhart and Noonan on Saipan in 1944."

Greene listened closely as the voices of Henson and Burks came from the recorder. At several points, he made notes on the pad, then leaned back and stared at the wall behind us.

When the tapes were finished, I produced photo-copies of the letters from Jackson and Maghokian regarding their findings in the Marshalls. Then I detailed in about twenty minutes the scope of the investigation and what we had learned.

"What do you want me to do?" asked Greene when I had finished.

"Help us find Captain Griswold," I said, "and give us an official Marine Corps position on all this."

The general stood up and walked around his desk.

"I'll try," he said. "I don't quarrel with your theory that Earhart and her navigator went down in the Marshalls, but I'm in no position at this point to give you any confirmation of it."

"Why isn't General Schmidt here today?" I asked.

"General Schmidt?"

"Yes. I talked with him last week in San Diego, and he said he was coming to Washington for this conference."

Greene sent the colonel out of the office to check on whether General Schmidt was expected. A minute later he came back with the statement, "General Schmidt is not on the list of expected guests."

That ended our long-awaited conference with Greene. Apparently we were no closer to an admission of involvement on the part of the Marine Corps than when we entered his office.

"I don't get it," said Ewing Hass. "The general tells you he doesn't quarrel with your idea of Amelia and Fred landing in the Marshalls, but hasn't yet given you much help. Well, don't worry. We're not done yet."

Back at the hotel I called Admiral Nimitz and reported.

"It's not too strange," he said from California. "Remember General Greene carries a lot of responsibility. There must be something the Marine Corps doesn't want known about this. Why don't you call General Schmidt again? If he won't talk, have him call me and I'll try to persuade him to give you the information."

General Schmidt answered the phone, but was not explicit about why he had not come to Washington as planned.

"I just decided this whole thing is best left as it is," he said. "I don't doubt your word about Admiral Nimitz, but I haven't anything to say."

At that moment, a woman's voice came on the line.

"I think he ought to tell you."

"Who's that?" I asked.

"This is Mrs. Schmidt," the voice answered. "I think it's time this whole thing was brought out into the open."

General Schmidt paused for a moment, then said, "Mrs. Schmidt has been after me to tell you."

"Well, won't you, sir?" I said. "These people deserve some justice after all these years."

"All right. I'll talk with you," he said, "but not over the telephone. Can you come here to San Diego to see me?"

"You bet I will," I said. "How about a couple of days? Say Saturday?"

"All right. We'll sit down and talk about it then," Schmidt concluded.

Between then and the Saturday departure, we covered the bases. At Central Intelligence Agency headquarters in Virginia, Paul Chretian showed me a two-inch background the Agency had compiled on me, thanked me for withholding the NTTU-Saipan story until the CIA pulled out, sympathized with our quest for an Earhart solution, and closed the door. Secretary McNamara "helloed" and "goodbyed," and had nothing to contribute. President Johnson was interested, asked questions, and indicated he would like to see a solution, but the "President's office can ask but not order individuals to release classified or security information. Keep me informed."

A chance conversation with Colonel Justin Chambers, Marine Corps Congressional Medal of Honor holder, did open a small gate. Chambers had served with the 4th Marine Division both at Kwajalein and Saipan.

"While I was on Saipan," he said, "I did hear that a grave containing two American fliers, a man and woman, had been found. The report went to higher echelon."

The day before we left for San Diego, General Greene's office found a Captain Griswold, who had been in Intelligence with the 18th Marines, 2nd Division, on Saipan in 1944. His full name was Tracy Griswold. He owned a construction company in Erie, Pennsylvania, having retired from the Marine Corps Reserve as a major in 1963.

During the six years of seeking answers to the enigma of Amelia and Fred, I have spoken to several thousand persons by telephone. Almost without exception it has taken several minutes to identify myself and properly introduce the subject before a discussion could begin. Such was not the case with Major Griswold. When I gave my name, he knew who I was.

"Yes . . . yes, I went ashore at Red Beach One at Saipan," he said, "and we did quite a bit of work south of what was Garapan City. You know, checking souvenirs and Jap houses, picking up Intelligence material. I just don't recall, though, having dug up any remains. Who did you say the men were who identified me?"

I told him.

"I don't remember them. I just can't remember anything like that. Are you sure they were talking about me?"

"Mr. Griswold, did your family have anything to do with the Griswold Stove Manufacturing Company?" I asked.

There was a long pause, then he said in an awed tone, "Yes . . . as a matter of fact they did. How did you know that?"

"I didn't," I replied. "Henson and Burks said they remembered you saying it."

"Well, I'll be darned," said Griswold. "Say . . . Mr. Goerner . . . could you possibly come over to Erie so I could talk to you in person?"

"I'm sorry, but I have to leave for San Diego tomorrow. If anything clicks in your mind, give me a call at KCBS in San Francisco."

That evening, Griswold called me at the Mayflower Hotel.

"I've thought a bit already," he said. "I'm starting to put a few things together, but I just can't recall having opened any graves."

"That would be a hard thing to forget," I said. "Especially if you recovered the remains of people as famous as Earhart and Noonan."

"Yes. That's right. Are you sure you can't stop here in Erie?"

"Not this trip," I replied. "Why don't you do this for me, though. Send me a picture of yourself taken in 1944 and another as you are today. I'll show the photos to Burks and Henson, and maybe we can determine that way if you were the officer they remember."

"All right," said Griswold. "I'll sure do that."

(I have called Griswold six times since April 1965 and to this writing, February 1966, no photographs have been received.)

The next day, Ross, Matt, and I flew to San Diego and an odd confrontation with General and Mrs. Schmidt.

"I'm sorry, gentlemen," said the general, "but there's no way I can help you."

"But we flew here from Washington, D.C., on the promise you would talk to us about Earhart," I said. "What's changed your mind?"

"There are many people who can tell you things about Earhart," replied Schmidt, "but I'm not one of them."

"Then why have us fly out here?"

"Well, you television and radio people have a lot of money. It won't hurt you any."

I could not believe what I was hearing, and when I looked at Mrs. Schmidt for assistance, she shrugged her shoulders in a helpless way.

"May I borrow your phone?" I asked.

I placed a call to Admiral Nimitz, briefly explained the situation to him, then asked General Schmidt to talk to his old comrade. As they talked, the general's respect and love for Nimitz was clear to all of us.

But: "I can't, Chester," he said. "I can't help them."

When Schmidt handed the phone back to me, Admiral Nimitz said, "I'm sorry, Fred, I tried. Come over to the house when you get back to San Francisco, and we'll talk about it."

Several days later Admiral Nimitz said to me, "I can't understand it. The Marine Corps is covering up for something or someone. Perhaps the State Department blocked it. The door is being closed on you for a reason. Keep trying. Don't give up."

Senator Kuchel and Ewing Hass in Washington were not ready to concede anything, either.

"Write a letter to General Greene, Fred," said Ewing, "and clearly ask the questions you want answered. Send us carbon copies and we'll see that something is done. We have one big recourse left. If satisfaction isn't forthcoming, we'll refer the whole business to Congressman John Moss and his Committee which investigates the illegal withholding of information by the government. I think John would love to get his hands on this one."

On April 16, 1965, I addressed the following questions to General Greene:

1. Does the Intelligence Division of the Corps possess any classified or unclassified files regarding Amelia Earhart and Frederick Noonan?

2. Did the Corps possess any such files or information at any time?

3. If so, to what department of government or individual in or out of government were the files or information given?

4. Does the U. S. Marine Corps officially support the theory that Earhart and Noonan landed in the Marshall Islands and were captured by the Japanese?

5. Does the U. S. Marine Corps officially support the theory that Earhart and Noonan were later taken to Saipan Island by the Japanese?

6. Does the U. S. Marine Corps officially support the statements made in the enclosed photo-copied letter from Mr. W. B. Jackson of Pampa, Texas?

7. Does the U. S. Marine Corps officially support the statements made in the enclosed photo-copied letter from Captain Victor Maghokian?

8. Does the U. S. Marine Corps officially confirm or deny that three Marines of the 2nd Division disinterred the remains of two individuals from a grave outside a native cemetery on the Island of Saipan sometime during the latter part of 1944?

9. If the Corps confirms this happening, what were the circumstances of the recovery? Were the remains identified? What was the disposition of the remains?

10. Does the U. S. Marine Corps officially support or deny the statement of Colonel Justin Chambers, USMC, Ret., indicating: "A report was made regarding a gravesite on Saipan which contained 'the remains of two Americans, a man and woman, fliers.' I saw this report, and it was sent along to higher echelon."

11. If the Corps confirms this report, what was the final disposition of the report and where is it now?

12. What is the official position and attitude of the U. S. Marine Corps toward the five-year investigation of the Earhart matter by CBS, the Scripps League Newspapers, and the Associated Press and the findings of that investigation?

May turned to June, June to July before General Greene answered, after much prodding from Senator Kuchel's office. Four days before the answer came, Paul Mantz died in the open cockpit of a weirdly constructed plane which he was flying across the Arizona desert. In a stunt scene for the motion picture, *The Flight of the Phoenix*, his craft struck a sand dune, cartwheeled, and ground him to death beneath its weight. Another link with Amelia was gone.

On July 12, 1965, General Greene's answer finally arrived. Here's how he answered the questions:

1. The Intelligence Division of the Marine Corps does not possess any classified or unclassified files regarding Amelia Earhart and Frederick Noonan. In this connection, it should be recalled that the flow of intelligence information at the time of the Marianas (sic) Campaign was from Marine Divisions through Corps and to the Joint Intelligence Center, Pacific Ocean Area (JICPOA).

2. & 3. The Marine Corps has not possessed any such files or information at any time as far as can be determined.

Questions 4 through 12—the Marine Corps takes no position on these questions.

No position? How could the Marine Corps *not* have a position?

In the months that followed, I debated whether to ask Senator Kuchel to go ahead and arrange the investigation, or to continue to wait—and to believe that the answers would come, eventually.

My decision was made in January 1966. Several weeks before he suffered the stroke which led to his death, Admiral Nimitz said to me, "I hope you will go ahead with your book, Fred. It could bring the justice that is deserved."

23

Now, in closing this account, let me make a full summary—a reconstruction—of what probably happened on that tragic last leg of the around-the-world flight of Amelia Earhart and Fred Noonan. From all the evidence that has come to my attention, and is presented in this book, I believe unqualifiedly that, in the essentials, this is the way it had to have been.

When Amelia and Fred took off from Lae, New Guinea, they did not fly directly toward Howland Island. They headed north to Truk in the Central Carolines. Their mission was unofficial but vital to the U.S. military: observe the number of airfields and extent of Japan's fleet-servicing facilities in the Truk complex, and prove the advantages of fields for land planes on U.S. held islands on the equator.

Flight strategy had been carefully developed during the around-the-world trip. A point-to-point speed of not more than 150 miles per hour had been maintained throughout. What Amelia and Fred had not revealed to anyone was that the Electra was powered by Wasp Senior engines capable of a 200-mile-per-hour cruising speed at 11,000 feet, and a top speed in excess of 220 miles per hour.

Oddly, the detour over Truk, though a longer route, bene-
fitted the flight plan. Instead of bucking the trade winds on the
Lae-Howland route, the winds would help them on the flight to
Truk and then supposedly would be light across their course
from Truk to Howland, leaving them a four- to six-hour reserve of
gasoline should Howland prove a difficult landfall.

Because the Electra was heavily loaded, the first hours of
flight were slow, but by late afternoon, when the mountains of
Truk broke over the horizon, the plane was light enough to
climb to its best altitude for speed. Amelia headed high across
Truk lagoon, noting the airfields on Etten and Moen Islands,
and the vast Japanese repair docks along the shores of Dublon.
Since a foreign aircraft had never been seen over Truk, the
Japanese were caught completely by surprise. Amelia and Fred
constantly scanned the skies about them, but no Japanese planes
were in the air. With her altitude and speed, Amelia was confident the Electra could outrun any pursuit.

With the first part of the mission accomplished, Fred gave
Amelia the heading for Howland. But now they were flying into
weather problems with which Americans were completely un-
familiar in 1937. Conditions varied from hour to hour, sometimes
minute to minute. Huge towering white clouds obscured the sea.
For periods the winds would be calm, then a series of tropical
fronts churned the air into nearly continuous squalls and
thunderstorms. Fred struggled to get star sights, but the clouds
and overcast blocked every attempt. Amelia fought to keep the
Electra level so the caging mechanism could control the tumbling
gyro compass. At last she found herself flying dead reckoning
by magnetic compass. The plane was still too far away to receive
homing signals from the *Itasca,* or for the newly developed U. S.
Navy direction finder on Howland Island to get a bearing from
her signals. Beside that, if she asked for bearings too soon, the
mission might be given away. It would be difficult to explain
why she was flying into Howland from the northwest instead of
southwest, and there was also the danger the Japanese might
get a fix on her signals. She would keep her radio transmissions
brief until the Electra came into logical range of Howland.

The tropical storms increased as the night wore on, and
neither Amelia nor Fred could gauge the amount of head wind

or drift. Amelia radioed no position report because she did not have one, and even if she had produced one, she could not have sent it.

At 5:15 A.M. Fred figured they were within two hundred miles of Howland, and it would be safe to ask for a bearing. Amelia radioed the information to *Itasca* and asked for a position on 3105 kcs from the special Navy DF set up on the island. Thirty minutes later, she repeated the request and indicated that they were within a hundred miles of Howland.

Actually, Noonan had not been able to calculate the head winds the Electra had encountered, and the plane was still more than four hundred miles from its destination.

By 7:00 A.M. Amelia was sure they had overshot Howland in the darkness, and she began to circle in the big Lockheed, hoping to pick up *Itasca*'s signals on her own direction finder loop. At 8:00 A.M. she received *Itasca* briefly but could not get a minimum. Then about 8:40 Fred succeeded in shooting a sun-line—157–337—and in desperation, Amelia radioed that to *Itasca*. They had no reference point with which to place themselves along the sunline, but at least it was something.

At that point she switched her radio from the nighttime 3105 frequency to daylight 6210, and decided to use an already calculated emergency plan. Gas was low, two hours remaining at most, and there was no time to waste. In her discussions with Eugene Vidal and William Miller, she had said, "If we don't pick up Howland, I'll try to fly back into the Gilberts and find a nice stretch of beach. If I have to do that, let's hope I choose an island that has fresh water."

Amelia turned the Electra north and west, still thinking she had overflown Howland. Actually, she was heading away from their destination. At approximately 10:30 A.M., when hope was near extinction, she sighted a small island, part of a larger atoll. She made one low pass, and saw that the water was shallow between reef and beach. It would be better to try a wheels-up landing on the water inside the reef than to risk a major crash on the narrow inclined beach.

Fred fastened himself securely in the cabin as Amelia brought the plane around once again and gradually lowered the flaps to full. The glide was long and smooth. Lower and lower the

Electra dropped until it skimmed the surface of the lagoon. Amelia held it up as long as she could, then the wings lost their lift and tons of aircraft dumped into the water, sending spouts geysering a hundred feet on both sides of the fuselage.

The around-the-world flight had ended, not in the Gilbert Islands, but at Mili Atoll in the southeastern Marshalls, territory mandated to Japan.

Amelia was uninjured, but Fred had struck his head against some metal in the cabin and was unconscious. Amelia pulled him clear, wiped the blood from a deep cut on his forehead, and bound the wound with bandages from the plane's emergency kit. A few minutes later, Fred regained consciousness, but had trouble standing. AE made him as comfortable as possible, and began to estimate their situation. If the emergency radio gear and battery in the cockpit worked, they should have nothing to worry about.

Amelia waded ashore to confront a dozen natives, the only inhabitants of the island, but none of them spoke English. By sign language, she managed to communicate that they should carry Noonan ashore. Then she waded back to the plane, climbed into the cockpit, and began to send S.O.S. messages. She still did not know where she was, but she had no doubts of rescue.

Around the world the story of the disappearance was on every newspaper's front page. The consternation at high levels of government in Washington was considerable, when word circulated quietly that Amelia had tried to reach Howland by way of Truk. The Japanese now had little doubt who had violated their top-secret air space.

For the next twelve days, the race was on to see which nation could find Amelia and Fred first. The United States had no chance really, because it could not enter the Marshalls. When Noonan recovered enough to shoot a star sight, he and Amelia must have known what faced them.

On or about July 13, 1937, a Japanese fishing boat moved into the island, and took AE and Fred aboard, transferring them later to either the Japanese seaplane tender *Kamoi* or survey ship *Koshu*. They were taken first to Jaluit, then Kwajalein, and finally to Japan's military headquarters in the Pacific, Saipan.

The kind of questioning and hardships they endured can be imagined. Death may have been a release they both desired. The most depressing aspect of the ordeal for both of them must have been the fact that their country could do nothing to rescue or ransom them.

Now, twenty-nine years later, what is going to be done to clear the record completely, to remove all the aspects of doubt and suspicion and bewilderment from a heroic story that the public has a right to know in full, so that two human beings may be properly honored for their courage and their contribution?

For one thing, this manuscript will be given to Senator Thomas H. Kuchel of California with the request that every effort be made to produce final, unqualified answers, if need be, by Congressional investigation.

Because of people who dare to reach out, like Earhart and Noonan, we now orbit men around our earth and turn our eyes to the stars and what lies beyond. Amelia Earhart and Fred Noonan chose their destinies, not waiting as most of us do for our decisions to be made for us. Amelia and Fred may have listened too closely to the commands of their own egos—sought too desperately the immortality of the hero image—but was that not better than to have been born deaf?

INDEX

Ackerman, Ken, 151–53
Ada, Juan, 237
Adams, Colonel, 281–82, 289
Akiyama, Josephine Blanco, 1–6, 9, 42–43, 45, 48, 59, 284
Akiyama, Maximo, 2–3, 9–10, 39–42, 46, 48, 51–60, 61, 93
Alexander, R. W., 85–86, 177
Andrews, Roy Chapman, 20
Arnold, Father. See Bendowske, Arnold
Arriola, Gregorio, 235
Ashworth, Robert L., 191
Attao, José, 235
Austin, Bernard, 306–7

Baker, Lieutenant Commander, 76
Ball, Raymond C., 296
Barrat, Genevieve, 287
Basa, José, 51
Bauer, Bill, 166

Beebe, William, 20
Bellarts, Leo G., 199ff
Benchley, Robert, 21
Bendowske, Arnold, 48, 54, 80, 97, 99, 151, 153, 222–23, 231–32, 243, 246, 267ff
Benny, Jack, 170
Berkeley, Randolph, 282, 288–89
Berle, Milton, 36
Bingham, Sidney V., 29
Bizarri, Lola, 137
Black, Richard Blackburn, 194–95, 204–6, 210–11, 214, 288
Blanco, Mrs. Antonio, 284
Bogan, Eugene, 164, 166, 221, 258, 260, 279
Briand, Paul L., Jr., 64–65
Bridwell, Paul W., 40–43, 44, 47–48, 50, 57–59, 94ff, 105–6, 110–11, 113, 125, 149, 154, 156–57, 183, 186, 222, 279, 284

Brittain, M. L., 79
Bromley, J. R., 176
Broun, Heywood, 21
Brown, Pat, 2
Bufkins, R. L., 87
Burks, Billy, 272–73, 276–77, 292, 293, 297ff, 311–12
Burks, Mrs. Billy, 299
Burns, Eugene, 166
Byrd, Richard E., 17, 20, 288

Cabrera, Joaquina M., 236, 239–40
Calvo, Oscar, 45–46, 47–48, 51, 80–81, 93, 97
Camacho, Eddie, 222ff
Camacho, Gregorio, 49
Camacho, José Rios, 51
Campbell, Robert Leslie, 196
Capelli, Bonjo, 188
Capelli, Edward, 188
Cartee, Horace L., 168
Chambers, Justin, 310, 314
Chapman, Frederick, 172–73
Chiang Kai-shek, 139–40, 142
Chretian, Paul, 310
Clay, Lucius D., 296
Clyde, Paul Hibbert, 90
Coleman, Peter, 257ff
Connally, John, 133–34, 136
Conover, Sylvan, 45, 48, 52, 54, 80, 97ff, 105, 108, 109, 111–13, 124–25, 151, 153–54, 183, 222ff, 243, 246, 250, 267ff
Cooper, Lieutenant, 76
Cooper, Merion, 20
Copeland, John, 156
Cosigny, Jean Marie, 37
Coye, John S., Jr., 125, 148, 150–51, 184, 216, 219–21, 222, 225
Cronkite, Walter, 154, 164

Damrosch, Walter, 21
Daniel, Bill, 222
Day, John F., 9, 188–89
Day, Linn, 2
Dehrig, Marge, 202
Devine, Thomas E., 69–70, 82, 87, 95, 103, 105, 107ff, 155, 186–87, 214, 217, 224, 231–32, 267–68, 270, 275, 279ff
Dewey, Thomas E., 291
Díaz, Antonio, 51, 234, 237
Díaz, Concepcion "Chande," 234–35
DiMaggio, Joe, 36
Dimity, E. H., 266–67
Dinger, Robert, 8–9, 64–65, 67, 222, 235
Distad, Marshall, 257
Dougall, Richardson, 286
Dowdell, James S., 93–94, 96, 282ff, 307
Draper, George, 157–59
Drewry, Elizabeth B., 295–96
Duenas, Father, 45
Dundes, Jules, 82, 85–87, 128–30, 144, 148–49, 154, 159, 177ff, 214, 220
Dunham, Ken, 65
Du Pont, Ethel. See Roosevelt, Mrs. Franklin Delano, Jr.
Durbin, Deanna, 169

Earhart, Amy Otis (Mrs. Edwin Stanton, mother of Amelia), 12–13, 16, 135–36, 262
Earhart, Edwin Stanton (father of Amelia), 12–14, 16, 21, 23
Earhart, Muriel Grace. See Morrissey, Mrs. Albert
Echols, E. D., 145
Eisenhower, Dwight David, 67, 145, 296

Elieu (native of Majuro), 164ff, 257–60, 262, 279
Elliott, Edward C., 24–25
Ellis, Earl Hancock "Pete," 88–89, 247–48, 252, 259
Engle, Clair, 86–87
English, Franklin, 85

Faussig, J. K., 285
Findley, Gordon, 221–22, 252–53
Finerman, Wilmore B., 169
Fitak, Alvan, 307
Furman, F. O., 34

Gallup, George, 137
Galten, Bill, 159–60, 199, 200, 202–3
Galvan, Francisco, 52, 80–82, 98, 112–13, 223ff, 250–51
Galvan, Vicente, 47–48, 232–33ff
Game, Ross, 214–16, 219–20, 222ff, 267, 271ff, 280, 293, 303, 306, 308
George, Betty Elizabeth, 171, 184
George, Harry S., 171
George, Lloyd, 17
Gervais, Joseph, 8–9, 64–65, 67, 222, 235
Gibbon, William, 247–48
Goding, M. W., 216–17, 220, 221, 225, 240ff, 267, 269
Gordon, Louis "Slim," 18
Gorrell, Max, 256
Gorski, John, 125, 151
Graham, Robert, 254–56
Greene, Wallace M., Jr., 270, 273, 279–80, 281–82, 289, 303, 305–6, 308
Greenfield, James L., 304–5
Gregorio, Brother, 45, 102–3
Grimsby, Roger, 180–81

Griswold, Tracy, 272ff, 289, 297, 301, 304, 309, 311–12
Grow, H. B. (Jasper), 164
Gruening, Ernest, 194–95, 211
Guest, Frederick, 17
Guest, Mrs. Frederick, 17, 18

Hagerty, James, 67
Halverson, Robert, 253–54
Hampton, Ruth, 205, 211
Harvey, Warren W., 79–80
Hass, Ewing, 282, 304, 305–6, 309, 313
Hasse, Warren, 277–78
Hatch, Norman, 281–82
Hatlen, Ted, 131
Haviland, Margaret, 37
Hayes, Arthur Hull, 128, 144
Hearst, William Randolph, 36
Hecht, Ben, 20, 21
Heggenberger, Albert, 17
Heine, Dwight, 260–62
Henson, Everett, Jr., 271ff, 293–94, 297, 300ff, 311–12
Hermle, L. D., 252
Herre, W. C., 90
Hewitt, Don, 154
Higashi, Roy, 172–73, 265–66
Hill, H. W., 257
Hilliard, Harriet, 36
Hippe, Leroy, 42, 58, 83–84, 94, 106, 184, 222
Hirshfield, H. G., 236, 307
Hoffschneider, Albert, 246–47
Hoffschneider, Daisy, 246–47, 250
Hoover, Herbert Clark, 20
Hoover, Mrs. Herbert Clark, 23
Hoppin, Jessie R., 259
Hoshina, Zenshiro, 67
Hubbell, Carl, 36
Hull, Cordell, 35
Humbred, William C., 307

Ireland, Mrs. Harry B., 33, 130–34, 148, 155, 158, 179, 269

Jackson, W. B., 277–78
Johnson, Martin, 20
Jons, Remedios, 269

Kamakaiwi, James, 205
Kamiyama, Albert, 238
Kanna, Ralph R., 172, 173–74, 219, 265–66
Katz, Matthew, 267, 269, 280, 293ff, 306
Kelleher, J. F., 188
Kennedy, John Fitzgerald, 145, 216, 243
Kenner, Lieutenant Commander, 76
Kent, Rockwell, 20
Kilts, Floyd, 171
Kingsford-Smith, Charles, 17
Kinkead, Robin, 151, 155
Kinley, Robert, 185, 186–87, 232, 273
Kinner, William, 15
Kirkpatrick, "Candy" Bob, 300
Kirmer, Bob, 183
Koop, Ted, 86–87, 128, 151
Kotobuki, Nakajima, 67
Kuchel, Thomas H., 86–87, 280, 282, 289, 303ff, 319

Lee, Walter, 203–4
Lewis, John L., 36
Lindbergh, Charles A., 17, 18, 19, 20
Livingstone, Mary, 170
Lohman, Joseph, 130
Love, Lieutenant, 206

Maatta, Vivian, 191–92, 198
MacBain, Merle, 183–84, 185, 203
McCone, John, 267

McCown, Theodore D., 130, 151, 155–56, 160–61, 167ff, 183
McElhatton, Dave, 1
McIntyre, Marvin H., 195
MacMurray, Fred, 37
Maghokian, Victor, 278–79
Magikura, Shunzaburo, 252
Magofna, Gregorio, 54–56, 98–99
Mahan, John, 163–66
Maitland, Lester, 17
Manning, Harry, 27–30
Mantz, Paul, 5–8, 24, 27–30, 57, 62–66, 132, 160, 202, 210–11, 314
Marshall, Herbert, 37
Martinelli, Mary B. See Ireland, Mrs. Harry B.
Marx Brothers, 36
Matsumoto, José Y., 2, 42, 44–45, 48, 51, 59, 97, 107, 238
Miller, Rudolph, 278
Miller, William Thomas, 191ff, 287, 295, 317
Mitchell, Billy, 89
Mitscher, Marc A., 252–53
Montijo, John, 14
Moore, Jonathan, 304
Morgenthau, Henry, Jr., 196
Moritsugu, Richard, 172–73, 219, 265
Morrissey, Albert, 134–36, 158
Morrissey, Mrs. Albert (sister of Amelia Earhart), 12, 16, 127, 134ff, 147, 153–54, 158, 179–80
Moss, John, 313
Mozley, Don, 66, 155–56
Muller, H. J., 13
Muller, Joe, 163
Muller, Rudolph, 163
Murfin, Admiral, 79
Murphy, Robert Ashman, 20

Naito, Sunao, 255

Nimitz, Chester W., 219, 242, 252, 254, 263–64, 265, 297, 305ff

Nimitz, Mrs. Chester W., 265

Noonan, Frederick J., 1, 4–10, 27–37, 53ff, 61ff, 70–72, 77–78, 80, 81, 91ff, 108, 110, 112–13, 120, 128ff, 152ff, 168ff, 230ff, 262ff, 303ff, 309ff

Noonan, Mrs. Frederick J. See Ireland, Mrs. Harry B.

Noyes, Leigh, 74

Nuno, William, 172–73, 265–66

Oakes, Paul, 156

Ohashi, Maria, 51

Otis, Amy. See Earhart, Mrs. Edwin Stanton

Paderewski, Ignace Jan, 20–21

Palamo, Tony, 80–81, 98, 230, 250, 251

Paley, William, 9

Pangelinan, Francisco, 235

Pangelinan, José, 99, 101–2

Pangelinan, Juan, 235, 268

Parkyakarkus, 36

Patton, Joseph M., 236, 307

Peck, Gregory, 5

Penaluna, William, 2, 3, 10

Penner, Joe, 36

Phillips, F. Clifford, 168, 169, 269

Picardi, Mike, 106

Pierce, Mark A., 91

Pierpont, Robert, 216, 281

Pillsbury, John, 148, 263–64, 265, 280

Powers, Francis Gary, 266

Putnam, David Binney, 20

Putnam, Dorothy Binney, 19

Putnam, George Palmer, II, 17–24, 31–32, 37, 205, 210–11

Putnam, Palmer C., 22

Quintanilla, José, 222ff

Rapkiewicz, Francis, 170

Read, Lieutenant Commander, 17

Reyes, Juan Guerrero, 51

Reyes, William, 237–38

Richter, Roy, 243, 248–50

Rico, Alex, 187

Robinson, William A., 20

Rogers, John, 17

Roosevelt, Eleanor, 6, 202

Roosevelt, Franklin Delano, 79, 90, 91, 150, 194, 195ff, 211, 290–91, 295 ff

Roosevelt, Franklin Delano, Jr., 36

Roosevelt, Mrs. Franklin Delano, Jr., 36

Roppul, Adolpho, 107, 109

Rose, Stan, 286

Ruegg, Fred, 148

Russell, Rosalind, 37

Sablan, Elias, 47–48

Sablan, Gregorio, 49, 51

Sablan, Josepa Reyes, 50–51

Sablan, Manuel "Deda," 48, 233, 235

Sablan, Oswald, 48

Sablan, Vicente, 8, 235, 236

Sakisag, Pedro, 51

Salas, Ben, 233, 235

Salas, Jesús, 50, 284

Salinger, Pierre, 216

Saltonstall, Leverett, 127, 134, 135–36

San Nicholas, Matilde Shoda, 99–100, 101

Schmidt, Harry, 244–45, 305, 306, 309–10, 312
Schofield, Frank H., 89
Scott, James, 155, 160, 168, 177
Seman, Felipe, 235
Seman, Joaquin, 235
Sheft, Casimir, 3–4
Shelly, John F., 176
Skinner, Cornelia Otis, 21
Smith, Daniel F., Jr., 82, 86, 127, 148 ff, 157, 176, 220–21
Smith, Yancy, 158
Snook, Neta. See Southern, Mrs. William Irwin
Snyder, Willis, 151, 152–53, 155
Southern, Mrs. William Irwin, 14, 187–88
Spruance, Raymond, 257
Stanley, Robert M., 70–71, 74, 78
Stanton, Frank, 128–29, 134–35, 136, 144
Stultz, Wilmer L., 18
Sumikawa, Michi, 252
Sutter, Ensign, 76
Swift, Ross, 216
Swords, Collins, 168
Sylvan, Father. See Conover, Sylvan
Sylvester, Arthur, 86–87, 128, 136

Taitano, Antonio, 54–56, 98
Tardio, Father, 45, 102
Telei, José, 247
Temple, Shirley, 169–70
Teusler, Rudolph Bolling, 91
Thaden, Louise, 20
Thieben, Lore, 187

Thompson, Warner Keith, 76, 204ff
Tibbets, Paul W., Jr., 249
Tinus, W. C., 213
Tole, Charles James, 166–67, 221, 279
Tracy, Spencer, 4
Truman, Harry S., 122, 139–41, 145, 291, 297
Tsunoda, Hitoshi, 174, 176
Tudela, Francisco, 51

Vidal, Eugene, 198, 317
Villa-Gomez, José, 233, 236
Villa-Gomez, Juan, 48

Wales, James E., 190–91
Wales, Mrs. Sidney M., 190
Watanobe, Masao, 255
Webster, Don, 154
Webster, Maurie, 9, 82, 297
Weiser, Harry, 169–70
Wendt, Waldemar, 39–41, 60, 62, 64, 94, 96, 125
Whitelaw, Sy, 9
Wiles, Ernest E., 170–71
Wilkins, Hubert, 20
Williams, Ted, 36
Winter, Frederick, 138, 142–45, 158, 267, 283
Woollcott, Alexander, 20
Wyatt, B. H., 255

Yamaguchi, Ken, 294
York, George, 39
Young, James, 35
Younger, J. Arthur, 175–76